The C

More New York

More New York Stories

The Best of the City Section of
The New York Times

Edited by

Constance Rosenblum

NEW YORK UNIVERSITY PRESS
New York and London

Dear Kit, I attended a program @ The Tenement museum where a few peo. read their articles from this book Nos. 16 & 50 - much to my surprise - entranced me - (since they 'r about baseball!!) & I immediately thought you would like them.
Love,
Pam

NEW YORK UNIVERSITY PRESS
New York and London
www.nyupress.org

Library of Congress Cataloging-in-Publication Data
More New York stories : the best of the City section of the New York times / edited by Constance Rosenblum.
p. cm.   Continues: New York stories. New York : New York University Press, © 2005.
ISBN 978-0-8147-7654-4 (cloth : alk. paper)
ISBN 978-0-8147-7655-1 (pbk. : alk. paper)
ISBN 978-0-8147-7673-5 (ebook)
1. City and town life—New York (State)—New York—Anecdotes.
2. New York (N.Y.)—Social life and customs—Anecdotes.
3. New York (N.Y.)—Biography—Anecdotes.
4. New York (N.Y.)—Social conditions—Anecdotes.
I. Rosenblum, Constance. II. New York times. III. New York stories.
F128.55.M66 2010
974.7—DC22   2010023628

New York University Press books are printed on acid-free paper, and their binding materials are chosen for strength and durability. We strive to use environmentally responsible suppliers and materials to the greatest extent possible in publishing our books.

Manufactured in the United States of America

C 10 9 8 7 6 5 4 3 2 1
P 10 9 8 7 6 5 4 3 2 1

Contents

Acknowledgments   **xiii**

Introduction   **1**

Part One Characters

1 Mr. Maxwell and Me   **7**

It Was the Mid-60's, and She Was the Dutiful Secretary of an
Esteemed Editor at *The New Yorker*. In a Few Short Years the
World Changed, and She Was the One in the Editor's Chair.

FRANCES KIERNAN (August 1, 2004)

2 Strumming toward Self-Awareness   **11**

For Years, She Had Seen the Fliers Promoting His Lessons.
Then She Inherited a Guitar and Gave Him a Try. Once.

LAURA LONGHINE (April 17, 2005)

3 Her Private Serenade   **15**

His Cheerful Whistling Floated through the Window of Her West
Village Apartment, and Captured Her Heart. If Only He Knew.

JOHANNA BALDWIN (August 7, 2005)

4 Tom's World   **19**

Sometimes, We Know a Place through One Person. When He
Dies, the Whole Neighborhood Goes Pale with the Loss.

ROY HOFFMAN (July 30, 2006)

5 In Noah's Room   **23**

The Life and Death of a Gifted Young Man with an Unquiet Mind.

JOHN FREEMAN GILL (September 17, 2006)

6 The Days and Nights of Maurice Cherry   31
Twice a Day, Every Day, He Traveled Back and Forth by Bus
between Chinatown and the Casinos of Atlantic City, Not to
Gamble but to Avoid a Life Lived Almost Entirely on the Street.
CASSI FELDMAN (August 5, 2007)

7 Werner Kleeman's Private War   38
Though Today He Lives Quietly in Flushing, Queens, More than
60 Years Ago, as an American Soldier, This Holocaust Survivor
Returned to His Native Germany to Arrest the Nazi Who Had
Arrested Him.
RICHARD FIRSTMAN (November 11, 2007)

8 The Chicken and Rice Man   45
Every Day of the Year, Jorge Muñoz Feeds the Mostly Homeless
Men Who Congregate under the Roosevelt Avenue El in Jackson
Heights, Queens. "He Got No Life," His Sister Said of Him. "But
He Got a Big Heart."
ADAM B. ELLICK (November 25, 2007)

9 A Life, Interrupted   52
The Young Woman, Who Had Been Missing for Nearly
Three Weeks, Was Floating Face Down off the Southern
Tip of Manhattan. Miraculously, She Was Rescued.
But the Explanation for What Had Happened Raised
Questions That Would Take a Long Time to Answer.
REBECCA FLINT MARX AND VYTENIS DIDZIULIS (March 1, 2009)

10 When Johnny Comes Marching In   60
The Man in Camouflage Walked into the Literary Bar in the
East Village, His Army Backpack Slung over His Shoulder.
And No One Said a Word.
HELEN BENEDICT (April 12, 2009)

Part Two **Places in the City's Heart**

11 Razzle-Dazzle Me   67
Times Square Is Successful Because People Wait in Huge Hordes,
in Numbers the Size of Entire Towns in North Dakota, for the
Light to Change.
ROBERT SULLIVAN (June 13, 2004)

12   New York Was Our City on the Hill   72

The City Held Out Unlimited Promise. But the Reality
Was a Struggle—for Money, Identity, and a Future.

EDWIDGE DANTICAT (November 21, 2004)

13   Here Is New York, Right Where We Left It   77

Before Manolos and Green Apple Martinis There Were Homburgs
and Short Beers, among Countless Evocative Remnants of an
Earlier Era That Endure, Often Uneasily, in the Glitziest City
on Earth.

DAVID McANINCH (February 27, 2005)

14   Comfort Food   85

For a While, He Was a Regular at Frank's Gourmet Deli on Smith
Street in Carroll Gardens. But Some Connections, like Apartment
Leases, Are Only Short-Term.

JAKE MOONEY (May 29, 2005)

15   The Great Awakening   88

In the Last Quarter Century, from Riverdale to Tottenville,
Waves of Change Have Washed over New York. In Brooklyn,
the Transformation Seems Almost Tidal.

SUKETU MEHTA (June 19, 2005)

16   The Worst Ballpark in the World   94

With the Plan to Build a New Home for the Mets, Shea's Days
Were Numbered. Yes, the Stadium Sat on an Ash Heap and Was
Pestered by Planes. Yet There Was No Denying Its Goofy Charms.

KEVIN BAKER (July 3, 2005)

17   A Toast, with a Shot and a Beer   99

A Couple of Wise Guys, a Musician or Two, and a Jukebox Set
on Julio, in a Crummy Little Bar of the Sort That Has
All but Vanished from the Upper West Side.

MITCH KELLER (August 21, 2005)

18   The Secret Life of Hanover Square   103

By Day, the Downtown Neighborhood Was a Ho-Hum Business
District. But as Windows Were Lighted and People with Grocery
Bags Emerged, the Area Revealed Its Hidden Face.

MARK CALDWELL (September 11, 2005)

19 New York's Lighthouse   107

The Building Is the Distinctive Image of Mythic New York,
the City of Film and Fiction, and Yet Irresistible.

MARK KINGWELL (April 23, 2006)

20 Call It Booklyn   113

With More Marquee Authors than You Can Shake a Mont Blanc
Pen at, Brooklyn May Be the City's Grimmest Borough for the
Up-and-Coming Writer.

SARA GRAN (September 10, 2006)

21 Breathless, Buoyant   120

No One Knows a Park, Its Smells and Seasons, Its Contours
and Crannies, like a Cross-Country Runner.

ALEXANDER ACIMAN (May 20, 2007)

22 In the Courtyard of Miracles and Wonders   124

Ever since Arriving in the City, He Yearned to Visit the
Cloistered Haven off West 11th Street. One Starlit Night
He Got His Chance.

DAVID MASELLO (December 16, 2007)

23 Stranger in a Strange Land   128

On a Sojourn in a SoHo Hotel after a Flood in His Brooklyn
Heights Apartment, Much Looked Familiar.
And Somehow Not.

ALEX ROSE (August 3, 2008)

24 Hard Times along Gasoline Alley   132

The Men Who Hang Out near the Service Stations on Atlantic
Avenue Will Pump Your Gas, Fix Your Brakes and Maybe
Tell You a Story.

JAMES ANGELOS (August 17, 2008)

25 A Game of Inches   139

With the Opening of a New Yankee Stadium,
Would Stan's Sports Bar Be Just a Little
Too Far from the Action?

KATHERINE BINDLEY (March 29, 2009)

Part Three Rituals, Rhythms, and Ruminations

26 Please Get Me Out of Here Please   149
New Yorkers Knew All about the Three-Day Ordeal
of the Chinese-Food Delivery Man Trapped in an
Elevator in the Bronx. They Had Been There,
If Only in Their Dreams.
COLIN HARRISON (April 10, 2005)

27 The Starling Chronicles   153
The Baby Bird Was Small and Smelly, Unlikely to Live Long.
But She Fell from Her Nest into a Cradle of Love,
and Soon She Became a New Yorker, with Wings.
LAURA SHAINE CUNNINGHAM (February 12, 2006)

28 A Chance to Be Mourned   160
After the Death of One of Its Own, a Homeless Group Searches
for Easier Ways to Grieve for New York's Nameless and
Unclaimed Dead.
EMILY BRADY (November 12, 2006)

29 Doodles à la Carte   168
Once a Week the Cartoonists of The New Yorker Assemble
for Lunch in Midtown, There to Enjoy a Little Sketch,
a Little Kvetch, and a Lot of One Liners.
CAROLINE H. DWORIN (January 14, 2007)

30 Unstoppable   175
Riding a Bike without Brakes on the Streets of New York May
Sound Insane. But to the Zealous Adherents of Fixed-Gear
Bikes—Fixies for Short—They Are a Thing of Beauty and
a Way of Life.
JOCKO WEYLAND (April 29, 2007)

31 The Urban Ear   182
New Yorkers Swim in a Sea of Sounds, Most of Them
Reassuringly Familiar. Then Once in a While Comes a
Very Different Noise.
MAX PAGE (July 22, 2007)

32 Children of Darkness — **186**

They Plumb Tunnels, Trestles and Other Abandoned Places,
Often Illicitly, and in Those Shadow Cities Find the Pulsing
Heart of New York.

BEN GIBBERD (July 29, 2007)

33 Tunnel Vision — **193**

Ever since Childhood, She Had Fantasized about a Hidden World
below the City Streets. In These Dreams, She Was Not Alone.

KATHERINE MARSH (November 4, 2007)

34 The Unthinkable, Right around the Corner — **197**

The Convoy of Police Cars Races down the City Streets, Sirens
Blaring, Red Lights Flashing. They're There to Protect. But
They Also Terrify.

FRANCINE PROSE (January 27, 2008)

35 His City, Lost and Found — **201**

Raised in Manhattan, He Is Fascinated by the Changes to His
Native Borough. Yet from His Garret across the River, He Does
Not Mourn Its Transformation.

NATHANIEL RICH (February 3, 2008)

36 Any Given Monday — **208**

These Men Don't Dunk. Yet Every Week for 33 Years, They Have
Sought to Slow the Passage of Time on the Hardwood Court of a
Gym on the Upper West Side.

SAKI KNAFO (February 24, 2008)

37 Lemon Zest — **214**

The Scott's Oriole, a Fluffy Yellow Visitor Never Before Sighted
in New York, Had Come to Union Square, Where It Seemed
Utterly at Home.

JONATHAN ROSEN (February 24, 2008)

38 Tree Proud — **218**

The Mayor Pledged to Plant a Million Trees. Sometimes It Takes
Just One to Steal Your Heart.

RANDY KENNEDY (June 1, 2008)

39 Faces in the Crowd   222
Circling the Jogging Loop in Prospect Park alongside
Skinny Ginsberg, Big Tony, and Other Creatures
Born of a Fertile Imagination.
MAC MONTANDON (October 26, 2008)

40 Fertility Rites   226
As She Traveled about the City in Search of an Elusive Gift,
a Remarkable Thing Happened.
JENNIFER GILMORE (January 11, 2009)

41 His Kind of River   230
The Indians Called the Hudson "The River That Runs Both Ways,"
and Its Majestically Freaky Nature Makes It Easy to Love.
DAVID HAJDU (March 22, 2009)

42 Soul Train   234
When You're Listening to the Music of the Subway, It's Easy
to Forget Where You Are and Where You're Going.
And You Don't Even Care.
ROXANA ROBINSON (May 17, 2009)

Part Four **Excavating the Past**

43 A Mother Lost and Found   241
Had Some Real Estate God Decreed That the Daughter
Would End Up in the Greenwich Village Town House
Where Her Mother Had Lived 46 Years Earlier?
ELLEN PALL (May 8, 2005)

44 Battle in Black and White   246
Half a Century Ago, the Author's Grandparents Helped Wage
a War to Integrate Stuyvesant Town. Even Today, Echoes
of This Little-Remembered Struggle Linger.
AMY FOX (March 26, 2006)

45 Morrisania Melody   254
Long before Fires and Violence Thrust the South Bronx into
the National Spotlight, One Small Patch of the Community
Played a Critical Role in Forging Musical History.
MANNY FERNANDEZ (April 30, 2006)

46 BoHo, Back in the Day   **262**

In the 70's, the Bums on the Bowery Were Gallant,
and an Impressionable Young Woman Could Rent
a Sun-Drenched Loft for a Song.

DOROTHY GALLAGHER (October 1, 2006)

47 Was He the Eggman?   **266**

A Dashing Turn-of-the-Century Wall Streeter May Have
Invented Eggs Benedict. Or Maybe Not.

GREGORY BEYER (April 8, 2007)

48 When He Was Seventeen   **274**

You Could Almost Buy a Legal Drink. Parents Didn't Hover
So Much. And If You Were Not Really Tougher than
Kids Today, You Certainly Felt like Your Own Man.

CHRISTOPHER SORRENTINO (September 16, 2007)

49 A Long Day's Journey into Lip Gloss   **280**

How Sephora Ate Her Theater, and Why She Hates to See
Blusher Displays Where Sam Shepard's Losers Used
to Slouch.

LESLIE NIPKOW (August 17, 2008)

50 Always, the Crack of the Bat   **284**

Stadiums, in the End, Are Just Window Dressing.
The Play's the Thing.

WILLIAM ZINSSER (March 29, 2009)

About the Contributors   **289**

About the Editor   **295**

Acknowledgments

AS was the case with the previous collection of essays from the City section, this book exists because of generosity on many fronts. Yet again The New York Times was kind enough to allow these articles and essays, along with the accompanying images, to be collected in book form. Alex Ward, the paper's editorial director of book development, was supportive every step of the way. All my colleagues at the City section, past and recent, helped make these pieces look and sound terrific.

You'd think that a book composed almost entirely of previously published material would be a cinch to assemble. Not exactly. In this regard, I'm especially grateful to Maura Foley and Richard Weigand, the section's most recent photo editor and art director, respectively, for helping collect the photographs and illustrations that accompany these pieces. And I owe special thanks to Dabrali Jimenez, the section's news assistant and general friend, who did the lion's share of helping me pull together the book's various elements and rescued me from computer hell more often than I care to admit.

As with the first collection, if it weren't for Eric Zinner, editorial director of NYU Press, and his support for this project, there would be no book. Most of all, and as always, I'm grateful to the writers who allowed their essays to be included in this collection. It was an honor to publish their work, and I hope this book expresses my gratitude to them.

Introduction

IN 2005, NYU Press published "New York Stories," a collection of 40 essays from the City section of The New York Times, a part of the Sunday paper distributed on newsprint in the five boroughs and electronically around the globe. Those pieces, which dug into the crevices and crannies of life in New York City in search of nuggets of insight and observation, were a disparate lot. Their subjects ranged from the allure of a Greenwich Village basketball court to the voyeuristic aspects of life as an urban window washer to the daily rhythms of a panhandler on the F train.

But these works had one thing in common. They captured the mood of the city during a particularly poignant era—the years framing the events of September 11. It's a cliché to say that nothing was the same in the years that followed the attacks on that luminous sky-blue morning, yet it's impossible to look back on that period and not classify events as either Before or After.

As I write this, the city is reeling from events that have been searing in a different way. The economic maelstrom that began buffeting the nation and the world in the spring of 2008 hit New York City with particular vigor. This is partly because the financial industry, the epicenter of the crisis, is based in Manhattan, but also because the city itself, a destination almost from the moment of its birth for both immigrants and sons and daughters from around the nation, was suddenly, agonizingly, on the ropes. To make it in New York, the idea embodied in the jaunty Frank Sinatra anthem to the city, was suddenly very hard if not verging on impossible for the newly minted college graduate, the immigrant from halfway around the world, and even some born-and-bred New Yorkers, who for the first time contemplated pulling up roots from the city that had been their families' home for generations.

Though many lives have continued unchanged, many more were drastically altered. Yet life in the city went on, and in the City section, we continued to take the pulse of the metropolis and tell its continuing, ever changing story.

The observation that there are eight million stories in the Naked City is the hoariest of clichés. Yet it's the rare New Yorker who does not have a compelling tale to tell, and part 1 of this collection, "Characters," offers profiles of some unforgettable individuals. We meet the Colombian immigrant who lives in Jackson Heights, Queens—the Chicken and Rice Man, as we called him—who has literally devoted his life to feeding local itinerant workers. We are introduced to a street person who spends most days and nights riding the bus between Chinatown and Atlantic City because he has no place to live.

Some of the lives are tragic, like that of the troubled young man who took his life on the morning of his 21st birthday. Some are tinged with tragedy, like that of the young woman who was swallowed up by the streets of Manhattan and rescued more than two weeks later in the waters off Staten Island through what can only be described as a miracle. Some of the stories are joyous, like the one about the whistler who roamed the streets of the West Village, spreading unexpected cheer amid the bleakness of winter.

In part 2, "Places in the City's Heart," we visit memorable corners of New York—not just the big-ticket locations like the Empire State Building but also less familiar sites like Potter's Field on Hart Island, where the unknown dead are laid to rest; the outer-borough strip called Gasoline Alley, where shady but friendly characters will hand you a line while pumping your gas; the old Shea Stadium, oddly mourned despite its flaws; and the nondescript deli in Carroll Gardens, Brooklyn, that stole a resident's heart when he wasn't even looking. Bars especially seem to keep the creative juices flowing, as they have throughout the city's history. So does Brooklyn: Is it the face of the city's future? Better than Manhattan? Home to too many writers? All of the above?

Part 3, "Rituals, Rhythms, and Ruminations," is composed of pieces that seek to capture the texture of local life, the phenomena we see out of the corner of the eye, like the battalion of flashing police cars that has become a staple of post-9/11 iconography. The inhabitants of some of these worlds are hiding in plain sight, like the intrepid cyclists who cruise the city aboard brakeless bikes. The inhabitants of others are invisible unless you know where to look for them, like the stealthy urban explorers Ben Gibberd describes in his piece "Children of Darkness."

The city's history is endlessly, compulsively fascinating, and in part 4, "Excavating the Past," are works that mine some of that history. Sometimes the stories are personal, like the one told by a daughter who discovered that decades earlier her mother had lived in the very apartment in which she herself once lived. Sometimes the stories take the form of social history, as in Amy Fox's account of the landmark racial battles at Stuyvesant Town, the middle-income bastion on Manhattan's East Side where she grew up. Sometimes the history is richly cultural, as with Manny Fernandez's account of the musical legacy of Morrisania, that Bronx neighborhood that spawned a cornucopia of memorable styles. Sometimes the history is wonderfully quirky, like the debate over who really invented Eggs Benedict, the quintessential New York brunch dish.

As was true last time, the roster of contributors is studded with illustrious names, among them Kevin Baker, Helen Benedict, Edwidge Danticat, Dorothy Gallagher, David Hajdu, Colin Harrison, Frances Kiernan, Suketu Mehta, Francine Prose, Nathaniel Rich, Roxana Robinson, Jonathan Rosen, Christopher Sorrentino, and Robert Sullivan. The collection includes works by two writers who were represented in the previous volume; Laura Shaine Cunningham's essay on a lost starling and David Masello's on a hidden courtyard in Greenwich Village were just too good to pass up, even as we sought to fill this volume with fresh names. The book also includes pieces by the most recent crop of regular writers for the City section. Although the job market for journalists is currently in freefall, they're so gifted that we're confident they'll make names for themselves down the line.

If you enjoy what you read in this collection, you might want to check out the many exceptional essays we loved but did not have room to include, such as Elizabeth Giddens's meditation on her house with a past, Sloane Crosley on her real estate woes, Joseph O'Neill on the corners of New York, Phillip Lopate's interview with longtime architecture critic Ada Louise Huxtable, Ed Park on the 9/11 echoes that refuse to go away, Brooke Hauser on the prom of many nations, Thomas Mallon on his first New York apartment, Michael Powell on New York City's two Roberts (Moses and Caro), Nicole Krauss on the life of a modern-day walker in the city, and Alice Mattison on the subway lines New Yorkers really crave. Luckily, in a virtual world, nothing ever truly dies. These articles will live forever in cyberspace; check them out on The New York Times on the Web.

The story of the City section has a bittersweet ending. In May of 2009, after a run of 16 years, the section published its final issue, falling victim to the same economic forces that were pummeling the rest of the planet and were hitting the world of publishing, especially newspapers, with particular force. But happily, the paper as a whole continues to arrive on doorsteps (and computer screens and mobile devices) with unfailing regularity. And thanks to the generosity of NYU Press, along with the writers, photographers, and illustrators who have allowed their work to be used in this book, the section lives again—sort of—between the covers of a book. That's a satisfying legacy.

Constance Rosenblum

May 2010

PART ONE

Characters

1

Mr. Maxwell and Me

It Was the Mid-60's, and She Was the Dutiful Secretary
of an Esteemed Editor at *The New Yorker*.
In a Few Short Years the World Changed,
and She Was the One in the Editor's Chair.

FRANCES KIERNAN

William Maxwell *(Anthony Loew/"Over by the River and Other Stories," Knopf, 1977)*

The author on Riverside Drive in 1967. *(Courtesy of the author)*

I N December 1966, long before secretaries were called assistants, I began working for William Maxwell, a New Yorker editor much admired for his own novels and stories as well as his talent for bringing out the best in his writers. Now, four years after his death, he is revered not only for his literary gifts but also for his generous spirit and great aptitude for friendship, two qualities not easy to come by in the world of New York letters. "A William Maxwell Portrait (Memories and Appreciations)," a collection of essays by fellow writers that will be published this month by W. W. Norton, makes much of this point.

What I saw the first day I was ushered into Mr. Maxwell's office was a middle-aged man whose face was utterly unremarkable save for brown eyes that seemed to take in everything. I saw him as old, although in fact he was in his 50's. I had no idea who he was. All I knew was that he, along with Roger Angell, was the editor I'd be working for.

That December, the Vietnam War was heating up, and the women's movement had yet to catch fire. I was 21, with a degree in English literature from Barnard, and had been earning $90 a week as The New Yorker's 20th-floor receptionist.

My pay was not unusual for a young woman with a liberal arts degree who could type reasonably well. I had been warned that receptionists and secretaries did not go on to more glamorous jobs at The New Yorker, but I was engaged to marry a young doctor, and after a few years I planned to retire anyway. I think, in fact, that I was promoted from receptionist to secretary as a sort of engagement present.

William Maxwell's office was at the north end of the 20th floor in the magazine's old building on West 43rd Street, just off Fifth Avenue. It was large enough to easily accommodate an old-fashioned desk, a long library table, several chairs and a couch covered in beige ticking.

The secretary I was replacing was retiring to the suburbs with her new husband, the way I was planning to retire one day. Her cramped office served as an anteroom to Mr. Maxwell's. In one corner were a couple of wire baskets overflowing with manuscripts. Above the desk was a shelf with a dictionary, a thesaurus, some packets of restaurant sugar, an electric kettle, a stack of blue and white cups and saucers, a tin of shortbread biscuits and a box of Twinings English Breakfast tea.

Official hours were 10 to 6. Often Mr. Maxwell was at his desk by the time I arrived, and always his desk was piled high with manuscripts, galleys and letters waiting to be answered. At noon he headed off for a quick lunch at the Century Club, two doors down the street. By 12:30 he was back again. From 12:30 to 2, he napped on his couch, during which time I was free to do whatever I wanted. Mostly, I went shopping.

Ordinarily the door to Mr. Maxwell's office was open by 2. If it remained shut, it was my duty to knock. My next task was to make tea, which was served to him and any visitors he might have, with the tea bag still in its cup and two shortbread biscuits. It never occurred to me to resent this part of my job. If pressed, I would have said that I could happily work for William Maxwell forever.

That June, my two bosses joined forces and bought me a wedding gift from Tiffany's. By fall, however, my new husband had been drafted and sent to a base in California. There was no way I could stay behind. After enduring 23 months of Tupperware parties and friends' baby showers, I returned to find that by some miracle my old job was once again vacant. The secretary who had replaced me had gone back to school. I, too, would be going to school, but only two nights a week, with the hope of earning a graduate degree in English.

For two years Mr. Maxwell and I jogged along nicely. By example, he taught me what it meant to write a good sentence and to edit with a light pencil. He also taught me that a gentle manner does not necessarily imply weakness. The only part of my job I found burdensome was keeping track of half the unsolicited fiction, carefully noting each story's arrival and departure in a black loose-leaf notebook. Submissions were sorted by the author's last name; I had A to K. After the reader who took care of my half of the alphabet was let go for reasons of economy, I sometimes had up to four overflowing wire baskets in my office.

By 1972 my attitude toward being a secretary was changing. Although I had mixed feelings about the women's movement, I was hardly indifferent to its demands for equal work for equal pay. My best friend had become a radiologist. All the young women who had arrived at the magazine with me had long since left for better jobs elsewhere.

•

FINALLY, one Monday morning, I arrived at work to learn that a fiction secretary down the hall, a woman younger than I, was being promoted to a job in the checking department. I had no desire to follow in her footsteps. But that afternoon, as the clock approached 6, I got up my courage and ventured into Mr. Maxwell's to ask if perhaps I could help with the unsolicited reading, at least until the reader who was doing double duty got caught up. He paused for a moment, then replied, "I don't see why not."

Over the next few weeks I found one publishable story and then another. Any story that was actually taken, I was allowed to edit, with Mr. Maxwell's assistance. Soon I was passing along promising writers to Mr. Angell as well.

As far as I was concerned, this state of affairs could have continued indefinitely. The day came, though, when the magazine's vice president insisted that my two bosses go to William Shawn, The New Yorker's editor, and make my de facto position official. My guess is he thought that would put a stop to what was going on before other secretaries got ideas.

An appointment with Mr. Shawn was set up; a meeting took place; and when Mr. Maxwell and Mr. Angell returned half an hour later, both men were shaking their heads. Anticipating their arguments, Mr. Shawn had announced that he saw no need to hire a second reader. Instead, he proposed making me an editor. While I was being trained for this new position, I would continue to read half the unsolicited fiction.

But there was one last question Mr. Shawn had insisted they ask. Both men looked embarrassed; clearly they knew better. Did I plan on having a baby soon? Not so far as I knew, I said.

Where I had least expected it, I had found a job with a future. The trouble was, Mr. Shawn was insisting I move down the hall to an office of my own. He had a point. No editor could possibly work as another editor's secretary. Of course I would still be seeing Mr. Maxwell. I could even buy my own tin of shortbread biscuits. But I was going to have to give up the electric kettle and the ticking-covered couch.

August 1, 2004

2

Strumming toward Self-Awareness

For Years, She Had Seen the Fliers Promoting His Lessons.
Then She Inherited a Guitar and Gave Him a Try. Once.

LAURA LONGHINE

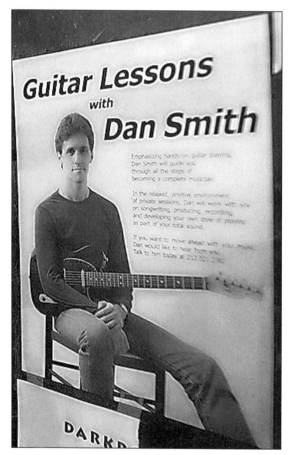

An advertisement filled with promise. *(Hiroko Masuike/The New York Times)*

N a sense, Dan Smith had been promising to teach me guitar for years. His fliers, adorned with the photo of a skinny, serious-looking young man holding an electric guitar, said it in bold capital letters: "DAN SMITH WILL TEACH YOU GUITAR."

I noticed a flier taped to the wall of the bodega near my first Manhattan apartment, on the Upper West Side. Over the next few years, I found them everywhere—on community bulletin boards, in restaurant entryways, on the sides of phone booths. A friend told me she once saw a whole wall of them, next to a shoe repair store.

I always had vague dreams of playing the guitar (who hasn't?), strumming away in my room and belting out throaty old heartbreaker ballads. Guitar fit very well with a certain romanticized vision of myself: lonely but appealingly sad, artsy and deep.

I didn't really have the voice to become a traveling folk singer, though. More to the point, I didn't have a guitar. So when I passed Dan Smith on the way to buy milk or cigarettes, I'd wonder briefly about him, idly imagine taking lessons someday, and move on.

Then my best friend moved to Los Angeles and, having long listened to my abstract longings for a guitar, left me hers. That changed everything. When someone gives you a guitar, you must learn to play it.

I had never bothered to take down Dan Smith's number, but once I made up my mind to call him, I saw a flier a few days later, in an Upper East Side doorway. "If you want to move ahead with your music," it said, "Dan would like to hear from you."

Taking guitar lessons from Dan Smith is like getting skin treatment from Dr. Zizmor; both are legendary self-promoters. So I set up an introductory lesson, even though Dan Smith, who speaks in a friendly but formal way that exactly matches what you'd expect from his picture, tells me he charges $100 an hour, almost what I earn in a day.

One chilly January evening I make my way to his apartment on the Upper West Side. In the lobby, a doorman directs me to an elevator at the end of the hall, past curving marble staircases. On the sixth floor I step out and am glancing around when I hear someone behind me. "Laura?" It's Dan Smith, leaning out of his doorway, an oddly familiar face. We shake hands.

In his living room, he tells me to take a seat and starts asking me questions.

What do I do? What are my plans for myself? When I tell him I'm a fact-checker (adding, quickly, that I'm also a writer), he asks where I want to go with that. I mumble something about wanting to be an editor, which doesn't make much sense. I find myself telling him that I am about to move in with my boyfriend, and then I wonder why I am telling him this. Dan Smith takes it all in with nods and reassuring repetitions of, "Sure, sure."

He asks me why I called him, and when I tell him I've been seeing his fliers for years, he straightens up. "Where?" he asks.

"All over," I say.

He grins. "That's the idea."

He had told me not to bring a guitar—I could play his—but asks about mine. Is it nylon or steel strings? I have no idea. I can't even remember the brand. "It's from the Matt Umanov Guitar Store," I offer, silently berating myself for arriving at my $100 lesson so woefully unprepared.

He hands me a Yamaha, and takes a Fender Stratocaster for himself. We go over tuning. "Don't worry if you don't remember everything," he says. "You'll kind of get it by osmosis."

In our phone conversation he had asked me what kind of music I liked, and I had mentioned Bob Dylan. So our first song will be "Knockin' on Heaven's Door," which has only three chords: G, D, and A minor.

Piece of cake. He tells me where to put my fingers for a G chord. But somehow, my fingers do not seem to stretch the way his do. It also quickly becomes apparent that my fingernails are getting in the way.

"It's completely up to you," he says, "but I do have nail clippers."

He washes a pair of clippers and brings them over with a small waste basket. As I trim my nails, he plays the song, strumming the chords on his Stratocaster and singing. After his rendition, we listen to Bob Dylan's rendition. Then I try again.

He tells me to relax my pinky, which is sticking into the air, twisted and tense. I try to relax it, while keeping my other fingers on the appropriate strings. It does not relax. With each chord, I send my fingers conscious commands. It's like having to tell your legs to walk.

Miraculously, in a matter of 10 minutes, I improve markedly. Occasionally real, right notes come out of the guitar. I decide that Dan Smith is an excellent teacher. I should take one more lesson. Maybe two. Then he lays out the rules.

•

YOU must pay your $100 in cash, at the beginning of each lesson, and take a lesson of an hour or more every week. If you cancel, you must still pay for that time, unless you can successfully reschedule. He concludes by saying, in his quiet, gentle voice: "I think we can work together. What do you think?"

I explain, awkwardly, what I've already explained on the phone, that I can only afford a couple of lessons just now. "I'd like to take at least another lesson or two," I say. "But I'm going to San Francisco next week."

"Why?"

"Well I have friends there, and there was a cheap airfare."

Dan Smith nods, and I immediately regret my revelation. I know what he's thinking. I can afford to fly to California on an apparent whim, but I can't afford guitar lessons?

"You have to think about how guitar fits into your life," he says. "Some people have a lot going on, and there's just no room for it.

"I'm not saying you're one of those people," he adds quickly.

No. I do not want to be "one of those people." Those sad dilettantes.

We try to schedule something for the following week, but it's hard. I try to explain how I have no control over my own schedule, which is true, but I feel as if I'm lying, and that he knows I am lying, to disguise my lack of commitment to the guitar.

"Why don't you just call me?" he says finally. I realize suddenly he has been standing for a few minutes. "I do have another student waiting."

In the hallway, a young woman with a hipster haircut is lounging against the wall. I hurry out.

Over the next week, I find myself actually considering the possibility of spending $400 a month on guitar lessons. Then I go to San Francisco, and suddenly two weeks have gone by and I have not picked up the guitar. My fingernails are growing back.

Instead of buying a guitar book, I start writing about my lesson, and when I call Dan Smith to ask him some questions, he says he doesn't have time for them. Reluctantly, he provides a few nuggets of biography—he is 34 years old, grew up in Newton, Mass., and has been teaching in New York for about 12 years—but he can't sit down for a formal interview. "Teaching is really taking up all of my time right now," he explains. It is, after all, what he does. Dan Smith teaches people guitar.

And I still don't sing.

April 17, 2005

3

Her Private Serenade

His Cheerful Whistling Floated through the Window of Her West Village Apartment, and Captured Her Heart. If Only He Knew.

JOHANNA BALDWIN

(Paul Degen)

T'S possible I had seen him before, but not until Christmas Day did I actually notice him. That's the day he became part of my life. Normally I would have been with my family. This season was different. Not only had I run out of money, lost someone I cared about and needed to be alone, I also wanted to stay home and write. That's what I was doing the morning of Dec. 25 in the top-floor apartment of the brownstone on West 11th Street when I heard him for the first time.

His music was coming from the east. It was a clear sound, joyous. It was a Christmas carol, although I can't remember which one. From the windowsill, I couldn't see much, even with my face pressed against the glass. The only thing I could see was his footprints. It had snowed all night, and the snow was still falling. I could hear a whistling sound moving past my building, but all I could see was the image of a man who was wearing a hooded parka and walking his dog.

Although the whistler and I never met, we spent the entire holiday season together. Nearly every day, he walked down my street whistling a different melody, mostly show tunes. He was the unexpected, unwrapped holiday gift. Anytime I heard him, I moved to my window to get a glimpse. The priority, of course, was to listen, until the sound faded and then turned a corner.

The first person I told about the whistler was my landlord, an attractive, gigantic bald man who, like me, also stayed in the city for the New Year. He seemed genuinely moved, as if he wished this had been his experience rather than mine. I realized that I had stumbled onto something unique. I had an enviable relationship with someone I didn't know. And in fact, I may not be the only New Yorker with a whistler; one was sighted in TriBeCa last winter.

I wanted to tell my two friends in the building but needed to wait until they were back from their holiday celebrations. They returned in mid-January, and then I waited until the whistler was approaching so they could be drawn in as I had been. When the opportunity came, I rushed downstairs to share the news. The two of them were on separate telephone lines the moment the whistler reached the front of the building. Overly excited, I told them everything I knew about the whistler, which was very little. At the same time, I pointed out the window, suggesting they hurry so that they wouldn't miss him. They looked at me with utter boredom, and continued their phone conversations. Then one of them yawned.

On one of the coldest February nights of record, I was having dinner on Perry Street with an Australian cinematographer and a producer friend when I heard him again. I told the women to listen, then began to tell them all about the whistler and his dog. Again, I didn't know what to say, except that the whistler lifts my spirits whether I'm working or not working, whether I'm having a good or bad day, whether our country is bombing another country or whether anyone has killed one of our soldiers recently.

The women went to the window, blocking my view, and their eyes brightened as they described the whistler back to me. Good-looking. Handsome, even. Why is he alone on a Saturday night? They suggested I introduce myself.

That didn't make sense. The whistler they were describing didn't sound like my whistler at all. I elbowed my way to the window to see for myself. And then I realized it. They were looking at the wrong man with the wrong dog. The man they were looking at wasn't even whistling. The real whistler, who is an older gentleman, had just disappeared off West Fourth Street.

The women suggested that I might be fixated on older men. Then the producer handed me a bag of leftovers and sent me home.

It's not a latent adolescent crush, I later explained to a friend on the phone. He's somewhere between his late 40's and early 60's. His sandy hair is thinning, but still looks good. He wears darkish glasses and dresses more formally than casually. He sometimes wears a bow tie, but on the one and only warm day of spring, he wore a T-shirt. I knew he wouldn't be wearing a T-shirt this spring day because there was a snowstorm outside. I figured I wouldn't even see him because of the ice coming down.

We continued talking on the phone, and somewhere between the subjects of money and men, we both heard him. The whistler was outside in the storm. I opened the window and stuck the phone outside so that as he whistled down the street, my friend and I could both hear him. She laughed, and I knew she understood what I did, that the whistler was the neighborhood alchemist who could transform an ordinary something into the extraordinary without knowing it.

Eventually it really did become spring. The whistler started wearing T-shirts, his steps seemed to be lighter, even his whistling was impossibly more upbeat. "Almost Like Being in Love" was his song of the day. If the whistler was happy about spring, I would try to be the same.

•

HAVING a relationship with someone you don't know is never disappointing. He will never say he is going to call you and then not call. He will never promise to do something for you and not do it. He will never say he is going to show up and then keep you waiting, or, worse, not show up at all. He will never ask you to do something you can't do. He will never let you down. He will never say the wrong thing.

The weeks of rain and thunderstorms did their best to stand in the way of summer's arriving. I'm not sure what confuses me more: relationships with people I actually do know or New York weather. Whatever the answer, the sun fought through the rain and finally won. We all knew we would see the sun again; we just didn't know when we would see it or how long it would last. Just as I'm pretty sure I'll see the whistler again. I just never know when.

Inevitably the day will come when I won't see him anymore. It won't be a dramatic day filled with emotion. There will be no letter or phone call, no flowers. There will be no abandoner and no abandonee. There will be no tears or blame, and the experience won't be entangled with frustration or hope. It will be as natural as the changing seasons, just like the day when a person looks back and realizes it's not winter anymore.

Whenever that day comes, I'll be grateful then as I am now. And yet I'll probably never thank him because I don't know the whistler and the whistler doesn't know me.

August 7, 2005

4

Tom's World

Sometimes, We Know a Place through One Person. When He Dies, the Whole Neighborhood Goes Pale with the Loss.

ROY HOFFMAN

Tom Mathison at Tortilla Flats in the early 1990's.
(Photograph courtesy of Kerry Moravec)

O N a brisk fall night, 2003, I wait for my friend at his Jane Street apartment so he can join me for a walk through the West Village. I watch him make his way slowly through the labyrinth inside his one-bedroom residence—10,000 books teetering floor to ceiling and bulging on shelves—as he slowly puts on his jacket.

"Need a hand?"

"No." He fumbles with the buttons. "Thanks. I'm O.K."

He is in his 50's, with thinning brown hair and a brushy goatee. He looks up at me through big eyeglasses, smiles, sighs. "Let's go," he says.

On the street he pushes ahead, stepping down a huge curb into the crosswalk, shuffling to the opposite side, then laboriously putting his left foot up and bringing the rest of his body along. A man passes by, calls out, "Hey, Tom." A young woman waves.

Over the course of many years, wherever I have lived—Chelsea, the East Village, Brooklyn or, now, faraway Alabama—I have dropped by Tom Mathison's to take a late-night stroll. I met Tom at a party in the 1980's, and when I later caught a glimpse of him in his neighborhood, I reintroduced myself and joined him for the first of our many rambles.

He became my tour guide along cobblestone streets where brownstones lean close to one another and corner bars are lively deep into the night.

A Wisconsin native with a dry wit and a doctorate in philosophy, he is a wise guide indeed. Not that he tells me much about his dissertation at Yale on Wittgenstein, or offers a tour-book history of Jane Street, Bethune, Horatio, Greenwich. Like a perambulatory Joseph Mitchell, he sketches the denizens of the small hours: the newspaper vendor who sells him the first early edition, the bartender who's laboring over a novel, the literary critic who carries on about French deconstructionists while drunk.

He complains rarely about his cerebral palsy, having once written: "My condition is congenital, essentially unchanging, a threat to neither health nor energy, and certainly no physical barrier to an entirely adequate imitation of everyday life. Yet much of the world still demands proof that I am not an alien being. This is the source of unending adventure in my life."

He is fearless, even as we cross streets at his methodical pace and I flinch as taxis loom at our shoulders. One night when he was alone, a robber pushed him down and plundered his pockets; within days Tom was back on the street.

This is, after all, Tom's world, the dozen blocks, like his thousands of books, where he finds freedom. He cannot drive. He does not like strangers to look at him twice. A child of the heartland, he no longer feels in sync there. Here, on foot or negotiating the subways as needed, he disappears happily into the labyrinth of the city.

And in the nightspots of his neighborhood he finds another home.

We arrive at a door front on Washington Street where music pounds, and we enter. In Tortilla Flats, jammed with partygoers half his age, he is greeted by a waiter, and he shuffles through the dancing, drinking crowd to a booth. We order beer, and he lifts his, shakily. "Ah," he says with a sigh as he takes a long swig.

Our plates are served. "Can I help?" I ask.

He shakes his head emphatically. The pretty waitress, knowing him, cuts up his Mexican food. He peers out at the youths who down shots of tequila and laugh and press together close. "Tell me," Tom says, looking at me through his big eyeglasses, "I'm not too old for this."

"You're not too old."

●

THAT winter Tom began to tire easily and his feet became swollen. He went for medical tests. I was far away when his mom and dad, Ruth and Lee, called me on New Year's Day, 2004, to say he'd been found to have leukemia.

Tom and I spoke often on the phone, but when I next traveled to New York, his parents had taken him south to Texas, where they were retired and Tom had a sister. I missed being able to pay a visit to my most nocturnal pal.

Those hushed blocks bounded by 14th Street, Houston, Eighth Avenue and the Hudson were emptier without him. Like a friend in any nook of the city not mine, Tom personalized the terrain. There were people I met, like Steve at Tortilla Flats and Janet at Cowgirl Hall of Fame, whom I identified as "Tom's friends." Restaurants that had come and gone, like the funky Gulf Coast near the Hudson, or the sleek El Teddy's in the far-off territory of TriBeCa, were "Tom's places."

The medical updates I received from Tom's parents seemed hopeful, then not. Up, then down. Then farther down. Tom wanted to leave Texas and return home. A friend he'd met at Yale, who had become a successful TV producer, had him flown to New York. He had further treatment; he was rapidly failing.

In early August 2004, I was back in New York. In his room in hospice at Beth Israel Medical Center, I found Tom small in his bed, straining forward from his pillow to talk to me. He had always spoken with a slur, but his voice was weaker. I sat next to the bed and, eager to be upbeat, caught him up to date on my family and friends. We talked about the streets he loved.

When the nurse arrived with his dinner on a tray and prepared to feed him, he looked up at me with large eyes through big glasses and said, haltingly: "No. You. Do it."

I lifted the fork, watched him eat slowly. He thanked me, sank back into the pillow and closed his eyes.

When I leaned over to give him a hug goodbye, I felt his brushy whiskers. I was back in Alabama when I got the word that a few days later he had closed his eyes for good.

Tom's books were donated to a school in the Philippines, and a memorial service was held for him at Cowgirl Hall of Fame, but the day it took place, Hurricane Ivan was bearing down on my Alabama home and I was unable to attend. A spring evening a year and a half later, I have my own.

Down Jane, over to Washington, by late-night stoop sitters and small cafes vibrant with talk, I walk Tom's streets. The lore he shared with me of bartenders and actresses and past-midnight amblers is joined now by one more story, his own.

From doorways call out voices of people who once dwelled there, still heard by those who knew them. Along the cobblestone streets tread the feet of those who, while vanished, still keep pace with old companions.

Tom, adventuring alongside me, his coat haphazardly buttoned, trudges faster as we near the river.

When I arrive at Tortilla Flats, I take a stool at the end of the bar, order a beer and through the din of the music and sway of the crowd, alone, toast my friend.

July 30, 2006

5

In Noah's Room

The Life and Death of a Gifted Young Man
with an Unquiet Mind.

JOHN FREEMAN GILL

Noah Simring, who took his life on the morning of
his 21st birthday. *(Courtesy of the author)*

IN the early hours of Saturday, July 29, on his 21st birthday, something broke or deflated or just gave out inside of Noah Simring.

After apparently staying up all night in his room, he made his bed carefully, changed out of the special pair of Lucky jeans a friend had given him, and put on old clothes. He then tried to leave the apartment where he lived with his parents, Ruth and Jim Simring, in a drab brick co-op on Third Avenue and 24th Street.

His parents, concerned by his irritable manner, prevented him from leaving until he agreed to let his father go along. The pair took the elevator to the roof, where Noah often went to smoke cigarettes. As his father pleaded with him to explain what was wrong, Noah suddenly said, "That's it; I'm out of here," and vaulted over the wall at the roof's edge.

His body landed in a rear courtyard, 19 stories below. His father called 911, and the police arrived on the scene before the family.

"It just seems like he made a mistake," his father said a few weeks later, his voice breaking. "And the only one that was permanent, that we couldn't help him with."

At a service held two days later at Riverside Memorial Chapel on the Upper West Side and attended by more than 350 people, a cousin read a poem that Noah wrote last December. The poem seemed to articulate the pain that Noah sometimes felt on sleepless nights when he was alone with his thoughts in his narrow ninth-floor room:

> They can see inside the open blinds,
> and while it is calming to be behind the window covers,
> I long for a traveler to point up here,
> Wave to whoever doesn't know, and
> Tell them.
> Tell them I am awake in a room open to the winter. . . .
> How days with open windows never end.

In his mother's view, that description of her son's room was, at least in part, literal. "He's always been extremely lonely," she said. "It's how he lived his life."

•

SUICIDE is well known as a leading cause of death among young people. What distinguishes Noah's short life is the considerable body of work that he created in an art form, music, that for him was a more natural means of communication than language. And what distinguishes his death is the determination of those who mourn him to preserve that music, and in so doing to allow his creations to outlive his final act of self-destruction.

Noah Simring was a shy and introspective young man with dark brown hair, contemplative blue eyes and an expectant smile. Although he often sat on the periphery of conversations, when he got going on a subject he felt passionate about, like music, he spoke with great intensity.

Starting early in his life, Noah had battled a darkly melancholy streak, and in the 10th grade he was given a diagnosis of depression, an illness his maternal grandmother had suffered from and one that for Noah seemed to worsen after high school.

In the summer of 2005, after he dropped out of the University of Vermont, his mental state deteriorated markedly, and he later began to hear voices. ("They're criticizing me," he confided to his older sister, Mia.) In the last months of his life, according to his mother, he was seeing a psychiatrist twice a week and was being treated with antidepressant, anti-anxiety and antipsychotic medications. He was also using cocaine, friends said.

Like many young people, Noah often spent long stretches in his bedroom, its door shut tight. On the outside of the door, in black marker, he had scrawled the words "Do Not Disturb—No Exceptions" alongside a metal clock face with no hands and a friend's drawing of a three-eyed monster hanging by the neck with its tongue lolling out.

But Noah, a born artist who was forever creating things—a picture of a vase of flowers painted with food coloring, a one-act play written on a paper plate, a suite of classical piano pieces about insects—also did something in his room that most young people don't. He recorded hours and hours of music.

An ardent audiophile, he eschewed digital recordings in favor of the sonic nuance of vinyl. His room was crammed with analog recording equipment, including a professional reel-to-reel Revox tape recorder and an assortment of vintage microphones. A tangle of black cables filled the drawers of his desk and snaked across the floor.

As a high school student at Horace Mann, in Riverdale, one of the city's elite private schools, Noah formed a rock band, Ghostcloud, with a schoolmate named Aaron Bernstein, a close friend and a fellow explorer of sound.

The first time he heard Noah sing and play guitar, it felt, as Mr. Bernstein put it, like "a kind of charisma, something drawing you into a world too gentle to touch, only listen to." Over the next five years, the pair spent countless nights in Noah's room recording eclectic rock music, whose sound ranged from thrashing, dissonant guitar sessions to ethereal melodies accompanied by Noah's mournful, intimate vocals. The range, said Sara Gruenwald, a friend who sometimes listened to their sessions, "was like going from a thunderstorm to a kiss."

Although Ghostcloud never performed in public, the two musicians took their recordings seriously. In addition to making two independent vinyl albums, one recorded in Noah's room and the other in a Park Slope studio called Seaside Lounge, the pair recorded four other albums in Noah's room. They finished the painstaking work of cutting and sequencing the quarter-inch tape of their final album just three days before Noah died.

As his family and close friends have struggled with their anguish over his death, several of them have found something approaching solace in trying to preserve as much of Noah as possible by producing the remaining Ghostcloud albums—not digitally but on vinyl, as Noah would have wished.

"Anyone who knew Noah would say his life was music," said Jeremy Snyder, one of two drummers who performed on "High Wire by Night," Ghostcloud's studio album. "And if his life equaled music and the music's still here, then that's Noah, and there's plenty to go around."

•

WHILE Noah was alive, his room was a place of private refuge. Beginning when he was a small child, he made visitors remove their shoes before entering, a ritual he never abandoned. Right up until the end, when his family wanted to communicate with him, he insisted that they slip a note under his door.

"He was volatile," said his father, Jim, a small, gentle man with brown eyes and a salt-and-pepper beard who, like his wife, is a dentist. "You could knock on his door and he'd let you in, or you could knock on his door and he'd make you feel terrible. You never knew what to expect."

In the hours after Noah's death, the father took off his shoes and went into his son's room. "I wanted to be in Noah's space," he explained. "I just kept looking at all the things in his room."

There was much to see. Its dominant features were electric guitars, amplifiers, speakers and the chaotic swirl of cables that choked the narrow space between his monumentally messy desk and his bed, which lay in a nook beneath dangling strands of crinkled cassette tape. The walls and cabinets, painted in a van Gogh palette of blue and green, were decorated with a photograph of the moon's surface, a circuit board from some disemboweled electronic machine, and surreal posters of the band the Residents, featuring a giant eyeball wearing a top hat.

Along the walls was an obsessively organized collection of hundreds of albums by musicians ranging from the indie band Sebadoh to the Russian composer Scriabin, one of whose complex sonatas Noah had been working all summer to learn on the piano.

In the poem read at his funeral service, Noah pleads from his room:

> Please, wind, blow in my favor this night,
> Move through like a ghost
> Before the snow melts, a calming soot to ease this worry.
> But the wind's answer blows through the city,
> No! From uptown instead, and smoke fills the room
> Swirling backwards with the gust
> And it is steady and certain.
> In, in, in, the room is frozen.

IF Noah's room was at times an anxious, solitary space, on other occasions it was an environment that helped forge powerful musical and personal connections between people.

"The band was integral and completely indistinguishable from our friendship," said Mr. Bernstein, who went from Horace Mann to Grinnell College in Iowa. "Noah was always very open about the music. People would come over, and he'd say, 'Play with us.' And if they didn't play an instrument, he'd give them one."

One visitor who felt welcomed in this way was Ms. Gruenwald, a Grinnell student whom Noah met through Mr. Bernstein. "Noah had this presence that was really awe-inspiring," she said. "His whole room had this ambience of creativity, and it all seemed to be systematized by some secret Noah system."

A week before Noah's death, Ms. Gruenwald visited his room for the last time, and he insisted that she jam with him and Mr. Bernstein by singing and performing on an antique mandolin—which she had no clue how to play. Afterward, Noah turned to her and said with piercing directness, "You have a beautiful voice." Although she had sung as a child, she had lost the nerve to sing years earlier. But Noah's encouragement inspired her to join a band as a singer. "I am completely in debt to Noah," she said. "He gave me my voice back."

In the weeks before Noah's death, Ms. Gruenwald found three identical antique keys, and to express the kinship she felt with the two Ghostcloud guitarists, she gave a key to each of them. Noah's still sits on his desk.

Nearby are shelves displaying dozens of antique cars, which Noah collected avidly as a child. It was while he was playing with one of these cars as a 2-year-old that his parents had an early epiphany about how unusual their son's mind was.

On more than one occasion, his mother recalled, he compulsively pushed a toy car forward and back over and over, fixing his gaze on a speck of dirt on one wheel. But just when she and her husband began to grow concerned, Noah announced that the front wheel was slightly smaller than the back wheel, so for every eight revolutions the front wheel made, the back wheel made seven. "Then we realized, he's beyond us," the mother recalled. "Way beyond us."

He retained this exploratory turn of mind throughout his years at Horace Mann, where he excelled at math. "He did not want to accept some easy formula, but loved exploring his own solutions, and sometimes they were very ingenious," recalled Rick Somma, who taught Noah 10th-grade algebra. "When he saw something, he saw it uniquely."

From a young age, Noah also showed a talent for music. Starting at age 8, he took second place three years in a row at the Cultural Heritage Competitions, a metropolitan-area piano competition at Queens College.

"He understood music when he was 8 or 9 that 15- and 16-year-olds didn't understand," said Alicia Jonas, his childhood piano teacher. But he could never learn to sight-read properly. "He had the brilliance, and also the weakness," Mrs. Jonas said.

After graduating from Horace Mann in 2003, he attended Wesleyan University and then the University of Vermont, where he lived in Chabad House, a Jewish student center, and adopted the rigorous religious rituals of the Hasidic Chabad-Lubavitch movement. But at both schools he had trouble settling in and making friends.

Last year, after his sophomore year, he dropped out of school and moved back home. At his mother's urging, he began taking classes at the New School. He also resumed the piano lessons he had stopped at age 12; in addition to learning to play Scriabin, he began composing his own classical pieces, including a sonata and a nocturne.

But in the eyes of some friends, he sometimes seemed burdened by a great weight of sadness. "He was very down because he saw beautiful things," said Jonah Bloch-Johnson, a friend from Horace Mann who studies music at Columbia, "and I think he couldn't quite get there sometimes."

Throughout the past year, while working at a Starbucks in Chelsea, Noah carried a musical composition notebook with him wherever he went and worked for hours on his sonata, either at the piano in his parents' living room, or on the subway.

"He wrote comments in the music almost like a poetic text that can be touched," said Mr. Bloch-Johnson, who has been sorting through Noah's unfinished compositions in the hope of editing them into works that he and others can perform as a memorial. In places where conventional composers typically write directions like "fortissimo," Mr. Bloch-Johnson discovered, Noah scribbled descriptive phrases like "sounds of night reconfigured," "warmth of sadness" and "descending stairs knowingly."

During his last year, Noah also weathered more than his share of emotional hardships. A young woman he was in love with broke up with him. In July 2005 his maternal grandmother, with whom he had been extremely close, died, and the experience of seeing her body in her apartment rattled him terribly; her funeral was on his 20th birthday. In addition, his mother, who developed ovarian cancer and was treated with chemotherapy starting when Noah was in 11th grade, suffered a recurrence of the disease last December and learned she would need further chemotherapy.

THROUGH it all, Noah continued to make music. In March, when Mr. Bernstein was home for spring break, the pair recorded marathon guitar sessions in Noah's room. Throughout July they worked with great intensity on their last two albums.

The evening of Wednesday, July 26, the two friends put the finishing touches on what was to be their final record, bringing it to a point at which it was all but ready to be handed over to a sound engineer. In the early morning hours, after Mr. Bernstein had gone home, Noah invited his father into his room and played him the tape of "Fountains of Rome," the first side of the album.

"It was sort of ethereal, and yet rich in texture and very depressed," Jim Simring recalled. "I said, 'I think it's pretty good,' and he said: 'This is what we've been working toward; this is what I created. This is the most depressed music I could make.'"

Just hours earlier, the music of Ghostcloud, and the experience of being with Noah in his room, had infused Mr. Bernstein with a feeling of elation.

While working on the album's second, more upbeat side, called "Luminosity," the two decided at the last minute to replace a slow, sad song with a livelier track. The effect, Mr. Bernstein said, was to give that side of the album a feeling of warmth and kindness. "It's luminous," he said, "and the experience of playing together was luminous, and that's why we called it 'Luminosity.'"

After the pair listened to the album, Noah turned to his friend and said, "This album is letting the world in; we're letting the world in now."

These words are among Mr. Bernstein's last memories of Noah. "I remember I was on his bed," he said, "and I just wanted to curl up and listen to it. I felt very calm and very safe."

September 17, 2006

6

The Days and Nights of Maurice Cherry

Twice a Day, Every Day, He Traveled Back and Forth by
Bus between Chinatown and the Casinos of Atlantic City,
Not to Gamble but to Avoid a Life Lived
Almost Entirely on the Street.

CASSI FELDMAN

Maurice Cherry at an Atlantic City restaurant. *(Lauren Lancaster/The New York Times)*

AS his bus exited the Garden State Parkway, Maurice Cherry gazed out the window, waiting for the precise moment when the gleaming silhouette of Atlantic City would swim into view. Suddenly there it was, lit up like noon even at midnight.

Most of the passengers seemed unimpressed. They woke up slowly from their naps, massaging their necks and groping around for their belongings. But Mr. Cherry, a diminutive 37-year-old wearing a baggy black Atlantic City sweatshirt, was thrilled.

"We're here," he said, flashing a jack-o'-lantern smile. "It's going to be a beautiful night."

Mr. Cherry had no plans to gamble. He is what is known as a rider, one of dozens of New Yorkers—often homeless or nearly homeless— who travel back and forth between Chinatown and Atlantic City or Connecticut each day, and sometimes twice a day. They sleep through the two-and-a-half-hour rides and make a quick buck off the casinos without handling so much as a single chip.

Casinos in the metropolitan area have always relied heavily on buses to lure gamblers from the region, but the Chinatown bus market is unusual. With a score of bus companies vying for customers, the casinos are forced to compete as well, by offering what amounts to a free ride—and then some.

On this particular night, Resorts Atlantic City was paying $25 to anyone who made the $13 round trip. The Atlantic City Hilton, reachable for $18 in bus fare, was offering $22 in cash and a $20 match-play coupon, which requires a gambler to pony up the same. Foxwoods, in southeastern Connecticut, had what was without question the sweetest deal: For just $10, a rider would get $50 in match-play coupons and a $12 food voucher. Though the casinos do not permit the sale of gambling coupons, a discreet rider can usually manage to sell them to a player at a discount.

The most dedicated riders virtually live on the bus, making two round trips a day. They leave early in the morning from an informal bus depot at Division Street and the Bowery, spend a few hours at the casino, then return in the late afternoon. As night falls, they are back on the corner, ready for their next journey. For some riders, the routine brings with it a sense of shame. "This is the bottom of the barrel," said one scrawny young man who was hunched against a chain-link fence as he waited for a bus. "There's not much further to sink."

Yet in the eyes of some who are familiar with the city's homeless population, this tactic shows creativity and resilience. Apart from providing the material benefits of an escape from the elements and a place to sleep, the daily excursions let the riders avoid the stigma of being homeless.

"They're making it on their own without putting their hand out," said Kim Hopper, a professor of sociomedical sciences at the Columbia University Mailman School of Public Health who has studied homelessness in New York since the late 1970's. "This is not charity. This is ingenuity."

Like the railroad boxcar jumpers of yore, these riders keep moving in order to survive, but with one crucial difference: After 10 hours and 500 miles each day, they are right back where they started.

•

MR. CHERRY is relatively new to the game of shuttling to and from the casinos, having learned of the system six months ago from his brother Dwayne, who frequents Mohegan Sun, in southeastern Connecticut. Mr. Cherry used to go there, too, but he said he was kicked out for plugging in his portable DVD player. "They said I was stealing electricity," he said, rolling his eyes.

Now he sticks with the New Jersey casinos, which hold a sentimental appeal. When he was a child, his mother organized group trips to Atlantic City from the housing project in Crown Heights, Brooklyn, where the family lived, but he was always too young to go. His mother also ran poker games in their apartment; by the time he was 6, he had learned to search under the table for dropped money—and to finish off the liquor left in half-filled cups.

"It wasn't 'The Brady Bunch,'" Mr. Cherry said of his childhood. And the urge to drink is with him still: Slouched in his seat in the middle of the bus, he sipped vodka, straight, from a plastic novelty cup adorned with flashing lights.

Life on the road is familiar to Mr. Cherry, who spent the past few years traveling around the country, working as a day laborer and visiting friends and relatives using Travelers Aid, a service that helps poor people pay for plane, train and bus tickets.

Before that, he was in and out of jail and prison for crimes including robbery, drug dealing and assault. His nickname, J.D., which stands for juvenile delinquent, was bestowed by his mother. "I've been to Attica, I've been to Sing Sing, I've been to Fishkill," he said. "I've been around the block."

Mr. Cherry has also been a victim. His face still bears the scars of an attack he says he suffered as a teenager at the hands of a romantic rival. And three years ago, he was hit in the head with a metal nightstick by a Metropolitan Transportation Authority police officer who had ejected him from Pennsylvania Station. News accounts of that incident described Mr. Cherry as homeless, but he does not see himself that way. "I'm a street person, but I'm not homeless," he said. "It's a fine line."

The officer admitted to the crime in court, and Mr. Cherry is now seeking a settlement, so he can, as he put it, "settle down, have me some kids, find me a good woman and just behave myself." As he waits, he travels to Atlantic City to listen to the ocean and avoid the police, who he thinks resent him for reporting the attack. "I really like it here," he said as his bus pulled into Resorts, Atlantic City's oldest casino. "I feel really, really free."

•

HOMELESS visitors have found inventive ways to get by in Atlantic City, and tips on strategies have spread quickly by word of mouth. They know where to sleep and where not to sleep, for instance, and how to avoid security officers. Yet the casinos are also learning their tricks. Many riders have been caught at least once selling gambling coupons, and a sign in a women's restroom in the Hilton reads, "No changing clothes in the bathroom!"

As riders get off the bus at Resorts, they are handed paper certificates worth $25 in cash, which they head straight into the casino to redeem. "It's the same people every night, day in and day out," said Michelle Garland, a Resorts cashier. "I guess it's the only way for them to get a couple dollars in their pocket."

The casino, a 70's-style carpeted maze rife with glassy-eyed gamblers, resounded with the unmistakable electronic melody of money being won and lost on slot machines. But Mr. Cherry was not even tempted to gamble. After redeeming his certificate, he walked from the casino to an Indian and soul food restaurant a few blocks away. After a $6.50 dinner of fried fish and macaroni and cheese, he strolled back along the Boardwalk, sea gulls circling overhead as if hypnotized by the white light beaming off the casinos.

Just after 1 a.m., he found a few friends sharing a case of Budweiser on a wooden walkway leading to the beach. They were quick to offer him a beer and, once he had drained it, to toss him a second one.

"We all look out for one another," Mr. Cherry said. "That's the thing about the group. If you don't see someone for a few days, you start to worry."

Indeed, the riders have formed a family of sorts, complete with feuds and alliances. They make dates to visit certain casinos, and trade bus tickets when one person wants to leave early and another wants to stay late. The camaraderie transforms what could be an excruciatingly lonely existence into an almost festive nightly adventure.

Around 2 a.m., Mr. Cherry wandered into the Trump Taj Mahal, a gaudy assemblage of gilded ceilings and giant chandeliers. A small group of riders had clustered at a bank of slot machines, sipping cocktails while dropping in an occasional quarter.

One of them, who gave his name only as Slick, explaining that he owed child support payments and did not want to get in trouble with the law, was nursing a Long Island iced tea. He happily accepted Mr. Cherry's doggie bag of leftover fish.

Although Slick is homeless, he has a steady job, lugging bolts of fabric into trucks at a warehouse in Newark. "I lost $80," he said between bites. "But I don't care. Tomorrow is payday."

Plopping himself down at a slot machine just long enough to give the impression that he might be gambling, Mr. Cherry ordered his free drink, in this case gin. Although free drinks are reserved for players, some waitresses seem willing to look the other way. A Taj Mahal waitress named Nancy Negron smiled coyly when asked if a good tip might persuade her to bend the rules. "That changes it a little bit," she said.

•

FOR the most part, the riders become invisible once they enter a casino, often scurrying off to a designated waiting area for bus patrons, where they can catch a few hours of sleep. The players are generally too preoccupied to notice nongamblers, and those who do rarely complain.

"If you don't use the bus shelter, you're not going to see them," said David Robinson, a pet store manager from South Jersey who had just finished a night of poker and blackjack at the Showboat Atlantic City and stopped to use a restroom near its bus lobby. Glancing at the riders asleep in their chairs, he added, "For me, no, it's not a problem."

While homeless people can be found at most of the bus lobbies, the one at the Taj is especially popular among the riders because its rows of purple, fabric-covered chairs are uninterrupted by armrests, making them ideal for lying down. Mr. Cherry calls it the "living room" because so many riders, at times 20 or more, can be seen splayed out there. "The only thing that's missing," he said, "is the 22-inch TV."

Just after 3 a.m., a frizzy-haired woman was working on a word-search puzzle, with her sleeping boyfriend's head on her lap. The woman said she had been coming to Atlantic City every night for years. "I like the lights," she said with a shrug.

One homeless man was camped out at the end of the room, in a spot he knew was unmonitored by security cameras. Even sitting upright, the man slept soundly, with his head tilted back and his mouth wide open. His backpack strap was wrapped around his wrist, a defensive habit learned years ago, when he used to sleep on subway trains.

In an earlier conversation, the man had described once waking up on the subway to find only the strap left around his arm; a thief had cut off the bag of his backpack. Though he has been kicked out of casinos by security guards, he said, he feels safer in Atlantic City than he did on the subway or in homeless shelters. "It's better than being on the streets, especially in the cooler months," he said. "And that's 10 months a year in New York."

Every so often, a security guard walked through the room, rousing riders and demanding to see their bus tickets. The guard, who declined to give his name, said he usually made two passes through the room each night, or more if other bus patrons complained about the sight, or smell, of the homeless riders. But other than wake them up from time to time, he said, "there's not much more I can do about it."

Michael Sampson, director of marketing administration for Trump Entertainment Resorts, which runs three Atlantic City casinos including the Taj Mahal, expressed similar resignation. "I've been in the business for 20 years," he said. "It's been a problem that we've dealt with for 20 years."

•

THE homeless among Chinatown casino-bus riders are indistinguishable from other frequent visitors to the casinos, many of whom do go to gamble, or simply to enjoy the trip. This fact makes it impossible to estimate the number of homeless people aboard the buses, but it also works to their advantage, making them difficult to weed out.

Peter Kim, whose company runs 13 buses from Chinatown to Atlantic City each day, estimates that 30 percent of his roughly 650 daily passengers are just along for the ride. "As long as they're not causing any problems," Mr. Kim said, "they are always welcome."

Some residents of Chinatown are less welcoming. Occupants of Confucius Plaza, a residential co-op that overlooks the pickup site, are urging the city to force the buses to relocate, complaining that riders—homeless and otherwise—bring litter, public urination and foul language to their street.

"I am pretty sympathetic to homeless people," said Justin Yu, vice president of the co-op board. "But the sidewalk is not a shelter."

For now, the bus operators have agreed only to move a block south, to Chatham Square. Their desire to maintain the status quo bodes well for Mr. Cherry. By 5 a.m., as this night was ending and the sky framed by the windshield of the bus faded from deep purple to silver, he was fast asleep on his way back to New York. An hour later, the Manhattan skyline appeared, resplendent at daybreak. When the bus pulled into Chinatown, around 7 a.m., Mr. Cherry trotted off to a corner store and bought two cans of malt liquor to drink as he waited for the 9 a.m. bus back to New Jersey.

Could he imagine growing weary of this endless cycle? he was asked. He shook his head.

"As long as Atlantic City is open," he said, "I will be coming out. You know what, honestly? I'm living the high life now."

August 5, 2007

7

Werner Kleeman's Private War

Though Today He Lives Quietly in Flushing, Queens,
More than 60 Years Ago, as an American Soldier,
This Holocaust Survivor Returned to His Native Germany
to Arrest the Nazi Who Had Arrested Him.

RICHARD FIRSTMAN

Werner Kleeman, Holocaust survivor and World War II soldier. *(Uli Seit/The
New York Times)*

FOR 56 years, Werner Kleeman's corner of the world has been a small house on a quiet street in Flushing, Queens, a brick, Cape Cod–style two-family house that is one of a row of similar homes built on a former potato farm during the Depression. Mr. Kleeman and his wife, Lore, raised their two daughters in the house, on 196th Place, and he made his living under the same roof.

He sold commercial-grade curtains and carpeting to institutions but never felt the need to move his business out of the house or to hire even one employee. He used the basement as his workshop and the upstairs kitchen as his office. He worked 90-hour weeks, which can happen when you do everything yourself.

At 88, he still hands out a business card that reads "Werner Kleeman, Interior Decorator."

Mr. Kleeman's wife died in 1979, and his daughters got married, had children and moved to Long Island, though both return to the neighborhood five days a week to teach in local schools. Now, most of his neighbors are Korean immigrants—"fine, good people, good friends," he says with the guttural inflection of his German roots—and the synagogue of which he was a devoted member and leader for nearly half a century, Flushing Jewish Center, has been replaced by a Korean church.

But Mr. Kleeman has stayed put. He remains tall and vigorous, with broad shoulders and a head of wavy white hair. He routinely breaks into a hearty, infectious laugh that makes it easy to imagine him as the bouncy young man in the photographs that appear in "From Dachau to D-Day," his recently published memoir.

Today is Veterans Day, but to him it will be just another day. "I don't parade at my age," Mr. Kleeman jokes. And he doesn't need a national holiday to remind him of his years in uniform. He thinks about them nearly every day.

As the title of his memoir suggests, Mr. Kleeman has a story to tell, one that transcends the boundaries of his life as a drapery salesman from Queens. It is a story that conveys, within one man's experience, two of the classic personal narratives of World War II. First is the story of the Jewish teenager in 1930's Germany who narrowly escapes the Holocaust. Second is the story of the American soldier who lands at Normandy on D-Day and lives to tell his grandchildren about it.

All this played out over a seven-year period that ended more than 60 years ago, but the pieces fit together to form the defining experience of Mr. Kleeman's life. And so here he sits, on an old sofa in his downstairs living room, matter-of-factly telling a visitor things that for decades he told almost no one.

•

WERNER KLEEMAN was the third of five children of a successful grain merchant in the Bavarian village of Gaukönigshofen. He was 13, a few months removed from his bar mitzvah in the village's small Orthodox synagogue, when Adolf Hitler seized power in January 1933.

Life for Jews in Germany deteriorated steadily. At 14, Werner was thrown out of school, and by 1936, the Kleeman family had been stripped of its livelihood by laws forbidding German Christians to do business with Jews.

With the situation worsening, Werner and his older brothers, Theo and Sigfried, began looking for ways to leave Germany. Theo emigrated to Palestine, while Sigfried went to the American Consulate in Stuttgart to apply for a visa to enter the United States. Werner followed suit when he turned 16, writing to ask a distant cousin in Nebraska to sponsor his emigration to the United States.

In the fall of 1938, after two years of waiting, Sigfried was informed that his visa had been approved, and on Nov. 9, he and Werner drove to Stuttgart to complete the paperwork.

They arrived not a moment too soon. Emerging from the consulate that afternoon, the brothers saw gangs of marauding Nazis destroying Jewish businesses, homes and synagogues. That night would be known as Kristallnacht, or Night of Broken Glass, the start of a two-day rampage against Germany's Jews and the first incendiary event of the Holocaust.

As Sigfried headed for a train to Switzerland, Werner spent the night hiding in the home of a local farmer, then headed back to his village to find his home in disarray: windows smashed, bedding slashed, floors strewn with shattered dishes and glasses.

His father was gone. Along with the rest of the Jewish men of the village, he had been arrested and turned over to Nazi officials by towns-people the family had known for years.

"Within one day, the whole community turned against us and the other Jews," Mr. Kleeman said. "The anti-Semitism was building up for a long time, but you didn't expect it to explode so suddenly and so brutally."

Mr. Kleeman had not been home for long before a local innkeeper, a Nazi party member, showed up to arrest him as well. He was taken to a jail in a nearby town and put in a cell with his father. A week later, Mr. Kleeman's father and some other older men were suddenly released on the basis of their service in the German Army during World War I. A few weeks after that, Werner Kleeman was aboard a bus headed for Dachau.

Later on, there would be no escape from the Nazi concentration camps. But the 30,000 men seized during the Kristallnacht rampage, the first victims of the Nazis' mass imprisonment of Jews, had a way out. At this early stage, the Germans were releasing prisoners with documented arrangements to leave the country.

Werner Kleeman was one of the lucky ones. In December, less than two months after his arrest, he received a letter from the British Consulate in Frankfurt informing him that he could enter England, thanks to the cousin in Nebraska, who had deposited money in his kinsman's name in a London bank. In early January 1939, Mr. Kleeman walked out of Dachau, went home, packed a suitcase and rode a train six hours to the coast of the Netherlands.

"The moment I crossed the border," he said, "I no longer considered myself a German."

•

It took a year for Mr. Kleeman's American visa to be approved, and another nine months for him to save enough money to buy the cheapest ticket for a ship sailing from Britain. In November 1940, after a 12-day journey across the Atlantic, he arrived in New York with two suitcases, $2 and the address of a cousin in Jackson Heights, Queens.

A year later, the United States entered the war. Immigrants were eligible for military service, and nine months after the attack on Pearl Harbor, Mr. Kleeman was drafted. As a member of the Army's Fourth Motorized Division, 22nd Infantry, he spent more than a year at various bases on the East Coast, training for the amphibious invasion of Europe.

In January 1944, the division shipped out from Fort Hamilton, Brooklyn. Mr. Kleeman found himself on another 12-day voyage across the Atlantic, headed back to England to fight the Nazis he had escaped five years earlier.

In Britain, he was transferred to division headquarters to serve as a post-invasion interpreter, an assignment in which he would forge several lifelong friendships, one of them with a counterintelligence man named Jerry Salinger, who wanted to be a writer.

"Jerry was just a nice little boy then," Mr. Kleeman said of the man who would become the celebrated J. D. Salinger. "He was kind of quiet."

The two men were together when their unit landed at Normandy on the afternoon of June 6, 1944, part of the second wave of the D-Day assault. Like every other serviceman who lived to tell about it, Mr. Kleeman has his own intensely personal memories of the war's most mythical collective experience.

He is reminded every day of a ferocious Air Force assault seven weeks after the landing, bombing so intense that it left him with permanent hearing loss. During those assaults, he took cover in a shed next to a stone house, where he found himself under a table with Ernie Pyle, the famous war correspondent.

"The bombs were crashing around us," Pyle later wrote. "We lay with our heads slightly up—like two snakes—staring at each other. We just lay sprawled, gaping at each other in a futile appeal, our faces about a foot apart, until it was over. There is no description of the sound and fury of those bombs except to say that it was chaos, a waiting for darkness."

•

FOR Mr. Kleeman, Normandy was more than a battlefield. It was a gateway to his past. Over the next few months, the Army pushed farther inland through France. Eventually Mr. Kleeman touched German soil for the first time since his harrowing departure six years earlier.

In the spring of 1945, just days after Germany's surrender, Mr. Kleeman received permission to travel to his hometown. He walked through Gaukönigshofen in stunned silence, seeing people he had known all his life but keeping his distance. The synagogue was a shell, a place for the town's fire brigade to store its equipment. From an old friend of his father's, he learned that all the Jews in the village had been taken by the Nazis, and none had come back.

Finally, Mr. Kleeman reached the home in which he had grown up. A 200-year-old house built like a fortress, the place was dilapidated and teeming with French laborers who were virtual prisoners of war; the photograph Mr. Kleeman took appears in his memoir.

Mr. Kleeman returned to the village a few weeks later, this time without the permission of his superiors. For several weeks, he worked for the United States Army captain in charge of the district's military occupation government. He also visited some of his former neighbors, among them an old man, "a very good friend of the Jews, a righteous Christian," Mr. Kleeman wrote in his memoir.

"We discussed everything that had transpired during those terrible years," Mr. Kleeman wrote, "and after we spoke, he told me he had something for me."

The man brought out a suitcase, and inside were a kiddush cup, a ceremonial wine goblet; a candleholder with a spice box in its base; and a 300-year-old "memorial book," handwritten in Hebrew—all items that the man had taken from the synagogue before it was destroyed. Mr. Kleeman would later donate the book to Yad Vashem, the Holocaust memorial in Jerusalem, but he kept the goblet and the candleholder.

That visit was an epiphany. It dawned on him why he had returned to his ancestral village. For weeks, he had seen the very people who had taken part in the destruction and persecution of Kristallnacht, and he had avoided them. Even though he was now the one in uniform and carrying a gun, he wrote, he "was still threatened and still scared." But now, he was ready to seize control.

Following military protocol, Mr. Kleeman traveled around the village with the local police, who dutifully arrested everyone he pointed out to them. In each case, he specified what the man had done, and the person was ordered to sign a confession. But there was one individual whom Mr. Kleeman wanted to arrest by himself: the innkeeper and Nazi party member who had arrested him that November day in 1938.

Mr. Kleeman appeared at the man's doorstep, gun in hand.

"He knew who I was," Mr. Kleeman said recently. "I didn't have to say anything. I put him on the hood of my jeep and took him to the same prison where he put me. A few days later, his wife comes to me begging. I told her, 'Out!'"

•

THESE days, Mr. Kleeman is eager to tell his story, but this wasn't always the case. When his daughters were growing up, and even in their early adult years, their father made clear that he didn't want to talk about his life in Germany before the war, or his experiences in the Army.

"We would ask and he wouldn't answer," his daughter Debby Schenkein said. "We were dying to know his story, but he just didn't want to talk about it. We wouldn't press him."

Not until 1984 did Mr. Kleeman first began speaking about those years. At an Army reunion in Pennsylvania that spring, an NBC News producer named Roberta Oster, who was working on a program marking the 40th anniversary of D-Day, persuaded him to do an interview with Tom Brokaw on the beach at Normandy. After the interview, Mr. Kleeman, accompanied by his older daughter, revisited his hometown in Germany. Little by little, the story unfolded.

Ms. Oster, moved by his experiences, encouraged Mr. Kleeman to write a memoir, but the project did not get off the ground until 2004, when his daughter Debby met Elizabeth Uhlig, a librarian-turned-writer who speaks German. Ms. Uhlig worked with Mr. Kleeman for two years, drawing out the details of his experiences. The book was published in August by Marble House Editions, a small press in Rego Park, Queens.

"The main reason I did it was that the children and grandchildren demanded it from me," Mr. Kleeman said. "I showed it to people before it was printed, and they all came back that it's very beautiful and down to earth. So it made me feel good."

Mr. Kleeman has found that telling the story of his earlier life has given his later years meaning. A reception for his book's publication was recently held at the Kupferberg Holocaust Resource Center and Archives at Queensborough Community College, and Arthur Flug, the center's executive director, hopes to keep Mr. Kleeman busy with speaking engagements. "I am happy to talk to anyone who wants to listen," Mr. Kleeman says.

Sometimes when he tells a piece of his story, he interrupts himself to go into another room, returning a minute later with a file or a book or a letter.

"This is the court record of the men I arrested," he said after one such foray. "A young man wrote a book on the history of Gaukönigshofen, and he found it in the courthouse. You see, they only used their initials—they were still being protected. Most of them only got a little time in jail."

November 11, 2007

8

The Chicken and Rice Man

Every Day of the Year, Jorge Muñoz Feeds the Mostly
Homeless Men Who Congregate under the Roosevelt
Avenue El in Jackson Heights, Queens. "He Got No Life,"
His Sister Said of Him. "But He Got a Big Heart."

ADAM B. ELLICK

Jorge Muñoz, right, with some of the day laborers he feeds. *(Oscar Hidalgo/The New York Times)*

EVERY weekday, starting as early as 7 in the morning and continuing until 7 at night, weary-looking men dressed in threadbare jackets and worn running shoes gather at the corner of Roosevelt Avenue and 73rd Street in Jackson Heights, Queens, under the gloomy shadow of the el.

Swiveling their heads as if watching a tennis match, the men scan each passing car, in the hope that a driver will stop and offer up $100 in exchange for a 10-hour day of grueling labor on a construction or demolition project on Long Island.

But offers of work are few these days, and competition for jobs is intense. As winter approaches, a man can easily spend the entire day shivering and desperately hungry, because these day laborers, many of them from Mexico or elsewhere in Latin America, are not only poor immigrants in need of work; many are also homeless, or nearly.

"We come here to look for work," said a 47-year-old Ecuadorean named Carlos Suarez as he hugged a cheap leopard-print comforter that serves as his bed. "There is none. What can we do?"

Mr. Suarez says that he has sometimes gone days without eating and has on occasion survived only on bread. But for the past three months, he has eaten at least one hot meal a day, thanks to a former illegal immigrant who, with the help of his mother, has become a guardian angel for these workers.

The man, Jorge Muñoz, is an elfin 43-year-old who goes by the nickname Colombia, a reference to the country from which he emigrated 21 years ago.

Every night around 9:30, he arrives at the intersection from his home in Woodhaven, driving a white pickup truck laden with enough home-cooked fare to feed the dozens of day laborers who congregate there.

For many New Yorkers, Thanksgiving is a weekend to indulge in a brief stint of volunteerism at a church or soup kitchen. For Mr. Muñoz, the holiday is just another night devoted to feeding his unofficial flock.

"Every single night, Jorge is here," said one worker, his leathery face peering out from a hooded sweatshirt. "Doesn't matter. Rain, thunderstorm, lightning. He do that from his good will, you know.

"He feeds everybody, make the stomach happy," the worker added. "He's an angel."

•

WHEN Mr. Muñoz's truck pulled in, several workers pressed their faces to the tinted windows, hoping to catch a glimpse of dinner. Hopping into the back of the truck, Mr. Muñoz began untying steaming containers filled with hot chocolate and foil-covered trays of homemade barbecued chicken. As the workers accepted Styrofoam containers stuffed with hearty portions of chicken and rice, they thanked him as respectfully as if he were a parent, never mind that the 5-foot-2 Mr. Muñoz, with his buzz cut and boyish grin, could pass for 20-something.

"God bless you," one burly worker said as he dug into his meal. "I haven't eaten in three days."

Mr. Muñoz replied with a smile, "You can eat here every day at 9:30."

The relationship between Mr. Muñoz and many of the men he feeds is personal. "Uribe, you want more coffee?" he asked as he saw a familiar face. "Simon, do you want seconds on this pasta?"

In a way, Mr. Muñoz seems to need these men as much as they need him. His unofficial meal program gives meaning and focus to his life. He is as eager to help his motley clientele as they are to be helped.

"I know these people are waiting for me," he said of the emotions that fuel his quixotic and perhaps obsessive crusade. "And I worry about them. You have to see their smile, man. That's the way I get paid."

THE operation through which these workers have been fed without charge began three years ago and is financed mainly from the $600 a week Mr. Muñoz earns driving a school bus.

His life revolves almost entirely around preparing and serving the meals. All the cooking is done in the small house with gray vinyl siding where he lives with his 66-year-old mother, Doris Zapata, and his sister, Luz, who works for the Social Security Administration.

He telephones home from the road a dozen times a day to plan the menus. He has few friends, and no hobbies.

"I haven't seen a movie in two years," Mr. Muñoz said one afternoon in his kitchen as he boiled milk for hot chocolate. "But sometimes I listen to music when I'm driving."

His sister described the situation more bluntly. "He got no life," she said, looking awkwardly away from her brother as she stirred a boiling pot of lentils. "But he got a big heart. He really does."

Mr. Muñoz also has stamina. Every morning he gets up at 4:45 to assess his inventory of food, which is made available in part with the help of friends and acquaintances. He doesn't have to go far.

A mammoth freezer that occupies nearly half the dining room is stocked with cooked meats and vegetables that he collects twice a week from Colombian acquaintances who work in the food industry on Long Island, but whose names Mr. Muñoz will not disclose so as not to jeopardize their jobs. The dining room table is laden with boxes of fresh but slightly wounded bagels and rolls donated weekly by Monteforte, an Italian bakery in Richmond Hill. From Tia Betty Mexica Bakery and Tortilleria in Woodhaven come bulging bags of sweet breads.

"One day Jorge just came in and asked for extra food for his guys," said Tomas Gutierrez, owner of Tia Betty. "Tortillas, breads—last week we made special tamales for his guys."

Mr. Muñoz's porch is walled with bulk-size bottles of ketchup and mayonnaise, and the living room is littered with the bounty from his weekly trips to Costco: 15 bags of spaghetti, six cans of tomato sauce, and boxes of plastic containers in front of the television. Mr. Muñoz says he has not watched the television in more than a year.

•

ALTHOUGH Ms. Zapata does not help deliver meals, she is an equal partner in her son's operation, and her involvement is born in part from her own experiences.

For the first years of her marriage, the family lived in a small city in Colombia. In 1974, her husband was killed when a passing truck sent a rock sailing into his head as he sat on a curb outside the coffee distribution factory where he worked. Although her parents visited monthly bringing food to feed Jorge and Luz, then 9 and 10, the help was not enough.

In 1984, after a decade of struggle, Ms. Zapata left her children with her parents and began the journey that eventually would take her to Bushwick, Brooklyn, where she found work as a live-in nanny, earning $120 a week.

Over the next two years she saved enough to bring her children to the city—all three are now United States citizens—but the osteoporosis and arthritis that have twisted her hands and hunched her back forced her into retirement seven years ago.

All these experiences have given her particular empathy for the workers her son feeds.

"We were immigrants and we were illegal," Ms. Zapata said one afternoon as she poured lemon juice into a bowl of rice. "So I imagine that the workers may also be going around in fear, hiding from the police, hiding from immigration."

Ms. Zapata thinks she understands the feelings that motivate her son, whom she calls Georgie. He always had a good Samaritan side, she said, which was on display when he was just 7 and a man came by their house asking for food.

Ms. Zapata told the visitor they had none. "But Jorge gave him his plate," she recalled. "I said, 'Jorge, you have to eat for school.' And he said, 'No, I'll just have bread.'"

●

THE mission shared by mother and son started three years ago when Colombian acquaintances who work in the food industry mentioned to Mr. Muñoz that excess food was thrown out at their workplaces. One evening around the same time, he noticed the knot of day laborers clustered under the el.

Stopping to talk, he learned that most of them sleep under the bridge across the Brooklyn-Queens Expressway at 69th Street or in the emergency room of Elmhurst Hospital, where they can stay until they are booted out at 5 a.m. To save money, they skimp on meals, and the little money they pocket is immediately wired to destitute relatives back home.

In the beginning, Mr. Muñoz's commitment to feeding these men was modest. Three nights a week, he stuffed each of eight brown bags with a piece of fruit, a cookie and a juice box, loaded the bags into his truck, and drove to the corner where the men congregated. Word spread, and within a year, Mr. Muñoz and his mother were churning out 15 hot dinners a night. Now they feed several dozen on a single evening.

"Once I started, I can't go back," he said as he headed off one recent evening. "Those guys are waiting for me. These guys, they got nothing. They live in the street. They have no family. They have no relatives, nothing. They just wait for me. And I say, 'O.K., no problem.'"

●

BECAUSE donations are sporadic and quantities unpredictable, cooking for a crowd in a kitchen the size of a parking space presents a nightly logistical challenge.

At 3 o'clock one recent afternoon, Ms. Zapata could be found staring dubiously at a tray of cooked, frozen barbecued chicken that had been donated by one of her son's benefactors. By 4, the chicken had thawed, but she estimated that it would feed only 20 people. Her son, who had just returned from his afternoon bus run, said 30 meals were needed. And so began the nightly process of ad hoc menu revision.

Time was of the essence. Mr. Muñoz tries hard to make sure the workers are fed at the same time every night; otherwise, he fears, he will lose them.

On a calendar pinned to the refrigerator, which bears 10 images of Christ, Ms. Zapata had scribbled the week's menus. Tuesday: baked pork with beans. Wednesday: burgers in barbecue sauce with hash browns. Thursday: pasta with beef.

As if seven nights weren't enough, on Fridays Mr. Muñoz collects donated waffles and pancakes, and he serves Saturday breakfast for 200 workers at seven locations in Queens. For Sunday dinner, on what he describes as his "day off," he and his sister make 40 ham and cheese sandwiches.

This afternoon, Mr. Muñoz and his mother scrutinized the week's menus to figure out what they could scrounge from storage without upending the rest of the week's schedule. After a quick survey of items on the porch, Mr. Muñoz decided on pasta with tuna.

Soon, pots on all four burners on the stove were bubbling with milk, pasta, and white and yellow rice. While waiting for the chicken to warm, Ms. Zapata and her children began sorting bills on a chair in a bedroom; no other space was available. Electricity runs about $120 a month, and gas $100 every two months.

According to Mr. Muñoz, the family spends about $200 a week on the meals.

"If I had a choice," he said, "I'd do a good breakfast with a proper budget. And I'd do lunch, too."

By 5 p.m. he was fading. He slouched against the kitchen wall and closed his eyes for a moment. Then he straightened up, poured his sixth cup of coffee of the day, and served himself a bowl of lentils over buttered rice. This was his dinner, and as the workers do, he ate standing up.

By 8:30, the truck was loaded. "Bye, Mami," Mr. Muñoz said as he gave his mother a kiss. "I love you."

En route, he stopped off at the International Ministerial Church of Jesus Christ in Woodside, as he does every night. When he arrived on the corner, the men lined up in single file in front of the bed of the truck, which functioned as a counter. He handed takeout containers to the men, who almost all returned for seconds. One man stuffed plastic boxes of orange juice into his pockets to tide him over until the next meal. Within 10 minutes, the truck was empty.

Mr. Muñoz tipped over the hot chocolate cooler. "I think there is a little bit left," he announced to one of the workers. "There is a little, brother. You got the last drop."

Hector Peralta, a ponytailed Mexican who came to the United States five years ago, has been eating Mr. Muñoz's dinners for four months. Without them, he said, he would go hungry. "We wouldn't even know what to do," he said. "This is my first meal since yesterday."

Gratitude goes both ways.

"I feel great when I see these guys with their smiling face," Mr. Muñoz said. "Because they got something to eat before they go to sleep."

November 25, 2007

Ana Toro contributed reporting.

9

A Life, Interrupted

The Young Woman, Who Had Been Missing for Nearly Three Weeks, Was Floating Face Down off the Southern Tip of Manhattan. Miraculously, She Was Rescued. But the Explanation for What Had Happened Raised Questions That Would Take a Long Time to Answer.

REBECCA FLINT MARX AND VYTENIS DIDZIULIS

Hannah Upp in Riverside Park. *(Nicole Bengiveno/The New York Times)*

THE young woman was floating face down in the water, about a mile southwest of the southern tip of Manhattan. Wearing only red running shorts and a black sports bra, she was barely visible to the naked eye of the captain of the Staten Island Ferry: When he caught sight of her bobbing head, it was like glimpsing the tip of a ballpoint pen across a busy city street. Less than four minutes later, a skiff piloted by two of the ferry's deckhands pulled up alongside the woman. One man took hold of her ankles while the other grabbed her shoulders. As she was lifted from the water, she gasped.

"I went from going for a run to being in the ambulance," the woman said several months later in describing her ordeal. "It was like 10 minutes had passed. But it was almost three weeks."

On Aug. 28, a Thursday, a 23-year-old schoolteacher from Hamilton Heights named Hannah Emily Upp went for a jog along Riverside Drive. That jog is the last thing that Ms. Upp says she remembers before the deckhands rescued her from the waters of New York Harbor on the morning of Tuesday, Sept. 16.

Rumors and speculation abounded about what befell Ms. Upp. She disappeared the day before the start of a new school year at Thurgood Marshall Academy, a Harlem school, where she taught Spanish. She left behind her wallet, her cellphone, her ID and a host of troubling questions.

It was as if the city had simply opened wide and swallowed her whole—until she was seen on a security camera at the Midtown Apple store checking her e-mail. Then she vanished again. And then reappeared, not only at the Apple store but also at a Starbucks and several New York Sports Clubs, where news reports said she went to shower.

Was she suffering from bipolar disorder? Running away from an overly demanding job? Escaping from a city that can overwhelm even the most resilient?

Other questions lingered. Did she forage for food? Where did she sleep? Most baffling of all, how did she survive for so long without money or any identification in one of the world's busiest and most complex cities?

That she was rescued, alive and well, is in itself amazing; most such stories do not have happy endings. But the explanation for what had happened raised even more questions than Ms. Upp's disappearance had—for her more than for anybody.

After her rescue, while she was recovering from hypothermia and dehydration at Richmond University Medical Center in Staten Island, she was told that she was suffering from dissociative fugue, a rare form of amnesia that causes people to forget their identity, suddenly and without warning, and can last from a few hours to years.

"It's weird," Ms. Upp said a few weeks ago over a cup of tea in a Hell's Kitchen cafe, the first time in the five months since her rescue that she had talked publicly about her experience. "How do you feel guilty for something you didn't even know you did? It's not your fault, but it's still somehow you. So it's definitely made me reconsider everything. Who was I before? Who was I then—is that part of me? Who am I now?"

•

THE answer to that last question, at least on the surface, is a bright, introspective young woman with an easy laugh and an expansive smile. Dressed this day for a job interview, she wore a black blazer and a knee-length skirt that contrasted with the slim silver hoop piercing her right nostril and the bright red metal wristwatch peeking out from beneath her sleeve.

She looked like any other recent college graduate negotiating the rapidly narrowing space between youth and adulthood. Her questions about her identity are, to some degree, no different from those of her peers who haven't had to deal with highly publicized memory loss.

"When you're just starting out, you have one job to your name: There's your professional identity and then there's who you are," she said. She may be questioning who she is after her experience, she added, "but everybody is." She laughed and added, "This is just extra."

Before she jogged out of her life that August day, Ms. Upp had a demanding schedule. The previous fall, after graduating from Bryn Mawr, she began teaching Spanish to more than 200 seventh and eighth graders at Thurgood Marshall Academy while studying for a master's degree in education at Pace University. It was a challenging job, but one she loved.

Ms. Upp also loved to travel. She grew up in a small town in Oregon, the daughter of two pastors (her mother, who lives in Philadelphia, and her father, who is in India, are divorced). While at college, Ms. Upp spent a semester in Buenos Aires, visited Ghana, Poland and Puerto Rico with the school's choir, and traveled with friends through Europe.

Last summer, she went to Japan to visit her brother, who is in the Navy, and to New Delhi to visit Piyali Bhattacharya, a close friend and former Bryn Mawr classmate.

"I asked her if she would be O.K. while I was at work, since she doesn't speak any Hindi and being a white woman in Delhi can be a bit daunting," Ms. Bhattacharya said in an e-mail message. "But as always, Hannah proved me wrong. She hopped off by herself, took a full tour of the Old City, admittedly the most difficult part of the city to navigate, and met me for coffee afterwards!"

THE medical condition diagnosed in Ms. Upp is so uncommon that few psychiatrists ever see it. Characterized in part by sudden and unexpected travel combined with an inability to recall one's past, dissociative fugue demonstrates the glasslike fragility of memory and identity.

Its most famous sufferer is the fictional Jason Bourne, the secret agent made flesh on film by Matt Damon. The Bourne character takes his name from Ansel Bourne, a Rhode Island preacher who suffered the earliest recorded case of the condition when he was en route to Providence in 1887. The preacher continued to Norristown, Pa., where he opened a store and lived with another family, until one day he "woke up."

The memory of how to perform mundane tasks like hailing a cab or even using the Internet remains intact. Victims lose only the memories tied to their identity.

"It's as if a whole set of information about one's self, our autobiography, goes off line," said Dr. Richard Loewenstein, one of the nation's few experts on dissociative fugue.

"We tend to experience our identity as a thing, as if it's a constant," added Dr. Loewenstein, who is medical director of the trauma program at Sheppard and Enoch Pratt Hospital in Baltimore, and has treated five patients with dissociative fugue. "But it's a lot less stable and has less unity than we want to believe."

Travel is a defining characteristic.

"People have been known to not only travel across cities or countries, but also across continents," said Dr. Philip Coons, a professor emeritus of psychiatry at Indiana University and the author of a book on the subject. "The explanation behind the fugue is that the person is running away from a bad situation, from a bad marriage or a bad financial situation."

WHEN Ms. Upp failed to return to her apartment after four days, her roommates contacted the police. After a week with no word, and fearing that she had been a victim of a kidnapping or another violent crime, her friends and family posted messages on blogs and started a Facebook page called "We're Not Giving Upp (on Hannah)," which was dedicated to tracking her down. Accompanying many postings was a photograph of a smiling young woman with warm hazel eyes, glossy brown hair and a white rose tucked behind one ear.

Despite the optimistic tone of the postings, her family was frantic.

"At first, you try to come up with any kind of possible theory that could provide a simple, harmless explanation of where she might be," her brother, Dan Upp, said from Japan. "But considering the circumstances, you really can't convince yourself that any of them are feasible, and you're left with the unavoidable conclusion that something is very wrong."

Ms. Upp credits the police with helping her piece together what happened during the missing weeks. Though details like where she ate and slept remain elusive to her, security camera footage and conversations with police detectives have provided some clues to the where if not the why.

According to police reports, Ms. Upp spent a lot of time in places like Riverside Drive, "where if you're in running gear, no one's going to look at you twice," she said. When she revisited Riverside Drive after leaving the hospital, Ms. Upp said, "it seemed to make sense to me. Not only is it one of my favorite places, but there's something soothing about the sound of water and just not feeling trapped in the concrete jungle."

Ms. Upp's doctors have helped her make sense of other clues, like her stops at the Apple store, where she was seen both checking her e-mail and speaking with a fellow Pace student.

"I was on a computer, but there's no evidence in my Gmail account of any e-mails being sent or read," Ms. Upp said. She did log in, something her doctors attributed to a muscle memory: How many times in our lives have we typed in our name and password without even thinking? "So their theory," Ms. Upp said, "is that I thought, hey, this is a computer, this is what I do with a computer." But once she opened her e-mail, she couldn't figure out who Hannah was and why everyone was looking for her. "So I logged out and left."

Her conversation with the Pace student had a similarly surreal quality. While Ms. Upp says she does not recall the meeting, a store security camera showed her speaking with the young man, who had asked her if she was the missing student everyone was trying to find. She said she wasn't.

News reports of her appearances at various New York Sports Club locations suggest that she was careful to keep moving, though Ms. Upp believes that the number of sightings was exaggerated. For one thing, she pointed out, she did not have her gym ID with her; for another, the gym knew she was missing and surely would have contacted the police had she appeared.

The one tangible clue to the extent of her travels was the large blister on her heel. In addition to the hypothermia, dehydration and a sunburn, the blister was the only physical record of her three weeks spent on the move, and it suggests why she eventually left the city's streets for its waterways: Her feet hurt.

"They think that just as I was wandering on land, I wandered in the water," Ms. Upp said. "I don't think I had a purpose. But I had that really big blister, so maybe I just didn't want my shoes on anymore."

•

CAPTAIN Christopher Covella, a mariner with 32 years of experience and more than 17,000 trips aboard Staten Island ferries to his credit, was in the pilot house of the John J. Marchi on Sept. 16, heading to Staten Island from Manhattan, when he saw something out of place.

"At 11:50 a.m. I noticed something in the water that didn't belong there," Captain Covella said. "All it was, was a head and it was slightly more than a quarter-mile away."

Slowing down the boat, he instructed two of his deckhands to prepare to enter the water near Robbins Reef, a tiny outcropping of land topped by a lighthouse just off the north shore of Staten Island. The two deckhands, Michael Sabatino, 28, and Ephriam Washington, 31, hung over the edge of the ferry in a 12-foot aluminum skiff as the captain edged his craft toward the island.

About 200 feet away from Ms. Upp, who was floating face down, the men were lowered into the water. When they reached her, Mr. Washington put his hands under Ms. Upp's arms, turned her face up, and, with the help of Mr. Sabatino, lifted her into the skiff.

"We realized that she was breathing and had no major cuts or bruises, so we decided to bring her back to St. George," Mr. Washington said. Three minutes later, they were at the Staten Island Ferry terminal.

After Ms. Upp's rescue, newspapers reported that she had jumped off a Staten Island pier in a suicide attempt. The reality, Ms. Upp said, was far less sensational, if almost as dramatic. Together with Captain Covella, she determined that it would have been impossible for her to jump off the pier and swim against the current to the spot where she was rescued. Instead, she believes that she left Manhattan from the Chelsea pier and kayak dock where she once attended a 9/11 memorial.

"From what I can piece together, I left Manhattan late at night," she said. "I've gone back over lunar records to figure out if there was a full moon then, which sounds right. At that point in the tidal records, the current would have been in my favor, so whether I was Olympic swimming or doggy paddling, I could have made it."

Made it, that is, to Robbins Reef, where she pulled herself ashore after swimming for several hours. She believes that she spent the next day sitting on the rocks around the lighthouse, a theory supported by the fresh sunburn she sported when she was rescued. She remained on the island until she returned to the water around 11 the following morning.

Then she was in an ambulance speeding toward the hospital. When her family and friends arrived, Ms. Upp said, "it was, wow, I'm happy to see you, but why are you so happy to see me?"

The day she was discharged, Ms. Upp posted a statement on the Facebook page her friends had created.

"I needed to publicly acknowledge my gratitude for everything, from search parties to people just caring," she said. "I did feel that I owed people at least some explanation," one that would put all the speculation to rest.

●

ALTHOUGH Ms. Upp was quickly courted by television talk shows, she decided to start rebuilding her life away from the spotlight. "Maybe people I've never met and never will meet will think I'm crazy," she acknowledged, "but maybe it's better than going on Oprah, you know?"

Initially, Ms. Upp said she believed that once she returned to her apartment, she would leave her ordeal in the past. But in some ways, it was just beginning. Never mind the reporter who showed up on her doorstep two hours after she arrived home; the larger question was whether she could resume her daily life without worrying about stumbling into another fugue. And would she forever be known as "that missing teacher"?

Ms. Upp considered leaving New York altogether, perhaps going to Japan to live with her brother. But, ultimately, she decided to stay.

"I didn't want my life to change in such a way that the things I enjoy I couldn't enjoy anymore," she said. "It was just, I can't let New York win."

Recovery has been slow. Simple social routines like seeing friends and taking a dance class have helped her re-establish her personal identity. Figuring out her professional identity has been harder. Ms. Upp is on leave from her teaching job, and though the post is still open to her, she is uncertain about returning. Was it significant, she wonders, that she disappeared the day before school started?

"There's a lot of room for self-doubt and confusion there," she said. "And, well, I don't know. I certainly would never have intended to do that, but it makes you wonder."

She wonders, too, about what caused the fugue state. So far, a possible catalyst has yet to emerge.

"That's the hardest thing," Ms. Upp acknowledged. "If I don't feel confident about the trigger, how do you start with prevention?"

She has learned, however, that fugues are usually isolated events.

"If you work through it, you can usually go on to live a normal life," she said. "Obviously, the hardest part is the period right after. It's textbook that you feel shame, you feel embarrassed, you feel guilt—all things I've definitely felt."

She has also experienced something rarely afforded to anyone in this city: the chance to slow down.

"If anything," she said, "I've gotten a time to really appreciate what normal life is like. I've never had a moment in my life where I've just stopped and said, hold on, let's re-evaluate everything."

Ms. Upp's friends have no doubt about her ability to move on.

"If Hannah doesn't want to let this incident eat away at the rest of her life, then it won't be an issue any more than the common cold is an issue to you or me," Ms. Bhattacharya said. "She's an incredibly strong woman who knows how to deal with a ghost and then release it."

And day by day, she works to put the "missing teacher" label behind her.

"My roommates and I have a code word to show that I'm not going to fugue again," Ms. Upp said. "My roommate had done this long interview with ABC, and the only thing they ended up printing was that I was a friendly vegetarian who likes to try new dishes. So if I don't get home one night, they'll text me, like, 'friendly vegetarian.' And I'll say, 'who likes to try new dishes.' And we know we're on the same page."

March 1, 2009

10

When Johnny Comes Marching In

The Man in Camouflage Walked into the Literary Bar in the East Village, His Army Backpack Slung over His Shoulder. And No One Said a Word.

HELEN BENEDICT

(Kyle T. Webster)

THE other night I was in a literary bar in the East Village, the kind of place where nervous poets, novelists and memoirists read their work to other nervous poets, novelists and memoirists, when in walked a tall, strapping soldier in full desert camouflage.

He said something to the bartender, downed a beer, hitched his huge Army backpack farther up his shoulder, sent a shy grin out to the room and left. Nobody looked at him; nobody grinned back—I glanced around to check. It was as if an unwelcome ghost had entered the room, a harbinger of bad news we didn't want to acknowledge.

I know it's the New York way not to stare. We don't stare at anybody, celebrities, crazies or ghosts, let alone soldiers. But it bothered me that everybody pretended not to have noticed him, and it bothered me that neither I nor anyone else had said hi or welcome or how are you doing?

I felt a class and political chasm open right there in the bar as I sipped my white wine. Here we were, a room full of writers, students and other privileged Manhattan types. And there was he, a young soldier reminding us that we are indeed at war, but that it's not being fought by the likes of us.

It's only too easy to live in New York, particularly Manhattan, and almost never see a uniformed soldier, let alone talk to one. They are a rare sight even in the subway and the streets, let alone in the literary bars of the city. But that young soldier got me to thinking: Is the invisibility of soldiers in New York keeping us out of touch with the fact that we are at war? And is it keeping us out of touch with who soldiers really are and what they really think?

In smaller cities and rural towns all over the country, the war is present because soldiers are. Even in New Jersey, this is the case. All you have to do is hop the PATH train to Jersey City, about an hour from Fort Dix, to find yourself surrounded by soldiers.

In fact, I met a soldier because of the PATH train once. A middle-aged Nicaraguan was sitting next to me on the train, and we began the usual grumbling about delayed trains, which led to a conversation about the economy and the cost of the Iraq war, which then led to his telling me about his son. "He joined up to get his citizenship," he told me. "Now he is back from Iraq and he's all screwed up."

I expressed sympathy and I told him that I'd been reading a lot about the war lately.

"I don't want my son in this crazy war," he said, pulling his cellphone out of his pocket. "Call him, please. Tell him not to go back." And he thrust the phone at me.

A few minutes later, I found myself standing outside on the sidewalk with this man, talking to his very surprised son on his father's phone. I didn't tell him not to go back; why would he listen to me? But I did ask him how he was doing. I expected the usual gung-ho patriotism because that's what I heard all the time from soldiers quoted in the news. But he surprised me.

"I don't know; I feel weird," he said. "I'm completely different. My temper's changed. My marriage is falling apart—I'm getting divorced. I've forgotten how to be a father. My wife, she's not understanding because she wasn't there. I'm going to be redeployed to Afghanistan. I'm scared but I'm going because I don't know how to fit in here anymore."

●

ON the way back to Midtown that same day, I was surrounded by soldiers. We were in one of those quaint, rattle-trap minivans that ferry people from Midtown to New Jersey and back, and behind me a young man was saying: "Yeah, I joined 'cause all my friends were headed for gangs or jail and I didn't want that to be me. So I spend a year over there, come back, and they're all in gangs or jail. There's nothing here for me. I'm going to re-enlist."

After that, I began to seek soldiers out and talk to them. And almost every one of them said things I didn't expect and told me things I didn't know.

So when I saw that soldier in the literary bar, I had a hard time listening to the next nervous poet read at the lectern. I couldn't stop thinking that the soldier really was a kind of apparition, a physical manifestation of the fact that we're at war. A young American in his Army uniform, he was either on his way to kill others in our name, or on his way back from having already done so. This was the uncomfortable if barely conscious thought, I suspect, that made us turn our backs on him.

I'm not saying that New Yorkers are apolitical. Quite the contrary. Most of the people I know here are passionate about politics, especially about the war in Iraq. They have written articles, plays and poems about it, marched in the streets to protest it, voted for President Obama in the hope of ending it. Yet most of them don't know a single soldier. And because of this, many assume that soldiers and liberal New Yorkers will never be able to talk.

Soon, though, this chasm might start to narrow. With the Iraq war winding down, the economy driving up recruits and the new G.I. bill offering better tuition benefits, soldiers will be showing up everywhere: in our streets and subways, our classrooms and, yes, our literary bars.

I wonder what we New Yorkers will do. Will we continue to ignore them in disapproval or fear? Or will we be willing to greet them and listen to the surprising things they have to say?

April 12, 2009

PART TWO

Places in the City's Heart

11

Razzle-Dazzle Me

Times Square Is Successful Because People Wait in Huge
Hordes, in Numbers the Size of Entire Towns in
North Dakota, for the Light to Change.

ROBERT SULLIVAN

(Photo illustration by Ivan Chermayeff)

FROM the window of a plane at night, when everyone seems to be asleep and the movie is over and the cabin lights have been dimmed, when you're exhausted and have been away from New York long enough to miss it (even though no sane person would miss your rent), when your captain heads to La Guardia by heading up the Hudson, then Times Square, that clearly discernible ribbony intersection, is a beacon, a canyon of brilliantness, an electrified message, a flashlight that makes it possible to read your magazine in your window seat without even turning on your overhead light. From the ground, Times Square does not seem so concentrated, though it is a canyon, and I love driving into Times Square at night, coming down Broadway into the chasm of absolute illumination. And if you climb out of the Times Square station, you are in a room in which you accidentally left the light on.

In Times Square, it is as if an entire city has woken up at 2 a.m. and found the TV blaring.

Maybe on the back roads of Ohio, in a beautiful small town that has yet to be Wal-Marted out of existence, there is an old country restaurant in which a steaming apple pie is being placed on a well-cleaned counter, and if so, that is a picture of the heart of America, the romantic postcard. Times Square, on the other hand, is the picture of America's guts, the country's capitalistic machinations exposed like the plumbing on the Pompidou Center in Paris. See the lights, the ads, the logos all blinking, flashing, shouting, hawking, selling. Sales is the protoplasm running through Times Square.

•

THE birthday of Times Square is the birthday of its most recent naming, in 1904, when Adolph S. Ochs, the publisher of The New York Times, moved to the square, formerly known as Long Acre. Long Acre Square at the time was an exclusive residential neighborhood in decline, last known for what were referred to as silk-hat brothels, which just goes to show that the sale of sex predated Times Square. When the railroads and the subways built stations in Midtown, Midtown became the city's commercial center. The theaters followed, along with their signs, and Times Square became the Crossroads of the World.

In an unnoticed historical coincidence, one of its most famous advertising props, the Pepsi-Cola waterfall, which required 35,000 bulbs and 20,000 gallons of water a day, was at Broadway between 44th and 45th, where once there was a well-known spring. The spring bubbled along

Bloomingdale Road, the name for Broadway when Times Square was mostly a meadow on the farm of Medcef Eden, a friend of Aaron Burr's whose name is forever preserved in the name of an often rat-infested lane near the South Street Seaport called Eden's Alley. "The Lion King" rules Times Square now, along with Andrew Lloyd Webber's latest. (The adult entertainment industry, meanwhile, has moved about five blocks west, where businessmen sneak into and stumble out of the new Hustler Palace, which, with its lights and giant billboard and glorified logo, looks like something out of Times Square, a Disneyfied porn palace.)

And there are signs. There are electric plasma signs and fiber-optic lights. Kodak uses a 59-by-52-foot fluorescent vinyl panel and a Jumbo-Tron. The facade of Nasdaq's building is entirely L.E.D.'s, 18 million of them that glow to show a stock ticker and market news. The building at 1 Times Square is host to the mother of all tickers and makes more money selling space on the sign than it does on rent. Who needs pain-in-the-neck tenants, the building managers have said, when you've got the largest sign tower in the world?

Is the new Times Square better? Are the buildings aesthetically interesting? Is the commercial mix correct? The argument is always binary. Old Times Square: dirty, unsafe, bad. New Times Square: clean, safe, good. But the real question is: Why are so many people there? And the answer is that people want to be with people, whether they're buying jewels or eating hot dogs. People make people feel safe and unsafe; a crowd draws a crowd.

I can't believe that having the ubiquitous Virgin Megastore is better for Times Square, but it's certainly not worse. It attracts tourists who, while gawking, can be gawked at by locals, which is like bats dining on moths near a streetlight. And chain stores offer shopping, even if the shopping can feel pornographic, shopping without meaning, for immediate gratification, for the lust of it.

The continual debate over Times Square development ignores the almost mystical aspect of the mob, and it forgets a few facts. To write "City," a 1988 book that examines the maneuverings of pedestrians in New York and other urban places, William H. Whyte sat in front of an old hotel in Times Square and charted the movements of prostitutes, johns and pimps. Mr. Whyte described the Times Square subways as "the national cesspool"—he was working, remember, predevelopment, when Times Square was its most "Midnight Cowboy"—but he noted too that the street vendors, the watch sellers, the guy bumming a dollar, even the pimp, were all there for the crowds, and, contrary to what urban planners and developers sometimes think, are like canaries in the coal mine with regard to the health of the city. When they go, the people are about to go too, which is why it was good to see the guy in the giant shimmering hat, Mighty Ducks jersey and Mardi Gras beads offering rhymes for sale at 44th Street and Broadway the other day: "Yo, lady on your cellphone / Talkin' to you homey at home."

Times Square is successful precisely because everybody comes up out of the ground and nearly runs into each other on the way to everything. Times Square is successful because there are people in the subways at night, along with cops and new tile walls and a Jacob Lawrence mural. Times Square is successful because you can stand on Broadway at 4 a.m. and watch a guy in a rat suit walk by, carrying a backpack and looking straight ahead, I swear. Times Square is successful because people wait in huge hordes, in numbers the size of entire towns in North Dakota, for the light to change so they can cross the street.

If you stand on one of the concrete islands in the traffic stream, you can turn your head slowly, like a panoramic camera, and see a prose poem of publicity, a whitewater rapid of wordy words: "Razzle Chicago Dazzle Geodon oral capsules South Pole, the Authentic Urban Brand for the Real World Can Your Network Think for Itself? George Michael. Patience. The New Album in Stores Now Get the Attention You Deserve. TrimSpa Fetish. Get It While It's Hot 1800Mattress. Free Checking Delux. Live Your Dreams. Pass It On Change a Dog's Life. Just Ask Your Veterinarian. Deramaxx 'Glittering'"

GLITTERING, yes, and underlined visually by curves of fleshy flesh, by Madonna in a Marie Antoinette outfit, by guys with swords, by a medieval henchman standing ominously over a Honda motorcycle, by that thing you see so often in Times Square, and in life, such that it becomes like seeing a utility pole over and over along the side of a highway, the celebrity, from the Latin, celebrare, to frequent.

And in the tower at the southern end of Times Square, beneath the giant cup of soup, you see a giant TV screen, itself the combined advertisement of Panasonic and NBC, showing images of the phrase "Welcome to Times Square," and then images of Times Square itself, including the Panasonic and NBC TV screen. In the giant image of the giant image of Times Square, Times Square falls into its own rabbit hole, disappears in its virtual self.

I love Times Square and have for years, when it was seedy and I found my first full-time job and had a drink to toast it with my friend Dave in a now knocked-down bar called Dave's (no relation), when I always played a video game for good luck after dropping off unsolicited manuscripts to various publishing companies in the area, when I strollered my toddler son up from SoHo, where his mom worked, and we watched all the New Times Square construction and, once, saw a crowd ignore a stack of burning boxes as we searched in vain for a cop.

I was in Times Square on Sept. 11, 2001, and I saw the plume as I looked down Seventh Avenue. The crowd was small by Times Square standards, an unnerving thing in itself. At one point someone thought they had heard a shot and then screamed, at which point the crowd became a running mass and then a stampeding mob, even though there was no shot, no gunfire.

More recently, I poked around on the islands in the stream of Broadway and Seventh Avenue, as I like to do, especially at lunchtime. I lingered over the very low-tech terrazzo map of the city on the police information booth. I saw seven trees in front of the Marriott Marquis, quivering in the breeze like cottonwood on a riverbank. Then I ate lunch in Duffy Square, the square within the square. I watched a pigeon sit on the dung-covered pate of George M. Cohan, famous Broadway song-and-dance man. And I looked back at Father Francis Duffy himself, chaplain of New York's 69th Regiment, an Army unit with a theatrical connection, James Cagney's film "The Fighting 69th."

For me, Father Duffy guards the place, holding back the crass materialism like Hercules holding up the world, with hope, with his 17-foot-tall granite Celtic cross, half Catholic, half pagan, summoning the powers of God and gods and the logoless earth from whence the granite came.

Once, just after I moved away from New York for a while, I went camping alone in some Western woods, way up on a mountain, something I'd never done before. I did not sleep a wink, and in the middle of the night I became convinced that someone was watching me. When I finally looked out, I was certain I saw the granite face of Father Duffy, which, in the morning, turned out to be a stump. The experience made me realize that I could not bear to be alone in the woods and how much I missed its opposite.

June 13, 2004

12

New York Was Our City on the Hill

The City Held Out Unlimited Promise. But the Reality Was a
Struggle—for Money, Identity, and a Future.

EDWIDGE DANTICAT

The author, in Haiti, at the age of 2. *(Courtesy of the author)*

I F you are an immigrant in New York, there are some things you inevitably share. For one, if you're a new immigrant, you probably left
behind someone you love in the country of your birth. In my case, I was
the person left in Haiti when my mother and father escaped the brutal
regimes of François and Jean-Claude Duvalier in the early 1970's and
fled the extreme poverty caused by the Duvaliers' mismanagement and
excesses.

The plan was for my parents to send for me and my younger brother,
André, who were 4 and 2 years old at the time of their departure, when
they found jobs and got settled in New York. But because of United
States immigration red tape, our family separation lasted eight years.
The near decade we were apart was filled with long letters, lengthy voice
messages on cassette tapes and tearful phone calls, all brimming with the
promise that one day my brother and I would be united not only with
our parents but with our two Brooklyn-born brothers whom we didn't
know at all.

Still André and I were constantly reminded by our Aunt Denise and
Uncle Joseph, who were caring for us in an impoverished and politically
volatile neighborhood in the Haitian capital, Port-au-Prince, that we
were lucky our parents were in New York. If we dared to disagree with
that idea, the Faustian bargain our parents had faced would be clearly
laid out for us. They could have stayed behind with us and we could have
all gone without a great many necessary things, or they could have gone
to New York to work so that we could have not only clothes and food
and school fees but also a future.

As my Uncle Joseph liked to say, for people like us, the malere, the
poor, the future was not a given. It was something to be clawed from the
edge of despair with sweat and blood. At least in New York, our parents
would be rewarded for their efforts.

If living in one of the richest cities in the world did not guarantee a
struggle-free life, my brother and I didn't realize it. New York was our
city on the hill, the imaginary haven of our lives. When we fantasized,
we saw ourselves walking the penny-gilded streets and buying all the
candies we could stuff into ourselves. Eventually we grew to embrace
the idea that New York was where we were meant to be, as soon as the
all-powerful gatekeepers saw fit to let us in, and if we could help it, we
would never leave once we were again at our parents' side.

Our parents might have had utopian fantasies of their own when they
sold most of their belongings to pay for passports, visas and plane fares to

New York. I can't imagine making the choices they made without being forced, mapping out a whole life in a place that they'd seen only in one picture, a snow-covered street taken by my mother's brother, who lived there.

Later my parents would tell me that what kept them trudging through that snow to their factory jobs was their visions of their two New York–born children playing with the children they'd left in Haiti and the future that we might all forge as individuals and as a family.

•

WHEN I finally joined my parents in Brooklyn, in 1981, at age 12, I became acutely aware of something else that New York immigrants shared. If they were poor, they were likely to be working more hours than anyone else, for less money, and with few if any benefits.

For years my father had worked two minimum-wage jobs to support two households in two countries. One job was in a textile factory, where my mother also worked, and another in a night car wash. Tired of intermittent layoffs and humiliating immigration raids, my father finally quit both jobs when André and I arrived so he could accompany my brothers and me to and from school.

That same year, our family car also became a gypsy cab, a term that, when I first heard and researched it, led me to think that we were part of a small clan of nomads whose leader, my father, chauffeured other people around when he was not driving us.

Though my brothers and I weren't aware of it at the time, our financial situation was precarious at best. Once my parents paid the rent and utility bills and bought a week's worth of groceries, there was little left for much else. My father never knew from day to day or week to week how much he would collect in fares.

Winter mornings were more profitable than summer afternoons. But in the winter, our needs were greater: coats and boots for four growing children, and regular hospital trips for my youngest brother, Karl, who was prone to ear infections and, as one doctor pointed out to us, might have suffered through 25 different colds one long winter.

We had no health insurance, of course, and each of Karl's visits to the doctor, or those for my brother Kelly—the only child I knew who got migraines, which we later discovered were a result of some kind of pressure on his optic nerve—were negotiated down at Cumberland Hospital's payment services department when my father took in my parents' joint tax return.

I remember going to the same hospital's women's clinic with my mother for one of her regular checkups when I was 16. She had a headache, her blood pressure was high, and the doctor told her that she'd have to be hospitalized that day if she wanted to avoid a stroke.

"Doctor, I have children at home and work tomorrow," my mother said, before signing papers declaring that she'd been advised of the treatment for her condition but had refused it. On the bus home, I watched her carefully, fearful that she would keel over and die for our sake, but she made it home, and despite the persistent headache, she went to work the next day.

I don't know what a catastrophic illness might have cost our family financially. But it was something my parents always had in mind. My father tried to pay all his bills religiously so that if we ever needed a bank loan for a sudden emergency, we would have no trouble getting it.

What we would eventually need a loan for was our house, which my parents purchased 18 years ago in East Flatbush. The day we moved in was one of the scariest and most exhilarating of our lives. My parents invited groups of church friends over to celebrate and bless our new home, but at the same time, they warned my brothers and me that the biggest battle they'd face from then on would be to try to keep it. The mortgage was nearly double the amount they'd paid in rent, and some months my father drove his cab both at night and during the day to make the payment, which he then took to the bank, in person, during the final hours of the grace period.

＊

IT is the burden of each generation to embrace or reject the dreams set out by those who came before. In my family it was no different. My parents wanted me to be a doctor, and when I wasn't accepted by a Brooklyn high school specializing in the health professions, my father met with the principal and persuaded him to reverse the decision.

When I decided, after a brief school-sponsored internship at Kings County Hospital Center, that medicine was not for me, my parents were disappointed, but accepted my decision. My brother André has never forgotten the day he turned 14 and my father took him to the post office to buy a money order for the application fee for his first summer job. And over time we have all nearly wept when tallying small loans and advances from Mom and Dad on salaries spent way before they were collected.

Over the years, I have also come to understand my parents' intense desire to see my brothers and me financially stable. They had sacrificed so much that to watch us struggle as they had would have been, to quote a Creole expression, like lave men siye atè—washing one's hands only to dry them in the dirt.

These days, if you're an immigrant in New York, you might not consider yourself an immigrant at all, but a transnational, someone with voting privileges and living quarters not just in one country but in two. This was my parents' dream until they reached middle age and realized that with their decade-long friendships and community ties in Brooklyn, they didn't want to live anywhere else.

Last year, when my father became ill with pulmonary fibrosis—a result, some doctors say, of environmental pollution, to which he was especially vulnerable from working such long hours in his cab—he began to have long talks with my brothers and me, fearing that as the disease progressed, it might become harder and harder for him to speak. While I was writing this, we talked a little about how New York had changed from the time he arrived.

The most striking difference, he observed, is that these days, like most New Yorkers, he has to worry about terrorism, both becoming a victim and being blamed for it. He also worries about the high cost of everything from food to housing, about doors closing behind him, and thousands of families never having the kind of opportunities that we've enjoyed. When he first got to New York, all he did was work nonstop and pray to see his children and grandchildren grow up. Looking back, it feels like a simpler time, but maybe it wasn't. Then and now, he whispered wistfully, one can only hope that the journey was worthwhile.

On Nov. 3, after this essay was submitted, my Uncle Joseph died at age 81. More formally known as the Rev. Joseph N. Dantica, he died in Miami after fleeing gang violence and death threats in Haiti. He was detained by Department of Homeland Security officials after requesting asylum in the United States and died in their custody. The department said the cause was pancreatitis.

November 21, 2004

13

Here Is New York, Right Where We Left It

Before Manolos and Green Apple Martinis There Were Homburgs and Short Beers, among Countless Evocative Remnants of an Earlier Era That Endure, Often Uneasily, in the Glitziest City on Earth.

DAVID McANINCH

Smith's Bar, on Eighth Avenue in Manhattan. *(Shannon Stapleton/The New York Times)*

THE handwritten sign on the wall of Rose's Luncheon (no room for the "ette" on a storefront this narrow) is meant to be noticed. It's near the front door, opposite the eight-seat Formica counter and just above the Alka-Seltzer and Bayer dispensers, and it reads, "We Believe in God." Then there's the dusty gumball machine filled with fossilized Chiclets, the old letter-tile menu on the wall and, not least of all, the fact that no cash changes hands when the old guy at the end of the counter finishes his meal and amicably takes his leave.

When the subject of the place's history comes up, a lively argument erupts about whether Rose's Luncheon is, in fact, in the Bedford Park section of the Bronx or in Norwood, but no one gets too exercised trying to count the years Rose's has been around. "Too long," said a sighing Kathy, the co-owner and the successor to Rose herself, as she added to the departing customer's tab on a chit she keeps behind the counter.

A few things are certain: When you order tea with sugar at Rose's, they go heavy on the sugar. When you say thank you, it's returned with a bright "You're welcome, honey" that makes you think that the person behind the counter wasn't expecting such good manners from a stranger. Rose's may qualify as a charming relic of a lost New York, but to people there on a wintry day, it's just the place to go for a hot lunch.

This is an amazing thing about New York: In a city that is constantly razing the old to erect the new, or at least slapping on new paint and jacking up the price, there are quite a few places like Rose's, places that have remained quietly, stubbornly, implausibly the same for decades. As big-box stores land like awesome mother ships, as French brasseries pop up like dandelions, and as hordes of sexy nightlife-seekers transform formerly hard-bitten blocks into vague facsimiles of Bourbon Street, a surprisingly quaint version of old-fashioned Main Street America is somehow hanging on in arguably the most glamorous city on earth.

In New York, home of the $50 foie gras hamburger, you can still sit down and order pigs' knuckles for lunch and Jell-O for dessert. In the city of the $12 green apple martini, you can still put two quarters on a bar and get a glass of beer. In some parts of town, you can walk 40 blocks and not see a single Starbucks as you pass storefronts that seem miraculously stuck in the 1950's—a clunky urban diorama of outmoded signs and basic services that, for anyone old enough to have even a dim recollection of a streetscape devoid of day spas and flagship stores, evoke a weird and aching nostalgia.

These forgotten old lunch counters, taverns, hardware stores, cigar shops and the like—many in the boroughs outside Manhattan but some in Manhattan's very heart—remind us that an entirely different city thrives outside the relatively small circuit traveled by even the most peripatetic hip New Yorkers. And many of these New Yorkers intuitively understand that you can't have Glamorous and Stylish New York without the backdrop of Gritty Old New York. You can't have your Manolos without your Thom McAns, your tuna tartare without your Salisbury steak, your Absolut Citron without your butterscotch schnapps.

These off-the-radar places, a fading presence on the city's streets, also represent a reality that's easy to lose sight of in the sexualized, klieglighted playground of Manhattan: that New York is still mostly made up of regular people wearing regular clothes, eating regular food and going to bed at a reasonable hour.

ONE of the best preserving media for old-fashioned tastes and mores in this city turns out to be alcohol, or, more specifically, places that serve it. One such place is the remote Five Corners Bar in College Point, Queens. Located in what was once the city's German-beer-hall capital, the Five Corners opened in 1948, when, in a partnering strategy that presumably sounded less strange at the time, it was attached to a barbershop.

Nowadays the Five Corners is a place of gentle camaraderie that most urbanites would associate more with a country inn than a New York saloon. On one side of the bar sits a collection of ephemera that includes superannuated bottles of German brandy and little ceramic plaques bearing German aphorisms. On the other side sits a similarly odd collection of neighborhood denizens, including old-timers who still greet each other in German and are quick to point out that College Point once had more bars per capita than any other New York neighborhood. As for the barbershop, no one seems to remember when it disappeared.

Also in the category of places you wouldn't mind taking your grandmother to for a drink is Schaffer's Tavern, in the Westerleigh section of Staten Island. Unlike the Five Corners, Schaffer's is in a neighborhood that was once famous for its sobriety: A beachhead for the temperance movement, Westerleigh briefly went by the far more dour name Prohibition Park, and many nearby streets, like Neal Dow Avenue, are named for prominent prohibitionists.

Indeed, the spacious, well-lighted saloon, which is sparely adorned with old pewter steins and is largely free of the usual promotional beer swag, is run with a probity that seems to fit the neighborhood's history. Closing time is midnight, a rule that has been enforced without exception since the place officially opened in 1933 (the same year it stopped being a speakeasy). And when the co-owner, William Schaffer, a bald 61-year-old dressed punctiliously in shirt and tie, comes over to refill your glass, you feel compelled to behave rather better than you do in your own home.

The same can't be said for every old-timey bar in New York, of course—even the most venerable places get their share of noisy drunks—but what some of these joints lack in quaintness they make up for in other small felicities. A loose interpretation of the smoking ban, for one thing. For another, the short beer.

This wonderful drink, which can still be had for 50 cents at places like Kelly's Tavern in Bay Ridge, Brooklyn, is a dignified holdover from an age before the mighty pint became the irreducible unit of consumption. The short beer is a mere half-mug, served more often than not in a small stemmed glass, and it remains the order of choice for scores of seasoned old drinkers who like to know they can still buy a round for the house once in a while. Behind the portal of many an unfashionable old bar awaits the not inconsequential delight of being able to enjoy a night of drinking in New York without using up a $10 bill.

For the truly old-school types, for whom drinking isn't exclusively a nighttime activity, there remains a handful of saloons that double as hot-plate emporiums, ghosts of a bygone day when the city's barstools were occupied at lunchtime by workers who liked a beer with their hot mid-day meal, or vice versa, and required both on the cheap.

Smith's Bar and Restaurant has held down the northwest corner of 44th Street and Eighth Avenue for 50 years, its name written in soot-coated neon script outside, in a style of sign once seen above countless New York bars and liquor stores but now largely extinct. While renovation has afflicted the separate dining room next door, the cavernous bar area of Smith's seems untouched by the wave of renewal that has brought the likes of Red Lobster and Bubba Gump to nearby Times Square.

A bright green menu panel above the steam tables opposite the bar advertises pigs' knuckles, knockwurst and lamb stew, and the Irish barmen, in ties and white shirts, serve their lunchtime customers—a scattering of men bent over newspapers and racing forms—with curt, dishrag-snapping efficiency. As traffic hurtles by on Eighth Avenue and Midtown sandwich shops fill with office workers clutching cellphones, the thick air of Smith's murky depths seems to retard one's movements and slow the day's cascade of thoughts.

●

THAT a place like Smith's still exists in Midtown is a testament to the bipolar nature of New Yorkers, who are obsessed with the new and trendy and yet fiercely protective of old haunts and habits. And while the former obsession is surely winning over the latter in most of Manhattan, a few vestiges of an older, perhaps humbler era survive mostly unnoticed even in the city's very crucible of renovation and improvement. These are places that have somehow avoided the two fates that ultimately await the majority of old-style Manhattan establishments: fame and veneration on the one hand or, on the other, obsolescence and obliteration.

For example, in a Midtown lunch scene dominated by street carts and soup and sandwich chains, you can still stumble across a place like Vasconcellos Coffee-Lunch, a shoebox-size Spanish lunch counter wedged almost invisibly between garment warehouses on West 37th Street and possibly the city's smallest sit-down restaurant.

Or take the traditional barbershops, redolent of Barbasol and stale coffee, that have held their ground on Manhattan's streets and, in some cases, beneath them: In the Columbus Circle subway station, two silently twirling striped poles beckon customers to the Peerless Barber Shop, which has been operating in the grimy arcade below Eighth Avenue for 40 years. You may not get the most luxurious shave of your life here, but such details seem to matter less when you're dozing in a soft chair, lulled by such time-tested phrases as "just a little off the top" and the percussion of the B train trundling along beneath you.

On Eighth Avenue and 40th Street, the old Knox Hats is gone, demolished to make way for the skyscraper that will house The New York Times, but one block south, in a store called Lovely Gifts, you can still find a full line of men's hats, row after row of fedoras, porkpies and homburgs that share space with the more standard acrylic knit caps.

In the Theater District, a few old French restaurants—Tout Va Bien, on West 51st Street, or Pierre au Tunnel, on West 47th, to name two survivors—remain stubbornly rooted in the days before America's culinary awakening, the days when French cuisine meant an unwavering menu of coq au vin, cassoulet and saucisson, and fusion was just a science term.

●

STILL, for anyone who is seriously pining for the middle ages of the 20th century, especially when it comes to cuisine, the boroughs outside Manhattan generally offer richer, if harder-to-find, rewards. A person daunted by the vastness of these unfamiliar precincts might start on Avenue U in Brooklyn, a four-mile thoroughfare of austere Russian restaurants, kosher delis and huge diners with bewildering multipage menus offering everything from cottage cheese to twin lobster tails.

Here one can find cavernous old Chinese restaurants with easy-to-pronounce names like Ming's Place and Richard Yee's. The latter's menu aims to please even the most unreconstructed American palate; in addition to chow mein, chop suey and moo goo gai pan, it offers chicken salad and club sandwiches.

The boroughs outside Manhattan can also satisfy those hungry for nostalgia of a nonperishable nature. It is one of New York's cardinal charms that you can still shop for a lifetime's worth of goods and sundries without ever setting foot in a chain store, or even any place that remotely resembles one.

The 80-year-old Dembner's Hardware, at the north end of Victory Boulevard on Staten Island, is the living antithesis to the suburban retail model. No brightly lighted aisles, no expansive point-of-purchase displays, and no desultory quests for knowledgeable help; if Harry Dembner, grandson of the original owner, doesn't get to you soon after you walk through the door, one of his floor workers surely will.

You name the part, the screw, the washer, the bracket, the tool, and your helper disappears into the impossibly cluttered recesses of the store and reappears with your quarry. Business is done briskly, with minimal niceties, in the accepted New York way that is forever mistaken for rudeness. On a bright winter weekday, the cramped floor is crowded with customers and alive with banter; business seems great. Which, in fact, it's not, according to Mr. Dembner, though it's hard to imagine the store accommodating any more patrons than it already has.

A few miles away, on Bay Street in the Rosebank section of Staten Island, John De Luca presides over what appears to be, if this is possible, an even more cluttered enterprise than Dembner's.

De Luca's General Store is little more than a square vestibule, intruded upon on all sides by dangling merchandise, and a small countertop cleared off for conducting transactions. Whereas Harry Dembner seems to be all business, Mr. De Luca, a glassblower by trade before he left his native Sicily, gives the impression of a daydreaming tinkerer who one day happened to find himself running a hardware and housewares store.

A customer who arrives asking for "those little things that hang blinds" is dispatched quickly. (De Luca's doesn't have them.) Another guy comes in looking for thumbtacks, which Mr. De Luca distractedly locates before returning to the day's real business of conversation and recollection.

Even when it comes to clothes and grooming, a market long dominated by pharmacy chains, department stores and nationwide fashion retailers, New York still offers some wonderfully outdated alternatives, small-fry counterparts to Duane Reade, J. Crew or Saks. Tiny clothing stores subsist in the boroughs beyond Manhattan—Ripi Fashions in Belmont, in the Bronx, or Barton Sportswear in Ocean Parkway, Brooklyn—guilelessly advertising "Latest Style Dresses" and displaying underwire bras next to rhinestone-studded angora sweaters.

Old cut-rate emporiums like Evergreen Discounts on Queens Boulevard in Rego Park, Queens, continue to be a source of clean underwear and bedclothes for many New Yorkers. And in Marble Hill—a section of Manhattan that is physically connected to the Bronx—the small Drug Mart Pharmacy on Broadway has display shelves that are still arrayed beneath 50-year-old backlit panels labeled "Hair Grooming," "Shampoo," "Toys," "Books" and the bizarre "Baby Pants." Shampoo they still carry; the books, toys, and baby pants appear to be long gone.

TALKING to people who make their living in places like the Drug Mart or the Five Corners Bar or Rose's Luncheon is a bittersweet undertaking. Most of these shops and taverns and restaurants struggle in the shadow of their bigger and better-known competitors, and for the proprietors, the future tends to be a much less fertile subject of conversation than the past.

Of course, it is the perennial lot of nostalgic types to mourn the old dispensation. Even such an astute observer of city life as E. B. White yielded to the temptation; in 1949 he lamented that the city "neither looks nor feels the way it did 25 years ago."

"Men go to saloons to gaze at televised events instead of to think long thoughts," he wrote. "It is all very disconcerting."

Maybe. But also inevitable, as White probably knew. One thing the streets surely stand to lose when these frayed patches of New York's vast tapestry are finally replaced is a measure of their human scale. These remnants of a less mobile and more local New York speak of a more modest urban life in which goods and money traveled in smaller amounts between slightly less hurried parties moving in slightly smaller orbits.

No one goes to these old places to be seen or find the perfect pair of shoes or have a life-changing culinary experience or stock up on Turkish pistachios or toilet paper. If for nothing else, people go to these unfancy places because they embody a hidden truth about New York: that it is possible in almost any part of this monstrously huge, indifferent city to feel strangely at home.

February 27, 2005

14

Comfort Food

For a While, He Was a Regular at Frank's Gourmet Deli on
Smith Street in Carroll Gardens. But Some Connections,
like Apartment Leases, Are Only Short-Term.

JAKE MOONEY

Frank's Gourmet Deli in Carroll Gardens, Brooklyn. *(Chester Higgins Jr./The New York Times)*

I DON'T remember the first time I walked into Frank's Gourmet Deli on Smith Street, but it must have been a little more than a year ago, around the time I signed a lease a couple of blocks away in Carroll Gardens, Brooklyn. Getting to know a new neighborhood is always a process of locating and evaluating the essentials—grocery store, laundry, pizza place, A.T.M. with no service charge—and Frank's, a convenience store that stays open late and is stocked with the basics, falls neatly into that category.

I do remember the first time I met the man who owns Frank's. His name isn't Frank at all, it turns out, but Mr. Kim, and he is behind the cash register almost all the time. I didn't know any of this on the night of that first meeting; I just knew I needed a bag of ice to mix drinks for a friend from out of town. Every other place in the neighborhood was closed. Frank's was my only hope.

Mr. Kim's face behind the register was a welcome sight, and it was the beginning of what I like to think of as a beautiful friendship. Beautiful, but fleeting. I've been thinking about it lately because I just started a new lease on a new place, three subway stops away.

It isn't a bad walk in nice weather, but it's certainly far enough to make Mr. Kim's convenience store less convenient. I shop elsewhere now, either at the place across the street, where they once sold me sour milk, or at another store a block away. The store is clean and they have what I need, but I don't feel the same connection I felt with Frank's. As for Mr. Kim, I don't see him much anymore, and that's a shame.

Such is life when you're young, relatively unattached and semigainfully employed. A recounting of most of my friends' moves so far this decade reads like a yuppie "On the Road," minus all the hitchhiking and jazz. Try this one: Boston to Redwood City, Calif., to Staten Island to Astoria to the Upper West Side to Greenpoint to Columbia, S.C., to Greenpoint again, then to Park Slope. Or this: Atlanta to Morningside Heights to Park Slope to Dumbo to Red Hook to Carroll Gardens to Long Island City.

In all these places, relationships were forged and lost. Not necessarily the life-altering, capital-R kind of relationships, but important ones nonetheless—with the clerk at the deli who knows your usual order, or the bartender who starts pouring your beer as soon as she sees you walk in the door. Knowing these people makes city life a little less anonymous and a lot less overwhelming.

In Mr. Kim's case, it happened gradually. He greets most regular customers with an enthusiastic "Hello, how are you?" and after a while, I started to really appreciate that. It felt good to be recognized. Soon, Frank's was my fallback for all of life's little emergencies—and this despite the fact that I lived above a grocery store. Mr. Kim sold me NyQuil when I was sick, a banana and a cookie when I had an early-morning subway to catch and no time for breakfast, and a cold six-pack when I wanted to sit on my roof and watch the sun set behind the Statue of Liberty.

Through it all, he was as calm and professional as a doctor, never rolling his eyes when I agonized over which pint of ice cream to buy, never interrupting our small talk to question whether frozen pizza bagels or another six-pack was a good idea at 1 in the morning. Mr. Kim was there for a lot of the highs and lows of the last year, and whether he knew that or not, I always knew I could count on him as long as I had a couple of dollars and it wasn't ridiculously late.

And now, of course, I'm gone. I'm not sure that Mr. Kim noticed—he has lots of regulars, after all, and I would have felt silly telling him, given that we've never had a real conversation and I don't even know his first name.

Paradoxically, my sense that he was a big part of what made the neighborhood feel like home was never clearer than on the afternoon I moved my first load of furniture. I had rented a moving truck for way too much money and spent the day carrying bookshelves and mattresses through the rain and biting wind, and I was looking to relax. I trudged into Frank's and ordered a cup of hot chocolate, somehow failing to notice the posted sign by the coffee machine that read, "No Hot Chocolate."

When I realized what had happened I started to change my order, but Mr. Kim interrupted me.

"For a good customer, we will make hot chocolate," he said, as one of his underlings scrambled to get a pouch of powdered Swiss Miss off the store's shelves.

These were the nicest words I heard all day.

May 29, 2005

15

The Great Awakening

In the Last Quarter Century, from Riverdale to Tottenville,
Waves of Change Have Washed over New York. In Brooklyn,
the Transformation Seems Almost Tidal.

SUKETU MEHTA

(Aaron Meshon)

AT a party on the Upper West Side in 2000, a distinguished American author, and longtime Manhattanite, asked where I lived.

"Brooklyn," I told him.

He snorted. "Poor people live in Brooklyn." Then he turned away to get some meat.

Shortly after the party, to see if I could move from my rented apartment in Boerum Hill, I went looking to see what I could buy in a part of Fort Greene where cars parked on the street were still regularly stolen. I told the broker that it would be nice for my kids to have a house by a park. "We just sold a house by the park: $510,000," the broker said. But there was a catch. "It had no walls or ceilings."

What happened, I wondered, to the distinguished author's "poor people"?

Several years before, representatives of the giant warehouse shopping club Costco had approached the City Planning Department with a question: Would it be worth it to open a Costco in Sunset Park, an area of Brooklyn that had lots of the aforementioned poor people? The economic data wasn't encouraging. Lots of Asian immigrants lived in the area, and their median income was not high. Also, the site was half the usual size, so the Costco store would have to be built in two stories, with costly elevators and escalators.

But the city's statisticians advised Costco to go ahead. There was money in those undistinguished apartment houses and wood-frame houses, they said, more money than met the eye. Being an immigrant area, the neighborhood has a thriving underground economy, they said, and official housing data doesn't account for illegally subdivided units.

The store opened in 1996 and turned a profit in its first year. Nine years later, according to company figures, it is among the nation's highest-grossing Costcos, earning upward of $150 million this year, compared with $120 million for an average Costco. In fact, the store has been so successful, the chain is considering opening another giant warehouse in Brooklyn.

It has become a cliché to say that Brooklyn is booming. But the change has become so broad—sweeping up the yuppies of Fort Greene, the immigrant shoppers at Costco, the hipsters of Williamsburg—that it looks for all the world like a difference not just in degree but in kind. Long seen by that distinguished author and by so many others as a poor backwater, Brooklyn now buzzes with a momentum that would have stunned residents of its sleepy streets not long ago. The change has effects salutary (a housing boom, thriving cultural life) and perilous (soaring housing costs, displacement), but the one constant is that it is huge.

With 2.5 million people, the borough is bigger than San Francisco, Boston, Atlanta and St. Louis combined. The population is approaching the historical high of 1950, when Brooklyn was home to 2.74 million souls. Turn around, and you will see the renaissance. There isn't a single vacant storefront along Fulton Street in Bedford-Stuyvesant, and hordes of shoppers throng Pitkin Avenue in Brownsville. After decades of disinvestment in Brooklyn, major projects are in the works, among them the development of 175 waterfront blocks, complete with 40-story luxury apartment buildings, along the Greenpoint-Williamsburg waterfront; the construction of an 800,000-square-foot sports complex for the Nets in the Atlantic Yards; and, in Red Hook, the return of cruise ships, including the Queen Mary 2 and the Queen Elizabeth 2, to a major new pier and passenger terminal.

And while housing is exploding citywide—the number of housing permits granted citywide last year exceeded the permits granted in all of the 1990's—the two boroughs with the most housing starts in this bustling market are Queens and Brooklyn. Why so many homes? Brooklyn's prime appeal is relatively low cost. Let's not kid ourselves. If rents in Manhattan fell, half the hipsters in Brooklyn would rush the bridges; they're a floating population. But it can't be just that; otherwise Staten Island and the Bronx would also qualify.

People are also moving to Brooklyn because—who in the 80's could ever have guessed?—it has become so much safer. From 1990 to 2000, according to the state's Division of Criminal Justice Services, car theft in the borough plunged by 75 percent, robbery by 67 percent and homicide by 69 percent. In terms of mass transit, it's the best-connected borough after Manhattan, with 167 of the city's 468 subway stations.

•

As for me, I live in Park Slope because I'm a writer. It's in my union contract. Brooklyn has become the Iowa City of the East, an area chronicled and cataloged and celebrated in countless novels and poems, read and unread. The number of Brooklynites who identified themselves as "authors and writers" to the Census Bureau more than doubled to 3,111 in 2000 from 1,506 in 1990. By contrast, the number of "cabinetmakers and bench carpenters" dipped almost by half over the same period, to 334 from 602.

Because of all the creative types who call the borough home, the new Brooklyn is hip. One of the clearest signs of this was a 2002 cover article in Time Out New York that ran under the headline "Manhattan—The New Brooklyn" and tried hard to make the case that Manhattan was cool again. "The Upper East Side is just a dorm," I overheard a young Asian hipster say to a friend as they walked amid the milling crowds on Court Street. "I like it here. There's so much life."

Sometimes all of South Brooklyn feels like a giant set for a sitcom about trendy young people. On plywood barriers at a construction site on Fourth Avenue in Park Slope, I noticed a series of desperate public pleas for a change of heart by a departing roommate: "I ⊠ You Scout Please Don't Leave"; "Scout if you stay I'll be nice to you all the time. Even when I'm PMS'ing"; "Kate says if you stay, you can spend another night in her bed."

It was not always thus. The unnamed young Irish hero of the Gilbert Sorrentino love story "The Moon in Its Flight," set in 1948, returns to Brooklyn after a party with his sophisticated Bronx girlfriend in equally sophisticated Forest Hills. At the party, "He skulked in his loud Brooklyn clothes," the novelist writes.

"When he got off the train in Brooklyn an hour later, he saw his friends through the window of the all-night diner, pouring coffee into the great pit of their beer drunks. He despised them as he despised himself and the neighborhood. He fought against the thought of her so that he would not have to place her subtle finesse in these streets of vulgar hells, benedictions, and incense."

But the new Brooklyn has more than one face. "There are two Brooklyns," pointed out Arun Peter Lobo, deputy director of the population division of City Planning. "At the very least." Indeed, anything you could say about Brooklyn, the fourth-largest city in America, is true somewhere within its borders. Yes, it's full of hipsters; Rhode Island School of Design students hop on the bus to Williamsburg as soon as they graduate. Yes, it's full of parents, marching their strollers down Union Street to shop at the organic foods co-op. Yes, it's also full of immigrants.

Although Queens, the borough most thought of as the new melting pot, is home to more than a million immigrants, Brooklyn is fast catching up, with 932,000. About 38 percent of Brooklynites are foreign-born; if you include their children, their numbers jump to more than 55 percent.

This isn't the Jewish Brooklyn of Woody Allen or the Italian Brooklyn of "Moonstruck." There are people living in Brooklyn who have no idea what stickball is, what stoop-sitting is, who the Dodgers were or why they left Brooklyn. These people play cricket in Marine Park, barbecue suckling pigs in their backyards, listen to Russian matinee idols in Brighton Beach nightclubs, and worship not Kobe Bryant and Derek Jeter but Diego Maradona, an Argentine soccer player, and Sachin Tendulkar, an Indian cricket star. They are inventing their own Brooklyn, a Brooklyn their kids will be nostalgic about 20 years from now.

Willy Loman, too, still lives in Brooklyn. Desperate working folks, salesmen and otherwise, struggle to provide for their families, to make the commission; attention is still not being paid. Income disparities are as big as Brooklyn itself; in 2000, the median household income in the wealthiest census tract—in Brooklyn Heights—was $112,414. In the poorest tract, in Coney Island, the median income, at $7,863, was not even one-tenth of that. The housing crisis exacerbates this inequality, with the world divided between those who own and those who rent.

Another big division in Brooklyn is between neighborhoods close to the water, or to a park, and those away from the blue and the green. People live in the western parts of Brooklyn with their eyes fixed westward. There are people in Park Slope who can tell you where to get the best gelato in Manhattan but have no idea where to find the best roti in Brownsville. Well inland are the nonimmigrant poor, people who have been poor for a long time and aren't just off the plane from somewhere else, aren't hoarding hope for their children as they toil in sweatshops.

The new Brooklyn has not cured poverty or solved related problems like inadequate schools. Low-quality schooling hits poor and immigrant families the most because it depletes the only substantial capital they have: their children. The children, with their great promise, are these families' Microsoft before Windows, their I.B.M. when it was just a typewriter company. When a public school succeeds spectacularly, like P.S. 321, in whose Park Slope district house buyers must pay a premium, parents storm the gates, with varying success. So it's private school for many Brooklyn parents—at $20,000 a year. "It's become punitive living here," says a writer friend who was trying to raise her kids in Park Slope. She couldn't afford a house, even though her husband is a corporate lawyer. Eventually she left Brooklyn to ride horses in a mountain village in Spain, and is happier for it.

●

MOREOVER, the various redevelopment plans, grand as they are, are being fought block by block by people who will be displaced by them.

The Nets arena will sit in a spot that has among the best access to mass transit in the city—"every train but the F," as my landlord proudly said when I was renting an apartment near there in 2002. Traffic, already hellish on Flatbush Avenue, may get still more hellish as several thousand fans converge at game time.

So there are downsides to the new Brooklyn, but there is the boom—and beyond all the economic data, there is a very human pull to the borough. In the world's loneliest city, Brooklyn offers community. Everybody can find community in Brooklyn: the body-fluid artists in Bushwick, the Chinese restaurant workers in Sunset Park, the die-hard Marxists in the Park Slope food co-op. No matter how foreign or fringe you are, the borough has a support group for you.

One reason for this is that Brooklyn is famously a series of neighborhoods. Another has to do with the physical structure of that emblem of Brooklyn—the brownstone. Adjoining rear gardens facilitate communal interaction, gardening tips exchanged over a backyard fence. Maybe what attracts the hipsters to Brooklyn isn't just cheap rents. It's the closest they can get to the families they left behind, in Kansas, in Vermont, in Tokyo.

For me, Brooklyn became a neighborhood one steamy August night in 2003. It was the night of the great Northeastern Blackout. In Park Slope, volunteers were out directing traffic at every intersection, even if the drivers laughed at them and zoomed past. Other Brooklynites shared phones and flashlights, or helped the elderly down dark stairwells.

As night fell, the texture of the city changed. The street lamps were out, and people strolled about with flashlights and lanterns. There was a bright white moon high above the city competing with the red glory of Mars, the warrior planet, which hadn't been so close to Earth in 60,000 years. The ancient Brooklyn tradition of stoop-sitting enjoyed a sudden revival.

At midnight, the bars were still dispensing ice for our whiskeys. We took our drinks out on the sidewalk; we'd make our own laws tonight. Everyone's face was illuminated in flickering, flattering light, and everybody looked beautiful and desirable. The floodlit megalopolis was transformed into a series of villages lighted by millions of small lights, in whose glow Brooklyn was revealed to be what we had forgotten it really is: an impossibly romantic, a 19th-century city.

June 19, 2005

16

The Worst Ballpark in the World

With the Plan to Build a New Home for the Mets,
Shea's Days Were Numbered. Yes, the Stadium Sat
on an Ash Heap and Was Pestered by Planes.
Yet There Was No Denying Its Goofy Charms.

KEVIN BAKER

Opening day at Shea Stadium, 1983 *(Chester Higgins
Jr./The New York Times)*

FIRST saw Shea Stadium the summer it opened, 1964, when the world was still young. My parents were taking me to the World's Fair, which was just across the elevated line in Flushing Meadows, Queens. This was appropriate because Shea, like the fair, was supposed to be a showcase for the world of tomorrow. You could tell this because it looked breezy, and fun, and half-finished—all bright, garish colors, flimsy new materials and unadorned concrete and pipes and steel cables laid out in that functional, neglected-housing-development style that modern architects used to assure us was the best future we could hope for.

I remember that the fair proved disappointing once we got inside, with endless lines and nothing that seemed all that amazing. Perhaps the trouble was that even in 1964, the future was no longer what it once had been.

The same would prove true of Shea. In fairness, no stadium ever started life with more strikes against it: a baseball park without any real bleachers, built in the flight path of an international airport, on the site of a gigantic ash heap. The bad symbolism abounded. Shea sits amid a sea of junkyards and chop shops. Subway riders from the No. 7 train approach it along the curious "Ramp to Nowhere," a concrete walkway that appears to lead directly from the elevated station into Shea's green, beckoning right field—only to stop some 20 yards short, dribbling fans out onto a cracked asphalt sidewalk.

There has always been something tawdry and second-rate about the place, right down to the battered plaster-and-lath apple that rises grudgingly out of a gigantic top hat whenever a Met hits a home run. Since the eradication of all those football-friendly, synthetic-grass excrescences of the 60's, some would argue that Shea is the worst ballpark in the world.

But now, with the planned construction of a new Mets ballpark next door that may also be used for the Olympics, Shea's days are numbered. And so, despite the stadium's flaws, it needs to be said: Right from the beginning, even the worst ballpark in the world was a great place to be. I went to my first game there with my Uncle Bruce, in 1967, to see the Mets play the San Francisco Giants, and it felt like a carnival as much as a ballgame.

The Mets were in last place, but there was a full house, with many of the fans cavorting merrily in the aisles. A poker-faced individual named Karl Ehrhardt but known as Sign Man held up exclamations ("Yikes") after every key play, and for years on Banner Day, the fans were invited to march onto the field and show off their homemade signs. (My favorite: "I'd Bet My Testes on the Metsies.")

This was something altogether new in New York sports, fans defiantly embracing a team of scrappy, lovable losers. The attitude almost seemed designed to send up the lordly crosstown Yankees, with all their ponderous tradition.

Many in the crowd, including my uncle, were rooting for the visitors. In those days, thousands of fans still turned out in droves whenever their beloved West Coast transplants, the Giants and the Dodgers, stopped back in town. But most New Yorkers had moved on.

Bad as the Mets were, they had established an identity that jibed perfectly with the city's as the 60's wore on: embattled, ragged, but facing the long odds against them with brave wit and style. When the team miraculously won the World Series in 1969, behind a fine young pitching staff led by Tom Seaver, all New York reveled in vindication. Fun City, indeed.

•

BY the time I got back to Shea, in the late 70's, the first bloom was clearly off the rose, for both the team and the city, with their seemingly perpetual crises. New Yorkers enjoy being underdogs for only so long. The Mets had sunk to the bottom again, and even Tom Terrific had been banished for insubordination by the decidedly unlovable and unscrappy club president, M. Donald Grant. In those years, you could buy a ticket to the cheapest seats in the upper deck, and for an extra dollar an usher would take you all the way down to a lower section. At night, Shea had begun to take on a decidedly spectral mood, cavernous and empty, one more patch of blight and squandered chances.

In truth, the best was yet to come: the Mets of Doc Gooden and Darryl Strawberry, Gary Carter and Keith Hernandez, and Mookie Wilson, et al., a wonderfully cocksure squad that would set team records for wins and brawls, on and off the field, and would capture the 1986 World Series after playing some of the most astonishing games in postseason history. The fans flocked back, screaming and dancing between innings along with a scoreboard video tribute to the Three Stooges called "The Curly Shuffle."

That year, I watched from the upper deck as the Dodger pitcher Tom Niedenfuer surrendered a decisive grand slam to George Foster. Niedenfuer proceeded to hit the next batter, Ray Knight, with a pitch—whereupon the pugnacious Knight jumped up and raced for the mound. Within seconds, both teams had poured onto the field, embroiled in a melee very much akin to the Curly Shuffle.

Soon after, the great Mets teams of the 80's, and their flawed stars, went into an untimely decline. But another pattern had arisen, one of bust and boom, despair and irrational exuberance, that also reflected the New York of the 80's and 90's. And always, one could expect the amazing, the unlikely, the goofy.

During the remarkable 1999 National League Championship Series against Atlanta, I had the privilege to witness what was then the longest postseason game, a 15-inning affair that started in the afternoon and went far into the drizzling October night. The Mets trailed in the series by three games to one, and a loss would end their season.

But a sense of sheer euphoria grew steadily around the park as the game went on, even with Atlanta threatening almost every inning, and two Braves runners being thrown out at the plate. The organist led the crowd in a second "seventh-inning stretch" in the middle of the 14th, and everywhere you could see the grins of fans who were happy just to extend the season by another inning.

The feeling was wholly different from the one I have experienced during big, close games in Yankee Stadium, where everything is magnified by the burden of history. That sensation is more raw and visceral, and one that I cherish as well, but at Shea people seemed as if they were actually having fun, as if it really were a game.

As the game and the rain continued, and the weak of heart departed, my friends and I kept improving our seats, until we actually ended up sitting next to Bud Harrelson, the excellent former Mets shortstop, coach and manager. Here was a living link to the legacy of 1969, and 1986, as it might appear only at Shea. We sat next to Bud as if clinging to a lucky icon, and watched the Mets rally to win in the bottom of the 15th, on Robin Ventura's grand slam.

Even here, the quirky interceded. Ventura's hit was reduced to a "grand-slam single" when Todd Pratt, the runner just ahead of him, stopped and embraced him on the base paths. One could hardly picture Derek Jeter behaving in such a manner.

The Mets would go down to another, plucky defeat in that series anyway, and again the next year, in their one and only Subway Series against the Yankees. Shea has continued its slow rot, and my friends and I joke about the hokey promotions (Greek Night!), and the once infamously small, foul bathrooms that drove the Jets to New Jersey (good riddance), and the themed concession stands such as "Beers of the World," which might be more aptly titled "Beers of Your Local Bodega." Last year, we were unable even to sit in the seats we had purchased because of a steady rain of roof water on a perfectly cloudless night, bilge that seemed to be pouring right down through a hole in a steel supporting beam above us.

Mets officials were unruffled by the deluge, but who can blame them? They will have their new stadium by 2009, and if the recent stadium-building craze around America is any indication, it will be a much better (if more expensive) place to watch a game, combining modern comfort with all the trappings of official baseball nostalgia.

Until then, I will be happy to indulge my own nostalgia, sipping a Beer of the World, and gazing from the airy, open exit ramps of Shea toward the Manhattan skyline.

July 3, 2005

17

A Toast, with a Shot and a Beer

A Couple of Wise Guys, a Musician or Two, and a Jukebox
Set on Julio, in a Crummy Little Bar of the Sort That
Has All but Vanished from the Upper West Side.

MITCH KELLER

A beloved bar on the Upper West Side of Manhattan. *(Cary Conover/The New York Times)*

I N the bar I always went to in those days, some of the talk I overheard compelled me to scribble it down on a napkin so I wouldn't forget it. I'd be sitting there having a beer and watching the wrestling on TV when suddenly the guy sitting next to me would say to the guy on his other side: "The dummy drew a gun. The black dude who's always got to count the money first. There's no need of that stuff if you do business right. I don't need it with him anymore."

Or, on a night when the bar was packed, the alpha male of the regulars, a wiseguy and the real boss of the bar, might find his path to the men's room blocked by someone. After waiting patiently for the guy to move, the Boss would tap him on the shoulder and say, "What are you, a statue?"

"Pardon?"

"I said go to Central Park if you're a statue."

It was the sort of bar that used to be common on the Upper West Side but has now almost disappeared, the sort that young college graduates and professional people searching for a place to hang out would reject after one look in the window. Since I was often the person looking back at them from the other side of the glass, I remember the joint well.

It was just a hole in the wall, narrow and not deep, all filled up with maybe 20 people. There was no gimmick, no fanciful governing idea, no effort at all to attract customers. You went there to drink and smoke. Nobody cared if you came back or not. Nobody asked you what you did or where you lived. The décor consisted of a few posters and clocks given out by beer companies. The lighting was always low, the TV up in the corner always on with the sound off. Wrestling, much of the time.

I did my napkin jotting furtively because I didn't want people to think I was gathering information on them. Some of them were partaking of cocaine in the restrooms and made no secret of it. Furthermore, I had already had one difficult encounter and didn't want another. When I first started going to the bar, one of the regulars wouldn't stop glaring at me, and I learned why when he came up to me one night and said, "You're a cop, aren't you?"

"No."

"Yes, you are. You're a cop. I know a cop when I see one."

He wouldn't back off, and finally the manager of the bar had to pry him away from me and usher him back to his stool. But my restraint during the confrontation had scored enough points with the manager and some of the resident barflies to earn me a type of acceptance among them. It didn't hurt that I made a point of leaving good tips and of always asking the young women who tended the bar what they wanted to hear when I went to the jukebox. Those two things will make you welcome in any dive in the world.

The place was at its liveliest in the wee hours of a weeknight, when in 30 minutes it could go from almost empty to crowded. There were always one or two old goats who lived in rented rooms, and an Asian man in a suit and tie who stayed every night until closing, and a group of young Spanish-speaking guys throwing their money away.

There was an affable, perfectly groomed Hispanic gentleman with a pencil mustache who said he worked in an illegal gambling club on the East Side. In those days there were still some prostitutes working the blocks of Broadway late at night, and a few of them came into the bar on breaks and carried on like college girls. Sometimes a musician or two stopped in on the way home from a gig downtown.

The king of the jukebox was Julio Iglesias. Stevie Wonder and Michael Jackson were played a lot too, and there was some tropical stuff, but Julio ruled. I'd ask the young woman scrubbing glasses behind the bar what she wanted to hear, and she'd look up and say, "'To All the Girls I've Loved Before'!" or "Something by Julio!" To this day, two decades later, it would be all right with me if I never heard another "something by Julio" for the rest of my life.

The aforementioned Boss was a neighborhood guy in his 30's whose preferred upper-body garb was a strapped white undershirt. He wasn't tall, but he was broad and square across the back, and the muscles draping his shoulders and upper arms were heavy. He had no discernible neck, his large head seeming to sink between his shoulders as if it had been dropped there from the ceiling. He appeared every bit as proud of his emergent paunch as he was of his muscles. He had full lips and wet black hair and a pouty face in which defiance and suspicion had made a perfect marriage.

•

THE BOSS always seemed to have a roll of cash in his pocket as big as his fist, and he wasn't shy about letting people see it when he took it out and stripped off a few bills for another purchase. Among the female regulars he was far and away the most popular guy. He drank only Champagne, and it was not unusual for one of the women to reach for the bottle and pour him some more when his glass ran low. Even his insults—"What are those, glasses you're wearing, or milk bottles?"—were just laughed off.

He would talk to the women in a bluntly sexual way that would have gotten any other man in the bar either kicked out or punched out. But the Boss got away with it. "I already got enough kids," I heard him say. "I got kids I don't even know I have."

Even today, all these years later, whenever I'm back on the Upper West Side I find myself keeping one eye peeled for the people I used to see in that bar. I never see them, of course. It's possible I wouldn't recognize them if I did; appearances can change a lot over two decades. But I suspect they're as long gone from that neighborhood as crummy bars and $300 rents. People like that do not ride out the sort of change that the Upper West Side has undergone over the past 20-plus years.

I do remember the last time I saw the Boss. It was at least 15 years ago, but it has stayed with me just as all my misspent hours in that dark, vanished bar have. He was standing against the wall of a building on Broadway, hunched up against the cold, drinking coffee and smoking. He didn't seem to have much to do. To be fair, maybe he was just waiting for something or someone. But I remember thinking, looks as if the glory days are slipping away.

August 21, 2005

18

The Secret Life of Hanover Square

By Day, the Downtown Neighborhood Was a Ho-Hum
Business District. But as Windows Were Lighted
and People with Grocery Bags Emerged,
the Area Revealed Its Hidden Face.

MARK CALDWELL

The lights of Hanover Square, near Wall Street. *(Michael Nagle/The New York Times)*

NEW YORK at night is a city of low-key voyeurs and discreet exhibitionists. Not droolers and flashers, but more or less lawful strollers like me, looking for the curtainless window whose occupant pursues some puzzling activity, or by the passing diorama show of apartment and brownstone interiors. In Manhattan this is a pleasure abetted by the tacit cooperation of residents who keep their windows clean and their shades up, affording a view to passers-by even when they don't enjoy one themselves.

Congested high-rise avenues, overwindowed and overpowered by street glare, make poor territory for such louche but ultimately harmless gawking. Far better are the toylike scale of the West Village, or the grander but still manageable brownstones of side streets in Chelsea and Murray Hill.

And over the last few years, despite Sept. 11, a new spy-friendly neighborhood has materialized downtown in the moldering lanes west of Broadway, between City Hall and the ferries. Increasingly, people live here. And increasingly, if you choose the right time and have a patient eye, you can spy on them.

On a warm Sunday night last month, with most of New York supposedly decamped for upstate or the East End, I walked along Ann Street, just below City Hall. At first glance it resembled a Lower East Side block unflattened by chic: tenements, 1800's-vintage factories inscrutable as to what they once made, and three-story brick row houses, all seemingly held up only by newer commercial structures offering them a shoulder. It's poorly lighted here, sometimes pitch dark, channeling a mean street from the 1970's, and waiting like a stage set for the appearance of a mugger's ghost.

But the first people to materialize were obviously alive and steps from home: an old man and a small girl of 5 or 6, tethered to a pair of bounding greyhounds, which hauled them out from under a razor-wired plywood scaffold, then dragged them joyously into Theater Alley (a cluttered lane that opens off Ann and once ran behind the old Park Theater, the city's leading venue in the early 1800's).

•

THE members of this quartet weren't anomalies, as I've come to realize after a year or so of noticing the block's increasingly numerous and visible residents. In the daytime their lighted windows collapse into anonymous facades and their apartments seem to hide from the office workers and tourists milling below. But at night—though still uncommon, at most one or two to a building—they're unmistakable.

A living space never looks like an office or a workroom, even if its second-story ceiling displays to the sidewalk a ghastly fluorescent ring and the lumpy grime of an ancient paint job. In one row-house window on Ann Street, the telltale was a filled-up bookcase and the top of an occupied Aeron chair arching over a buzzing air-conditioner whose drips banged on the steel sidewalk hatchway.

Commercial buildings are being colonized, too, and that helps hide the neighborhood's homes, as with the co-op at 3 Hanover Square. By day you can't tell it from the office block it once was; its lobby remains as stark as a bank vault. But after dark the lights in its tall upper windows open them to the sidewalk and show that they, in fact, belong to duplexes that overlook the torn-up park in the square and offer a glimpse of the East River.

People seem to materialize, giving no clue where they came from or where they're headed—a gay couple, for instance, suddenly appearing with bags from the semimythical 24-hour neighborhood grocery I've been told about but which nobody I've spoken to can locate.

Far downtown's deceptive appearances and still-evolving social composition can often leave you baffled as to the meaning of what or whom you're looking at even when you're vouchsafed a view. Turning the corner at Pearl Street into Coenties Slip, I saw a silhouette, sitting at a desk or table behind a second-story window. It bowed down till its head disappeared, lurched bolt upright, then repeated the cycle five times. Eating off the table? Snorting cocaine? Peering at a spreadsheet? Who knows?

Just below Hanover Square, Stone Street, cobbled, closed to traffic, lined with outdoor tables belonging to a row of bars and restaurants, has become the town square to this emerging neighborhood. On workday evenings the community ambiance disappears under hordes of blue-shirted business types, out for an after-hours drink. But on Sunday the scene quiets, and the few people inside or out are clearly locals—a father sharing French fries with his two young sons, a man sitting alone with a Guinness and the paper.

Ulysses', on Stone opposite Mill Lane, is a wildly popular singles pub, especially on Thursday nights. But its staff has adjusted to the slower weekend pace, and has noted, too, the demographic shift. Karen Hansen, the Sunday-night floor manager, says the residents seem to be a mix without a profile: retired people, couples in their 20's, middle-aged professionals. She has talked to a rising number of prospective home-hunters looking for a neighborhood restaurant in a quarter that at first doesn't seem to have any.

In that respect, residential Wall Street is like no other recent urban resurrection, wary of engineered coolness and the publicity juggernaut that always seems to follow. Its old brick and old wood (like the red clapboards on the 1794 building at the corner of Water and Dover Streets, far below the arch of the Brooklyn Bridge and now housing a low-key cafe) qualify it as desirable, but have so far avoided the blandness of perfect remodeling.

·

EVEN a few happily vulgar glass apartment-tower invaders, looking like refugees from the Upper East Side or even Fort Lee, dilute what otherwise might be an overdose of antiquity. In sunlight these towers are nearly indistinguishable from offices or hotels. But later in the day, the doormen in the lobbies become visible and the residents, many apparently transients working temporarily for a financial or law firm, drift in and out. In the huge rental building at Gold Street and Maiden Lane, I saw one man sitting in a Hopperesque trance, motionless in his all-white corner living room, encased as if in a specimen box with two all-glass walls and two blank white ones.

Just 10 years ago he could never have figured as a slice of neighborhood life: the iconic weekend and nocturnal Wall Street was still a geometry of deserted canyons and buttelike office towers. Then, of course, came Sept. 11, the dislocation and despair that followed, and the battle of developers, planners and interest groups that for now seems to have overtaken the stage.

But even as the planning for ground zero drags on, Lower Manhattan has been changing according a momentum of its own, perhaps even attracting a class of urbanites who like their environs mercurial and their identities unpegged. The clutter of often squat 20th-century construction may have weakened the area's old, cold architectural strength, and the Internet has weakened Wall Street's imperial grip on business power. But the influx of residents has alchemically transformed these blocks at night, giving them the aura of a secret city—like Diagon Alley, Harry Potter's shopping mecca, invisible unless you know where to look and when.

September 11, 2005

19

New York's Lighthouse

The Building Is the Distinctive Image of Mythic New York,
the City of Film and Fiction, and Yet Irresistible.

MARK KINGWELL

The Empire State Building, the ultimate New York City beacon.
(Ruth Fremson/The New York Times)

IKE most people, I made a trip to the observatory of the Empire State Building on my very first visit to New York, when I was a gawky Canadian teenager fresh off the train from Toronto. My visit to that building, which will have been open 75 years on May 1, was romantic in more than one sense. I was with my first girlfriend, a petite girl with braces on her teeth. Though neither of us had seen "An Affair to Remember," the 1957 Cary Grant–Deborah Kerr weepie that immortalizes the building as the quintessential New York lovers' rendezvous, we knew that the top of the building was the ideal place to share a kiss, even if it was awkward and adolescent and jostled by other tourists hefting the bulky camera equipment of the predigital day.

The movie we saw later that day in Times Square—a matinee of "E.T. the Extra-Terrestrial"—featured a fistfight in the back of the theater, in the smoking rows, and my girlfriend and I broke up on the train ride back to Canada. But that moment on top of the building, looking out over the broad Hudson and Lower Manhattan's dense packing of brick and stone, sealed New York's grip on me, as it has on millions of others.

I would not visit the top of the Empire State again for two decades, probably a typical gap. You go once, and you may never go again. Natives may never go at all, which is a shame. The foursquare view from the top of the Empire State, even more than the sweep of Manhattan that was available from the summit of the twin towers, is one of life's great vistas. It may not quite be, as the building's primary booster and moving force, Al Smith, argued, better than air travel. But it must surely be what Ms. Kerr breathlessly calls it (twice): the nearest thing to heaven we have in New York.

•

IN business terms, the Empire State Building may be the most famous white elephant on the planet. Built against all logic during the Depression, it has never succeeded in its ostensible function as an office building. Early years of indifference gave it the label "Empty State Building," and vacancy rates have recently climbed again, from a low of 1.7 percent in 2000 to more than 18 percent.

The current rent of just $37 a square foot is well below Midtown averages of $48, and yet the building's owners still can't fill the place. (The small offices and antiquated infrastructure are part of the deterrent, despite projected upgrades; but so is a continuing feud between the two companies that control the building, Helmsley-Spear and Wien & Malkin, which complicates leasing arrangements. The dispute arose a decade ago when heirs of the building's co-owners since 1961, Harry Helmsley and Lawrence Wien—both now dead—could not agree on control.)

Meanwhile, some four million visitors a year make their way to the observatory on the 86th floor (a higher deck, near the building's 102nd-floor summit, reopened last fall after having been closed for years). Here, the weight of the building's significance seems to outstrip its financial woes, even its very material existence. Like all great monuments, the Empire State Building shelters meanings that extend well beyond its gorgeous Indiana limestone cladding and tiny throwback offices.

Consider just three of the many factors that make the building memorable: the idea of the skyscraper, the mythical functions of the tower and finally the peculiarly American dream-logic of the building's astonishing construction.

When the Empire State Building opened its rather modest Fifth Avenue doors on May 1, 1931—Al Smith, the former governor, was there, of course, with photographers, kids and a band—the event punctuated a period of architectural ambition and civic glee that the world is not likely to witness again.

In the span of two short decades, New York's congested street plan and material wealth, together with crucial developments in science and technology, tempered steel and the elevator, led to the invention of a new architectural form. From Lower Manhattan to Midtown, from Wall Street up to the 40's, Manhattan pushed into the sky the planet's first vertebrate buildings, shoving aside the squat crustaceans that had held sway for so long.

The Empire State had several distinguished predecessors during the 1920's. The "race for the sky" contest—between H. Craig Severance's Manhattan Company Building, way downtown, and William Van Alen's Chrysler Building—gripped the city's imagination in a manner that is hard to imagine now. When Van Alen won the race by hoisting the Chrysler's distinctive spire from a secret mechanism built inside the peak, the skyscraper and the idea of war over architectural one-upmanship seemed settled for good.

For many, the Chrysler remains Manhattan's best tall building, a Deco masterpiece, even though it was mocked mercilessly by contemporary critics, not least for the distinctive sheathing of its "Aztec pinnacle," to quote the poet Charles Tomlinson.

The race was not over, however. One of the most poignant pictures ever captured of the Chrysler—not by Margaret Bourke-White, that disciple of the Chrysler cult—shows the rising column of the Empire State construction at 34th Street through one of the triangular slash-windows of the uptown rival.

Taller buildings would come, in Manhattan and Chicago and elsewhere, but the Empire State would not be surpassed.

Even without its now distinctive (and never used) dirigible mooring of chrome-nickel steel and faceted glass, added at Smith's behest and over William Lamb's objections so that the building would have "a hat," the Empire State would have been taller than the Chrysler. The spire made it 1,250 feet high—a figure that would settle skyscraper hash for almost half a century. This span as world's tallest building is itself worth a meta-record in this age of Asian gigantism, where structures like the Petronas Towers in Kuala Lumpur straddle the summit of summits for, at best, a few years. (The world's tallest building at this writing is Taipei 101 in Taiwan, and at least three taller buildings are already planned in Shanghai alone.)

•

To some eyes, the Chrysler remains aesthetically superior: a function, in part, of Deco's nostalgic appeal and Van Alen's instinctive grasp of Gotham's Batmannish soul. In a comparison with the slimmer Chrysler, it is easy to underestimate the tough masculine beauty of Lamb's design for the Empire State.

Whereas the Chrysler displays a giddy modernism, the Empire State combines subtle Deco grace notes with an assured, almost classical sense of proportion. Its solid central shaft rises gracefully from cleverly arranged volumes at the base, lifting to an understated cap of layered sections. In a Vanity Fair feature of the day, Lamb was named one of New York's 10 "Poets of Steel," an honor denied to both Van Alen and Severance.

But even absent such aesthetic rehabilitation, the Empire State would be superior in meaning, the distinctive image of mythic New York: the New York of film and fiction, beckoning and false, corrupted and sometimes corrupting, but irresistible for all that.

The building is, obviously, a tower, indeed the central tower of New York. Thus it functions, as the modernist master Robert A. M. Stern once put it, as "the lighthouse of Manhattan." But like all towers, it is no mere structure or landmark. A tower speaks of and to the human ambition for transcendence, that restless desire to transcend what the Futurist theorist Emilio Filippo Tommaso Marinetti called "the vile earth." The paradox of the tower, any tower, is that it stands fixed to the ground even as it stretches up and tries, somehow, to achieve liftoff.

The Empire State is not Futurist in design, nor is it explicitly utopian. Indeed, its workaday offices and no-nonsense design are deliberately utilitarian in conception. Most people who visit the building pay no attention to its often underrented interior, a kind of urban time machine filled with diamond merchants, insurance companies and private investigators, among many, many others.

Nevertheless, with its machine-made grace, the Empire State Building towers above the island grid and fixes the scene. Standing at the center of Manhattan, it gathers up the city to itself and then redeploys it, out and down, to every spot from which it can be seen.

Towers spring from military desire as well as spiritual urges, and the central position of the Empire State might raise, as towers do, the specter of surveillance. Especially in these Patriot Act days, one can imagine that it drapes a visual net over New York, a sort of heaven-suspended security system.

And yet the grid it overlooks is, for all its constraints, a stage of freedom and spontaneity. Its very rigidity seems to offer new invitations to liberty. The streets crush and bend and mangle their straight lines, giving way to the wonky charm of the West Village, for example, or the Battery. The Empire State, meanwhile, resolutely resists any link to the security state. Its empire is not the one of watchful eyes and foreign invasions; rather, at its summit assemble the free citizens of the world, multilingual and blessed, who ascend to gather in their views and memories, not data or evidence.

The Empire State holds New York's eight million souls together in a way the taller World Trade Center never could, and even now, in dark memory, does not. The older building's unlikely birth in the middle of the 1929 Crash; its defiant optimism steered by Al Smith and the financier John J. Raskob, those quintessential self-made men; the astonishing assembly line of steel and stone that made it the fastest megaproject the world had seen; its gathering of workers from all nations and trades—all this combines to make the Empire State the ultimate dream building.

Monument and promise, folly and wonder of the world, it can be no surprise that no other tall building even dared challenge it for preeminence for almost half a century.

We sometimes speculate about a particular feature of a city, and wonder what things would be like if it did not exist. Especially because of what happened to those taller buildings downtown, the answer in the case of the Empire State Building is clear. Like our ideas of God and happiness, if the Empire State Building did not exist in the New York skyline, we would have to invent it.

April 23, 2006

20

Call It Booklyn

With More Marquee Authors than You Can Shake a
Mont Blanc Pen at, Brooklyn May Be the City's
Grimmest Borough for the Up-and-Coming Writer.

SARA GRAN

(Gary Hovland)

HAVE a theory about the F train.

I think that people who ride the F train, which stops in the heart of Park Slope, Brooklyn, and is therefore the train of choice for dozens of writers, editors and publishers, choose their subway reading material very carefully. You rarely see the folks who get off at Seventh Avenue reading anything pocket-sized, and never anything with an embossed cover, or anything that's advertised on the train itself.

Here is my theory: I think people who ride the F train know who their fellow riders are, and save the trashy reading for home. On the F, they pull out only their hippest and most intellectual pursuits. Like the mythological "disco cars" of the 70's, the last cars of certain trains that were supposedly reserved for using and selling drugs, the F is reserved for those who read books reviewed in The New Yorker.

You could say it's a coincidence that the F train is filled with literary fiction fans. I say it's a conspiracy.

Not, of course, that I would ever think twice about what I'm reading on the subway. I'm different. I didn't move to Brooklyn for my publishing career, for the chance to mingle with other writers or for the prestige of a 718 area code. On Saturday, I won't be attending the Brooklyn Book Festival at Borough Hall, Brooklyn's answer to the late New York Is Book Country festival. And I wasn't thrilled to learn that BookExpo America, the most important conference in the publishing year, will move some of its operations to Brooklyn in 2007.

It's not that I'm above any of those things (I'm not), or that I wasn't invited (although I wasn't), it's that I didn't move to Brooklyn for the literary culture, because I didn't move to Brooklyn at all. As I mentioned not long ago in my blog, I'm from Brooklyn, specifically, from Park Slope, the epicenter of Brooklyn's literary culture, and possibly the very worst place in the country for a writer to have been born.

I live most of the year in the South now. But I come back to Brooklyn often, and when I do, I stay with my parents in Park Slope because I can't afford to stay elsewhere. I love Mother and Dad, but I would prefer to stay anywhere else. Park Slope is a neighborhood almost exclusively populated by writers; to be specific, writers who are better than I am, are more well known than I am and sell more books than I do.

I don't want to give away the exact location, lest my crazed fans hunt me down, but let's just say my family home is in the vicinity of Tea Lounge on Seventh Avenue, the cafe where, according to his Amazon page, Rick Moody ("The Black Veil") likes to hang out and answer his e-mail. We're closer to the old McSweeney's Store (the one on Seventh Avenue that sold ferret wash and coat hooks shaped like bird claws in addition to books published by McSweeney's) than to the new McSweeney's Store (the one on Fifth Avenue that sells superhero supplies and houses the wonderful nonprofit 826NYC).

When I go home for the holidays, I would prefer to be someplace like Greenwich Village or the Upper West Side, where I can get books off my mind for at least a few minutes. But I am the only person in New York who can't afford not to stay in Park Slope.

Not that the writing isn't going well. I'm selling books, making film deals, moving copies in Germany. Anywhere else, that would make me quite a success and, needless to say, pay for an apartment. In Brooklyn I get pity (No National Book Award? No National Book Critics Circle? Not even nominated?), and when I come to town, I get a room in my parents' basement.

There's a rumor going around that Brooklyn is some kind of heaven on earth for writers. I think it started in The Believer, the magazine of optimistic writing founded by the same people who brought us the McSweeney's ferret-wash store (and which, by the way, should stop bothering with individual contributors' bios and just go with "the writers live in Brooklyn").

I think they've been a little too optimistic: right now, somewhere, a young kid, M.F.A. in hand, is dreaming of living in the borough famous as a nice place to visit but a great place to live. A place where she'll be next-door neighbors with an editor at Penguin, and the guy down the block will be an agent at Writers House. Books are plentiful and cheap in this magical borough, although what our young M.F.A. doesn't know yet is that this is because they've been remaindered.

I'll play poker with Jennifer Egan, our neophyte imagines. David Grand will drop by for coffee. I can write lyrics for One Ring Zero, the Brooklyn-based band with lyrics written by Brooklyn-based writers. I'll get a desk at the Brooklyn Writers Space, read my work at the bars on Fifth Avenue, and if I need a job—on that one-in-a-million chance that my writing doesn't make me rich—hey, there are about 50 bookstores on Seventh Avenue. That'd be a fun job!

•

SHE dreams, our young writer, of the day when she, too, can walk her blond Lab down Seventh Avenue on a Sunday afternoon, stopping at the organic bakery for a $7 loaf of whole grain winter wheat bread, and maybe give her new best friend Elissa Schappell ("Use Me") a call to see how she's coming along with the new issue of Tin House—the issue, of course, that's publishing our writer's own brilliant first works.

If the hip-lit magazines One Story or Small Spiral Notebook haven't already snapped up all her stories, that is. And when our hypothetical bright-eyed kid finishes her masterwork of a novel, she won't even have to stray too far to find a publisher, not with the upstart presses Akashic Books and Soft Skull right in the neighborhood.

I have one piece of advice for you, aspiring Brooklynite: Run out, right now, and rent "The Squid and the Whale," Noah Baumbach's small masterpiece of a movie about growing up in Park Slope among writers. Observe closely Jeff Daniels's character, the anti–Dave Eggers. He's not rich, he's not young, and his books aren't selling. He ends up on the other side of Prospect Park, divorced, ignored by the critics, still convinced he's smarter than everyone else and still looking for a parking spot. The character is said to be based on the filmmaker Baumbach's own father, the writer Jonathan Baumbach.

Let me tell you the hard truth: Brooklyn is the worst place on earth for a writer. The competition is fierce and sometimes deadly. The "local authors" shelf in your bookstore has Kathryn Harrison and Paul Auster. Take your laptop to your local coffee shop to do a little work, and you're likely to find Touré ("Soul City") sitting at one end of the counter and Norman Mailer at the other.

Jonathan Safran Foer and Nicole Krauss might be sharing the vegetarian special at a booth in the back, and don't be surprised to find Colson Whitehead and Darin Strauss commiserating about book tours over coffee and pie.

The phrase "anxiety of influence" takes on a whole new meaning when your influences are right there in the room with you, eating lunch.

Anywhere else in the country, people say, "Gee, you really published a book?" In Brooklyn, they ask when you're going on Charlie Rose and if you know Jonathan Lethem. If not, end of conversation, time to move on. Getting off the F train right now is a young woman whose first novel was just pre-empted by Vintage for high six figures. The New York Times Magazine is writing her profile, Marion Ettlinger is taking her head shots, and she's preapproved for a co-op on Prospect Park West.

You try writing a book under these circumstances.

On my most recent visit home, I dropped by a bookstore in Park Slope to sign copies of my latest book. Everywhere else in America, the author at her drop-by signing is greeted with warm handshakes and the offer of a beverage, sometimes even a snack. Much small talk is made. People ask you where you get your ideas and when you decided to be a writer, two questions that are unanswerable but, hey, at least you get to be the center of attention for a few minutes, sometimes as long as a quarter-hour if you really milk it.

If you know any writer with a swollen head, I advise you to send her to a drop-by signing at a bookstore in Brooklyn. In Brooklyn, another writer is just a big yawn, and the bookstore is worried not about providing a snack or even a beverage but about whether it can return signed books.

On the positive side, in Brooklyn no one asks me where I get my ideas and when I decided to become a writer. I like to think that to the astute Sara Gran fan, the rich well of my inspiration is so obvious that there's no need to ask. I choose not to consider the perhaps-more-likely possibility that they're too busy wondering where Siri Hustvedt gets her ideas and, hey, when did she decide to be a writer?

Young writer, you learn to live with the pain to your ego. But there is a better reason not to move to Brooklyn: you will find nothing to write about that another writer hasn't written about first. And if you move here, I will have even less to write about that another writer hasn't written about first.

As a Brooklyn native, I am in a race against the clock. Most writers get to approach middle age knowing that as they get old and dull and run out of interesting things to write about, at least they can return for inspiration to the halcyon days of childhood. But everyone else has already written about my halcyon days, because everyone has already written about Brooklyn.

•

MY BROOKLYN has been appropriated by those hipper than I, cooler than I—better writers than I, but that's hardly the point. The point is: Brooklyn is mine, and I am not inclined to share it. You might say it's a big place, and other writers have as much claim to it as I do. I say, unless you're from Oxford, Miss., you really don't understand.

Consider Seventh Avenue Donuts, formerly known as 24-Hour Donuts, a small doughnut shop and luncheonette in what used to be the south edge of, and now, according to any real estate agent worth his salt, is the dead center of, Park Slope. It's also the least Park Slopish place in Park Slope. Everything is served with ketchup, the seats are made of plastic, smoking was allowed until the last possible minute, and you needn't have won a MacArthur to be able to afford to eat there. I spent about 90 percent of my adolescence there.

In New Orleans a while back, I went to see John Wray read from his fine novel "Canaan's Tongue." To promote the book, and presumably for fun, he re-enacted a journey that one of the characters in "Canaan's Tongue" takes down the Mississippi in a raft. Mr. Wray was kind enough to share the fact that he named his raft Donuts, after a Certain Brooklyn Coffee Shop where he and some of his writer pals like to hang out.

Thank you, Mr. Wray. I appreciate that. All that time spent cutting school and hanging out in Seventh Avenue Donuts in the 80's is now wasted, because Mr. Smartypants decided it was his coffee shop, too, and has immortalized it as his own.

Another example: Like all good New Yorkers, I love the faded beauty of Coney Island, and over the years often thought, "Gee, wouldn't this be a great place to set a mystery novel?" (All good New Yorkers, of course, not only love Nathan's but also daydream about writing novels.) Apparently Maggie Estep ("Flamethrower") thought so too, which is why she sets much of her excellent Ruby Murphy mysteries here.

Well, forget about Coney Island, how about Williamsburg, where I lived in the 90's? Paul Ford, author of the newish "Gary Benchley, Rock Star," beat me to it. And prehipster Williamsburg? Well, it's hard to top Henry Miller, isn't it?

More or less all of the Greater Park Slope/Windsor Terrace area has been covered by Pete Hamill ("A Drinking Life") and Bernard Malamud ("The Assistant"), so we can scrap most of my childhood right there.

Some other things I always wanted to write about: St. Vincent's Home for Boys, that enigmatic downtown Brooklyn landmark (Jonathan Lethem beat me to that one in "Motherless Brooklyn"), the wonderful old Abraham & Straus on Fulton Street, where I went shopping for my new school clothes as a girl (Lethem in "The Disappointment Artist"), or the strange experience of living in pregentrification brownstone Brooklyn in the 70's (Lethem in "The Fortress of Solitude").

As I say, I'm in a race against time here. A. & S. and Coney Island and Seventh Avenue Donuts may have already been claimed by better writers, but surely there is something of Brooklyn left for me, and me alone—if I hurry. I think there's a block up by Garfield and Seventh—nope, that was in Paul Auster's film "Smoke." Down by the Gowanus Canal—oh, forget it, that whole neighborhood was done to death in "Last Exit to Brooklyn." I grew up next to a family of Mohawk Indians who worked in high steel, that might be something—never mind. Joseph Mitchell.

Bay Ridge? Gilbert Sorrentino. Brooklyn Heights? Paula Fox. Frankly, between the new anthologies "Brooklyn Noir One" and "Brooklyn Noir Two" and the forthcoming "Brooklyn Hardboiled" (none of which I was asked to participate in, not that I'm bitter), I think they've got the whole borough covered. Almost.

You could say that only the dead, and Jonathan Lethem, know Brooklyn. I say, I've got a block in Vinegar Hill with my name on it, and I'm getting to work.

September 10, 2006

21

Breathless, Buoyant

No One Knows a Park, Its Smells and Seasons, Its Contours
and Crannies, like a Cross-Country Runner.

ALEXANDER ACIMAN

The author, at left, in Van Cortlandt Park. *(Vincent Laforet/The New York Times)*

THE last practice I remember was during the period between summer and fall, before summer had entirely faded and before autumn had entirely set in. The leaves had just begun to litter the back hills of the cross-country course of Van Cortlandt Park in the Bronx. We had been sent out to run six miles, past the hole in the fence, past the fruit market just outside the park, past the big oak tree; we all knew this was going to be a long run.

The team had its own language. Our coach used to tell us to meet near the big tree by the little tree—in our opinion, an apt description. When we heard the command to run on our own, we would choose our course. Shall we go to Lebanon? No, no, wait, let's go past Crete. Yes, Crete.

The soccer team had no idea what Crete was; neither did the football team. Only we, the cross-country runners, knew that Crete was the area past the muddy highway, and Lebanon was an odd rock formation that looked like Scylla. Did you know the Continental Army made fires here to scare the British? someone always asked as soon as we passed the patches of sand on the main field.

It would happen right around the end of September. We would smell the familiar odor of the park, the whiff of rotting leaves lifting through sod and goose feces. It was fall, the core of our season, and we had the smell to prove it.

Every other team hated the rank aroma, but to us it was a "Welcome Home" banner in the park, or the Motherlandt as we called it, playfully adding a *t* at the end. The smell always made us grin as we passed the cobblestone bridges that hung above the old railroad whose spikes still stood bored into the ground along the Tibbetts Brook Park passage.

The smell belonged to fall; the smell belonged to cross-country. The park was our turf, our ground to roam. Nobody knew this as well as we did. Not even the better runners on opposite teams knew the secret inlets and rivulets we were so familiar with.

It was well known that our team was the only one that could navigate through every dirt road or hillside in the vast woodlands others naïvely called a park. It was only natural that we knew that area better than anybody else did because we spent several hours a day there practicing.

However, once we realized that fall had come, we knew that our season would fly even more quickly than it had the previous year. And before we could even fully realize that our season had begun, it would be time for our final race. Time flies when you run every day, one team member would muse. We must be getting faster.

Later on in the year, spring came. It was time again for track—all the same friends reunited and another outdoor running season. As soon as the season started in April, we would go on long runs just to compensate for all the time we had spent at the indoor running track, in the Armory on West 168th Street, where the hard surface had injured every one of us.

We all felt in our element again, comfortable with the park. We were being reacquainted with the old paths and the narrows we had known so well only a few months earlier. We found ourselves once again hopping chain-link fences to get onto a better course, offering up tactless impersonations of team members or using a clown's voice to imitate our coach's orders, and darting past the golfers to avoid getting caught trespassing on the softer dirt of the Van Cortlandt golf course.

•

I COULD hear the patter of our feet against the hardened mud, accompanied by the distant chants of "Yellow Submarine," our team anthem. Once we reached the end of the path, we realized we were all out of shape because the long winter had prevented us from running around the woods. We took a rest and sat down by the edge of the road; it had been months since we had run together. Our graduated captain would call us a Band of Brothers, we few, we lucky few, we band of brothers.

We watched cars swarm down the highway to our left as we picked the mud from our shoes with small sticks we had torn from the trees. It smells like cross-country, someone said. Yes, it does, someone responded. I didn't know cross-country had a smell, another would say. Well, you haven't been around long enough to know, have you?

Though some of us never truly showed it, we were all thinking of the park, the fall, and cross-country, both the sport and the team. We knew that only Van Cortlandt Park could stir within us the familiar feeling of contradiction, that even though lactic acid boiled in our tired muscles and we were training faster than we could even breathe, we were never more comfortable than we were when we ran.

Masochistically, we were at ease only when we found ourselves running up extra hills because one team member decided to talk back to our coach and we were all being punished. While other kids went home after school to start their homework, we'd throw on our sneakers and storm down the Old Croton Aqueduct. Now it was time to reunite, yet during a different part of the year, and for us, a different running season.

The park was ours again, ours to run. The spring rain was ours, the mud covering our legs up to our calves was ours. Leaning over, I looked down the path and saw two long miles of mud, dirt, sweat, blood, cramps, the Beatles, New Balance, the Olympian Steve Prefontaine, bad jokes, old stories and cross-country. Two miles back to school, and it didn't matter, because we were already home.

May 20, 2007

22

In the Courtyard of Miracles and Wonders

Ever since Arriving in the City, He Yearned to Visit the Cloistered Haven off West 11th Street. One Starlit Night He Got His Chance.

DAVID MASELLO

(Anne Watkins)

ON a cold Saturday night last fall, two of my closest friends and I ate dinner and watched a movie in an old town house on West 11th Street. While I was there, I had an experience I had been wanting for more than 25 years.

My friend Michael had been hired by the owners to live in the town house for a week to dog-sit, and he invited me and our friend Donna over for an evening. The three of us planned to rent "Sweet Bird of Youth," the 1960's drama starring Paul Newman and Geraldine Page, and watch it on the big-screen television while eating take-out falafel and kebabs from a favorite Middle Eastern restaurant. We drank good French red wine, and we were surrounded by four sleeping dogs who would periodically awaken and imprint a cold nose on our wrists, hoping for another belly rub or shard of pita bread.

One of the most unusual things about the house is the flagstoned courtyard in the back, reachable by a set of French doors. The courtyard is shared by a full block of houses along Bleecker Street, and other buildings that wrap around 11th and Perry Streets.

I had wanted to see the courtyard ever since moving to New York decades earlier, and especially after I rented an apartment on West 11th Street in the late 1980's. I had heard about its existence as if it were a reclusive silent-movie star or a sacred Indian burial mound whose entrance was known only by select archaeologists.

The courtyard itself has a mostly secretive history, and the residents who share it are adamant about keeping it theirs. The brick and wood house we occupied, which dates from 1818, is the sole remnant of the 55-acre estate that a prominent property owner named Abijah Hammond established in 1799. What is now West 11th Street was called Hammond Street, and the courtyard was simply a parcel of that open, hilly land, visible in an 1825 pen-and-ink view that is in the collection of the Metropolitan Museum.

"Behind these houses," a walking-tour guide had told me soon after my arrival in New York, pointing to the row of stoopless 19th-century houses along Bleecker Street, "is a private courtyard. And parties take place there, and everybody who knows about it wants to live in one of these buildings."

The town houses were, and still are, painted different colors—slate gray, cinnamon, red, white—and shops are located in some of their first floors. When I lived in the Village, a bird store occupied the corner of 11th and Bleecker; after hours, pedestrians used to stop in front of its windows to watch swarms of mice feasting on birdseed, and if the wind was right, the squawks of cockatoos and parrots could be heard in the middle of the night.

The night the three of us stepped into the courtyard, where we remained until the cold drove us indoors, it was more magical and intimate than any place I have seen in New York. If I could describe an ideal space, this might be it: a communal urban yard for a small neighborhood of people, its occupants visible but not heard, a discernible glow from lamps and blazes in fireplaces.

Our breaths unfurled in little gray clouds, and we smelled wood smoke drifting from chimneys. We were cocooned by the lamp-lit interiors of town houses, each revealing its domestic scenes in the manner of Broadway stage sets for 1940's drawing-room comedies: a couple sipping soup, a man on a couch petting his dachshund, children illuminated by the blue explosions of light from television sets. Overhead, we could see stars.

Behind all the addresses that shared this courtyard, the occupants have created private spaces that meld with the public—a wrought-iron table and chair whose scrollings were whitened with the early frost, sculptures anchoring a closely clipped square of lawn, as if the grass were a carpet that could be unfurled by wind, even a miniature crop of corn.

•

I KNEW that if I lived in this house that I was visiting only for an evening, I might never again feel the alienation that comes with sleepless nights. Here, I imagined, I'd get out of bed after a troubling dream, dress until I was warm, sit on a chair in the courtyard and perhaps fall asleep there, awakening stiffly with the morning light.

From the center of the courtyard, I could see, several doors east, the black dumbbell silhouette of 266 West 11th Street, the walk-up tenement building where I lived for eight years. My apartment was on the top floor, and after dinner I used to pace the roof, which came to feel like my own outdoor room. From the south end of the roof, I could discern the hollowed-out space of the courtyard, but I could see no details, just a void that opened amid the mesh of fire escapes and sumac trees.

The evening with my two friends had been a perfect one, without an agenda or plot—unlike the film we'd watched, in which Geraldine Page as a failing actress connives to land a write-up from the columnist Walter Winchell. I had experienced the courtyard as if it too were a friend. I don't know if I'll ever make another visit, but now I know what it's like to occupy it for an evening.

There are other places in New York I want to experience, like Turtle Bay Gardens, which is a Midtown version of the courtyard. I want to cross the verdigris sky bridge that spans West 32nd Street, and I'd like to lean on the lectern still used in the auditorium of Cooper Union, the one where Lincoln stood to deliver his "right makes might" speech.

But having paid a visit to the courtyard in the Village, I've accomplished at least one goal that I've had ever since I moved to New York from Illinois years ago as a young man. This is my home, and I want to know all the best places.

December 16, 2007

23

Stranger in a Strange Land

On a Sojourn in a SoHo Hotel after a Flood
in His Brooklyn Heights Apartment,
Much Looked Familiar. And Somehow Not.

ALEX ROSE

(Juliette Borda)

ELL me if you've heard this one.

A man from Minsk decides he wishes to visit the neighboring town of Pinsk. He packs a bag, bids farewell to his wife and boards the train, where he promptly falls asleep. When he awakens, he is struck by the astonishing likeness of Pinsk to Minsk.

He walks the streets noting that everything looks just the same as his home town, "only somehow different." Never does it occur to him that the strangely familiar shopkeepers and street merchants who greet him, or even the woman who bears an uncanny resemblance to his wife, are the very same people he has known all along.

I was reminded of this classic Jewish tale a few weeks ago, when my Brooklyn Heights apartment was flooded, my carpet spattered with rust-infused rainwater and chunks of gooey drywall, and I was temporarily relocated to a nearby Holiday Inn. Crossing the Brooklyn Bridge by cab, lugging my bags to the lobby, checking in at the front desk behind a line of international guests, I could already feel myself becoming disembodied from my once-familiar surroundings, a de facto tourist in my own town.

The hotel sits at the southwest corner of Lafayette and Howard Streets, an area real estate agents call SoHo, but one that otherwise bears little resemblance to the district we associate with that name. This row of three or four blocks is something of a no man's land, a sliver of negative space cloistered between four brand-name quadrants—SoHo, Little Italy, Chinatown and TriBeCa—with no token identity of its own. It was refreshing, if a bit disorienting, to walk through the ageless shadowlands of a city that seems to grow slicker and more anemic each day.

Unlike the ultrahip greasy spoon just north, a place like the Landmark diner on Grand Street, one block from the hotel, retains its unselfconscious, Old World charm, with its checkerboard tiles, Formica tables and exposed ducts. There are no glossy photographs of itself on the walls, no skinny-jeaned 20-somethings hunched at the bar with silver laptops.

Howard Street in particular has a quality reminiscent of city outskirts, a sort of "functioning ruins," similar to the landscape one finds in a Ben Katchor strip. This is particularly true at night. The crude industrial sprawl of Canal Street, with its foam rubber outlets and major appliance bargains, washes seamlessly into the artsy glitter of design stores and vintage boutiques on Grand.

I saw a red neon sign reading Pe Pai, which I assumed to be a Chinese transliteration. On closer inspection, I realized that the text actually spelled Pearl Paint, or would have if the other bulbs had been working.

•

ON my second day at the hotel, I tightened my gut and ventured into SoHo proper. Though I'd been there dozens of times in the past, my experience had always been circumscribed by whatever menial activity I was there to perform. I'd barrel across Prince Street, head down, iPod blasting, never bothering to appreciate the jostle and flux of life around me.

Now that I had no task but to observe, I found myself giddy with stimulation. Before long, I was behaving like the very tourists that New Yorkers notoriously revile, which is to say both overly alert and completely oblivious—squinting up at the buildings, stepping through vagrant urine, standing idly at crosswalks, craning my neck at every passing beauty. I inhaled the dizzying chorus of scents: exhaust from laundromats, sizzling pretzels, fresh sawdust from construction sites, astringent fumes from the sudsy cleaning agents rolling down the sidewalk.

Finally, I surrendered. Why not own the experience, I thought, and capitulate fully to the traveler mindset?

I swallowed my pride and bought a fanny pack.

I also called friends and had them take me through various neighborhoods, pointing out their favorite bars and parks and regaling me with tales of late-night debauchery. I sampled as many independent bookstores as I could find, hunting for hard-to-find authors and out-of-print editions. (The grand prize goes to St. Mark's Bookshop on Third Avenue.)

I shopped at high-end outlets on West Broadway, procuring, among other things, an $89 T-shirt. I ate like a king in NoLIta, wolfing down pulled-pork sandwiches on toasted sourdough and glorious baked eggs with fresh cilantro. I sucked down mojitos and bellinis in the afternoon. I browsed the upscale galleries.

The highlight of my stay was a walking tour through the East Village. A frizzy-haired grad student delivered an unapologetically leftist history of Lower Manhattan, full of robber barons, negligent landlords, bloody protests and glamorous unionizations. It was thrilling to imagine fin-de-siècle New York with its dirt roads and unbearable stench, the swells lining up outside the theater, middle-class women congregating in smoke-filled parlors, the madness of the Bowery with its decaying horse carcasses and clamoring el. For the rest of the day, I couldn't help seeing things in grainy black and white.

●

BUT eventually, perhaps inevitably, the exotic spell began to wear off. I'd learned the names of the obscure streets, the marvelous old businesses with their heartbreaking clearance sales. I'd started to recognize the inhabitants, the routes to the best coffee shops. At the same time, I longed for my own New York, the quotidian city of MetroCards and Leonard Lopate on the radio and free concerts in the park.

When I received word that my ceiling had finally been repaired, I checked out of my drab suite at the Holiday Inn and heaved my bags toward the No. 6 train. Suddenly, the sky darkened and a fierce squall lashed the streets. In a heartbeat, the environment was transformed. Models scurried under awnings, makeup drizzling down their cheeks. Men in Paul Smith pinstripes and D&G aviators stumbled into hydrants, tripped over dog leashes. Puddles formed, windows fogged. In the gloomy rush, New York could have been any other city: Warsaw, Tokyo, Minsk.

Then, just as suddenly, the thunderclouds parted and the rain came to a halt. The sun reappeared. The mist cleared, and within moments the neighborhood looked just as it did before. Only somehow different.

August 3, 2008

24

Hard Times along Gasoline Alley

The Men Who Hang Out near the Service Stations
on Atlantic Avenue Will Pump Your Gas,
Fix Your Brakes and Maybe Tell You a Story.

JAMES ANGELOS

A gas pumper who calls himself Flip outside a Hess station in Stuyvesant
Heights, Brooklyn. *(Andrew Henderson/The New York Times)*

THEY can be seen all along Atlantic Avenue—urban foragers of a sort, often bedraggled and always in search of a dollar. Many of them pump gas, but that is not the only hustle along the strip.

As one regular walks on sections of Atlantic, a traffic-clogged 10-mile road that runs from the Brooklyn waterfront to the Van Wyck Expressway in Queens, he holds a bottle of glass cleaner and offers to wash car windows. Outside an auto parts store, street mechanics replace brake pads and tune transmissions, using tools hauled around in shopping carts.

One recent evening, opposite a BP station at Vanderbilt Avenue in Prospect Heights, Brooklyn, a taxi with smoke pouring from under its hood pulled over to the sidewalk, and a burly man ran over and lifted the hot, browning hood to expose flames rising from the engine's alternator.

After patting the flames with a rag, the man poured water on the fire. With steam still rising from the engine, the man demanded of the cabby, "Where's my tip?" The driver forked over five singles, which apparently were not enough. "The engine could have exploded!" the man protested. The cabby pulled out two more singles.

But pumping gas is the most common hustle along Atlantic Avenue. Men, and often teenage boys, stand next to self-service pumps and, at a time when it can easily cost $60 to fill a tank, offer their services in exchange for pocket change, asking, "May I pump your gas for you?"

Whatever the hustle, as the road travels east and the neighborhoods along it get poorer, the number of self-styled entrepreneurs only grows. At three stops along the way, they can be seen making a living, or at least a few extra dollars, off the endless rumble of cars and trucks that pummel the avenue's rutted surface.

•

BENEATH the peeling roof of a Hess station at Ralph Avenue in Stuyvesant Heights, Brooklyn, framed on the north by the Brevoort housing project and on the south by Kingsborough Houses, are eight self-service pumps—and often just as many hustlers who come and go as their economic needs dictate. The competition can be fierce; one hustler, called DMX by other gas pumpers, described it as a battle between lions and tigers.

"Coming in! White truck!" DMX yelled one afternoon as he sought to claim an S.U.V. even before it turned into the station.

DMX, who was a station regular earlier this summer, is tall and wears a white headband. On his cheek is a three-inch scar, which he said was carved into his face during a fight in a prison upstate.

Like several other people interviewed for this article, many of whom lead cryptic lives, he declined to give his full name. But like nearly all the hustlers in the neighborhood, he has a nickname; he earned his because he can make his voice sound as raspy as that of the rapper of the same name.

Street etiquette dictates that once a hustler claims a car, he has exclusive rights to approach it. But sometimes this arrangement breaks down, as it did recently.

"Yo, why you step in front of me like that?" a gas pumper yelled to another as passengers in a sedan that had pulled up to a pump looked out the windows with stunned expressions.

Amid such competition, the gas pumpers sometimes turn to intimidation.

"I'm going to get every car that gets in here," DMX announced loudly at one point. "I got to eat.

"If they get in my way, I'm going to cut somebody."

Such hostility is in sharp contrast to the fawning attentiveness that DMX showers on customers. Smiling broadly, he refers to them as "my sister" or "my dude." For babies in the back seats, it's "Hey, cutie!"

"Once you get them smiling," he said, "you don't know what may come out of their pockets."

When a woman in a cream-colored PT Cruiser pulled up to Pump No. 2, DMX gazed into her eyes. "You all right?" he asked. "You look good." After pumping her gas, he received a dollar.

In this respect, the gas pumpers are not like the squeegee men, who were ubiquitous in the city during the 1980's and were notorious for intimidating drivers stopped at red lights by demanding payment for unsolicited services like wiping dirty rags across windshields. The hustlers of Atlantic Avenue approach customers with careful hesitance and usually accept rejection politely, often with a guilt-inducing "God bless you."

The station's employees work in a little white hut equipped with bulletproof windows. They have become accustomed to the gas pumpers, and have even developed a rapport with the regulars. The station manager, who said his name was Tony, said that he had called 311 a few times to shoo the hustlers away, but that he no longer bothered.

Police officers come and hand out tickets. But once they leave, the hustlers return. "It's unstoppable," Tony said.

An eight-hour workday can land a gas pumper about $50, and for the more energetic ones, maybe more. DMX, who lives nearby, said he spent his earnings on food and clothing. Other gas pumpers, some of whom have sketchier housing situations, say that they spend much of their earnings on crack cocaine. Flip, a stocky 43-year-old who habitually toots a silver harmonica, says he sometimes sleeps on the A train, keeping company with a four-inch glass pipe.

As Flip talked about his past one recent morning over a cheeseburger at a McDonald's next to the gas station, his eyes watered as he described what he called "all the positive things I was supposed to be." As a child, he enjoyed acting, and he said he was an extra on "The Magnificent Major," a 1977 children's special on NBC about a little girl who didn't like to read.

Mr. B, a skinny, 29-year-old regular at the station, also has a crack habit, though he says he is not addicted. "Psychology of the mind," he says, keeps him from being dependent on the drug. His glassy eyes roll slightly upward, and he often looks as if he is trying to suppress a grin. He likes to mention his grandmother. "Today is my grandmother's 90th birthday," he told two customers, each on a different day. "I'm going to see her later."

Both Flip and Mr. B take 30-minute breaks, drifting away from the station and returning dazed and sometimes a little paranoid. When Flip returned from one such break, he said, "I went to go see Oz." In fact, he had made his way to Kingsborough Houses, where, he said, he took the elevator to the fifth floor of a building, puffed on his glass pipe and then rode back down.

The same afternoon, Mr. B left the station and began walking along Atlantic Avenue toward the sunset, passing the weeds that grow through the cracks in the sidewalk. "He won't be back for a long time," Flip said with a laugh.

But Mr. B returned about an hour later. He stood silently next to Pump No. 8, looking lost in a tangle of dismal thoughts. Asked where he had gone, Mr. B flashed his famous grin and replied, "Eat, eat, eat, eat."

●

WHILE the gas pumpers rely on a mixture of intimidation, charm and charity to make a living, other Atlantic Avenue hustlers sell their automotive skills.

Outside an AutoZone store near Washington Avenue in Clinton Hill, Brooklyn, several street mechanics work under cars parked on the side of the road, installing parts purchased by the store's customers.

On a hot spring day, a 36-year-old street mechanic named Matthew Joseph lay precariously on the baking asphalt of Atlantic Avenue, near three lanes of westbound traffic that whizzed by as he jacked up the left front side of a Hyundai sedan. Mr. Joseph wore a black do-rag and a white tank top that exposed his muscular arms. After a few years of working on the side of the road, he is used to the traffic being only a few feet away.

Pulling off the tire, Mr. Joseph released a cloud of dust that looked orange in the sunlight, and began replacing the car's brake pads. Doing this sort of work, he usually earns about $150 a day, which helps him pay the $950 monthly rent for his one-bedroom apartment nearby. For this job, he charged the car's owner $40, about half what a garage would charge, he said.

Mr. Joseph is enthusiastic about fixing cars, and he likes to explain automotive problems to his customers, though his explanations are sometimes dizzying in their complexity.

"You have to see if your injector has an injector control module," he told a driver in a red minivan that afternoon. "If your injector has an injector control module, then you check to see if the control module for the injector maybe isn't firing."

"I feel you," the driver replied, though he looked confused.

Later that day, Mr. Joseph sat in the passenger seat of a blue Jeep, the brakes of which he had just replaced. The driver sped up and down Atlantic Avenue, testing the work.

"The front brakes is good," Mr. Joseph announced. "Beautiful. Beautiful delay. Hard and sturdy."

Mr. Joseph offered his cellphone number to the car owner in case there were any problems. "You could call me, too, all right," he said. "You'd be driving, even at nighttime, call me. I'm official."

Walter Malone also works near the AutoZone. He is in the auto body repair business, which he conducts on the sidewalk outside an old muffler garage. In addition, he lives in the garage, sleeping on a makeshift bed of mats and cushions protected from leaks in the roof by tarps. Mr. Malone, who often wears a red hard hat and silver chains around his neck, is deaf and speaks only in grunts.

One afternoon, a man who identified himself as Broadway pulled up to the garage in a rusty green pickup. Mr. Malone examined the truck carefully.

He pointed to the dented hood, making a hammering motion with his large hands, indicating that he would pound the dent out. He walked around the truck, making a "bah" sound when he found a problem and pantomiming how he would fix it. After the inspection, Mr. Malone rubbed together his thumb and index finger to indicate that this job would be costly. Using pen and paper, the two men eventually agreed to a price of $300. Broadway promised to bring back the pickup the next morning.

As it turned out, Broadway did not return. But before driving off, he explained that he had bought the truck for $200, and he planned to use it for, among other things, picking up mattresses left on the street and delivering them to a refurbishing business that would pay him $15 for each one.

"Everybody's got a hustle," Broadway said. "You can make a dollar in this here New York City."

•

THE gas pumping hustle at a Mobil station at Bedford Avenue, near the Bedford-Atlantic Armory and its homeless shelter, is a lot less cutthroat than the one at the Hess station a mile and half to the east. One day not long ago, a student from the nearby Science Skills Center High School named John Greene could be seen wandering among the station's 16 pumps after school. John, who was wearing a Bob Marley T-shirt, was craving a snack of nachos, but first he needed to raise the money.

"Can I pump your gas for you?" he asked over and over.

A large man who calls himself Big Earl pulled up to Pump No. 13 in a minivan that blared R&B music. "It's cool," Big Earl said in response to the boy's offer. John filled the tank with regular, and Big Earl handed him a fistful of change, nearly $2.

"Children are our resources," Big Earl said. "If we don't take care of our resources, we don't take care of our future."

Once John had collected $4, enough for two servings of nachos, he headed for the nachos machine in the station's convenience store. "It's my favorite," he said as he pressed the buttons that released chili and cheese from the plastic tubes of the dispenser. Two days later, he said, he would be back for more.

A more familiar face at the Mobil station belongs to a skinny and mysterious man with a graying beard who has been pumping gas and acting as the convenience store's de facto doorman for five years. Vishal Khosla, the station's manager, calls the man "Green"—no relation to the student John Greene—and says he likes having him around because he keeps an eye out for thieves and troublemakers.

Most days, Green arrives at the station at 7 a.m. He earns more than enough to pay his $10 daily rent for a room nearby, he said. When the weather gets too hot, he quits early, and is happy to be able to come and go as he pleases.

"I be good here," he said one afternoon, his linen polka-dot shirt rippling in the warm breeze. "I don't try to get over on anybody. Everybody gets to like me because I do good."

As he spoke, he opened the door for customers, receiving a dollar from one.

"If you do good," he said, "you shall prosper."

August 17, 2008

25

A Game of Inches

With the Opening of a New Yankee Stadium, Would Stan's Sports Bar Be Just a Little Too Far from the Action?

KATHERINE BINDLEY

Stan's Sports Bar, a longtime watering hole near Yankee Stadium in the Bronx. *(Todd Heisler/The New York Times)*

THIRTY feet. That is the distance between the entrance of Stan's Sports Bar at 158th Street and River Avenue and the faded black sign affixed to the side of Yankee Stadium that says "Bleacher Entrance." It is a third of the length between first and second base, easy strolling distance for the droves of Yankee fans who crowded in religiously each baseball season.

And for 30 years, this archetypal American sports bar, with wooden baseball bats as its door handles and sketches of Mickey Mantle and Lou Gehrig on its walls, has been a prime piece of Bronx real estate.

Until the Yankees moved across the street, and then it wasn't.

The old Yankee Stadium sits on the south side of East 161st Street and extends south to the corner of 157th. The new stadium sits on the north side of 161st Street and runs north almost to 164th.

Many dismiss the move as insignificant to local businesses, noting that technically, the new stadium is just across the street from the old one. But for Stan's, it's now a long block to the gates of the new stadium.

The move alone had the potential to diminish the number of fans the bar packs in before, during and after every game. And then came the upscale dining and drinking options within the new stadium, a steep increase in ticket prices and a recession that may leave regular visits to the ballpark a luxury ever fewer people can afford.

Ever since last September, when the Yankees played their final game in the old stadium, the combination of these factors has left a question in the minds of Louis Dene, the bar's 43-year-old owner, and his two managers, Joe Mondi and Michael Rendino. After the gates to the new stadium open on Friday night for an exhibition game against the Chicago Cubs, they wonder, what will all these changes mean for them?

"It's really a big mystery," said Mr. Dene, who bought the bar from his father, Stan Martucci, 11 years ago. "You can ask 10 people, and eight will tell you that the tradition and uniqueness of Stan's will live on. And the other two will tell you you've got all this corporate competition and people will have to come to Stan's with intent instead of stumbling upon it."

Mr. Dene estimates that the move will cost him 30 to 40 percent of his business. If there's one thing he and his staff have learned over the years, it's that theirs is a business whose fate has always been intertwined with that of a baseball team.

•

THE tradition itself began in 1979. Mr. Martucci and his wife, Barbara, were raising four sons in Willowbrook, Staten Island, and he was running Stan's Sports World, a memorabilia shop on River Avenue that is still in the family.

"My dad's love was for the souvenir end of the business," Mr. Dene said of Mr. Martucci, who died last March. "He wasn't a bar guy; he didn't drink."

But buying the building next to the souvenir shop, which was already a bar, seemed like a smart move.

Mr. Dene, it turned out, took a liking to the bar and restaurant business. At 25, he became its manager. Around the same time, he was coaching football for Susan E. Wagner High School in Staten Island, and he recruited his players to help as bar backs.

Mr. Dene now lives in Santa Barbara, Calif. Though he comes to town for every Yankee home stand, he leaves much of the bar's operation to Mr. Mondi and Mr. Rendino.

Mr. Mondi was one of those high school football players, an inside linebacker who was friends with the Martucci boys. Today, he lives in West Brighton, Staten Island, splitting his time between helping to run Stan's and working as a firefighter in Hunts Point in the Bronx. Mr. Rendino, who lives in Throgs Neck in the Bronx, worked as a firefighter in Morrisania until he developed lung problems after 9/11 and retired on disability.

·

FOUR weeks before game day, sawdust still speckled the ceramic tile floor of the empty bar. Snow lay on the ground, and there was no heat. Seated side by side in one of the blue wooden booths, Mr. Mondi and Mr. Rendino talked about Stan's back in the day.

"You have to die to lose your shift here," said Mr. Mondi, who at 34 has already put in 20 years at the bar. He recalled meeting at Mr. Martucci's house on game days as a teenager. From there, everyone packed into a 15-person van and headed for the Bronx. "All the kids from the neighborhood worked here," he said.

His partner, Mr. Rendino, a burly 34-year-old who was dressed this day in gray slacks and a blue button-down shirt, is the "face of the business," as he puts it, the one who attends community board meetings.

Mr. Rendino said he started working the door at Stan's in 1998. Mr. Mondi insisted that it was 1997. The two men batted this point back and forth before concluding that it might have been 1998 after all.

What they do agree on is that Stan's started out as a tough-guy bar, a rough-and-tumble joint.

"I remember we played the Red Sox in '91," Mr. Mondi said, "and right in that corner, some guy came in wearing a Red Sox jersey, and they ripped it off his body, they lit it on fire, and they urinated on it. Right here in the bar."

The South Bronx in those days was a crime-ridden place, and fans rarely lingered after games.

"When I first got here, it was like a ghost town," Mr. Mondi said. "People would come to see a Yankee game, and if the game started at 7, they would try to get here for 7 and they would leave the minute the game was over."

That began changing in 1996. More police officers were assigned to the area, the Yankees were getting hot, and for the first time in 18 years, the team won the World Series—and then three more World Series in the next four years. With the team's reinvention came the reinvention of the bar.

"You know what it was?" Mr. Rendino said. "It was Jeter, Knoblauch, O'Neill and Tino Martinez. It was a popular thing for girls in Manhattan living on the Upper East Side to get a season ticket package with their friends and come to 15 or 20 games."

As the Yankees became trendy, so did Stan's, and soon, fans were filling the booths before, during and after games.

Stan's is open for every home game, which comes to an average of 90 very busy days a year, give or take a few special events, like the pope's visit last April. That day, the flat-screen televisions, usually reserved for baseball, broadcast the pope celebrating Mass at the stadium.

"People were praying on our floors," Mr. Rendino recalled. Alcohol sales were lower than usual, but he and his partner thought it best not to kick out a bunch of worshipers.

●

TODAY, the version of Stan's with which most people are familiar is a place where the official capacity is 270 but it feels like 370. Stan's has all the characteristics of a classic sports bar: loud music, sticky floors, drunken fans. The décor is Yankee blue, accented with neon signs and white ice bins lined up for the bottled beers. On nice days, when the glass panes in the windows are removed, it's hard to tell where Stan's ends and the stadium begins.

But will those same fans turn south instead of north when they exit the subway? Will they walk that extra block?

Sitting in a booth near the back of the bar, Mr. Rendino attempted a diagram using two cellphones that sat on the table.

"The train station is here," he said. "The old stadium's here, the new stadium's here, the bar's here. It used to be, they get off the train, they walk by. Now they get off, and they go in the exact opposite direction. That's the problem. The one block is a problem."

•

THREE weeks and counting until the first game in the new stadium.

The radio inside Stan's was turned up, boxes of Brillo pads were scattered around the kitchen, and everything smelled like bleach. Staff members had gathered for a thorough spring cleaning, even though 10 minutes into the first game of the new season, they say, the place usually looks the way it did during the final 10 minutes of the last game of the last season.

As they worked, they discussed the changes coming this year. No one has ever come to Stan's for the food, but the managers may need to attract more people now, so they're adding more health-conscious items (the Philadelphia cheese steak sandwich will be offered with chicken). Advertising is another option being considered for the first time in the bar's history.

Teddy Tonge, who stands 6 feet 5, weighs 290 pounds and works as a bouncer, insisted that there was no cause for concern.

"This is established," he said.

He is already looking forward to keeping the fans in check. "Three chances and out," Mr. Tonge said, pointing a long arm northwest toward Highbridge, where he lives.

Others see the extra block as more significant, among them Tony Del-Carmine, a 38-year-old father of three who has been coming to Stan's for years. Mr. DelCarmine lives in Stamford, Conn., but one day not long ago, he came to the Bronx to check out the new stadium, then popped into the bar to see if there was anything he could do to help spread the word that the walk would be worth it.

"It's inevitable to wonder what's going to happen," Mr. DelCarmine said. Fans, he noted, have a certain mentality. "Clearly," he said, "the inclination is for them to go to the first drinking hole they can find."

•

THIS year, that first drinking hole could be the Dugout, which opened five years ago on River Avenue just north of 161st Street and may have just become the most coveted location on the block. Ten days before the first game at the new stadium, that bar's owner, Tyrone Robinson, 31, was preparing for what he expects will be his best season.

"Whatever Stan had on that side last year, I'll be getting that," Mr. Robinson said. "And I guess he'll get what I got."

Because of the new stadium, Mr. Robinson has expanded his 2,400-square-foot space by 4,000 square feet and is working on a roof deck. He is also ordering 180 cases of beer for the forthcoming exhibition games instead of the 90 he ordered last season. He's hoping to see business double.

In virtually every respect, the Dugout is the antithesis of Stan's. The only natural light is provided by the double glass doors at the entrance, making the space extremely dark. Deep red walls and a disco ball hanging from the ceiling give the place the feel of a lounge.

"There's a term I'm looking for," Mr. Robinson said, searching for how to describe the atmosphere. "Midtown comes to the Bronx—that's it."

And he expects that the higher ticket prices for games will change the nature of his clientele.

"It's a whole new caliber of people I'm looking forward to meeting," he said. "It costs more to get into the game, so we're going to meet people that are willing to spend a little more."

•

THAT same afternoon, Lou Lomonaco, 42, who lives on City Island in the Bronx and works as a high school guidance counselor, took a break from jury duty at the courthouse up the hill to peer inside the new stadium, where attractions will include a high-end steakhouse and a Hard Rock Cafe.

Mr. Lomonaco, who has been attending games since 1976, said he would do so this year only if someone invited him.

"My understanding is it's outrageous," he said. "I guess they have to support what they're doing here, but it's unfair to the average person like myself."

The managers at Stan's say that the average person is exactly their customer, and they fear that the Yankees might have priced that person right out of the Bronx. Still, they're confident they have the loyalty of their regulars, people like Rolling Rock Lou.

Lou, whose real name is David Bender, is 64 and lives in Somerset, N.J. Decades ago, Mr. Bender's friends decided that he looked more like a Lou than a David. He drinks only Rolling Rock, and so the staff at Stan's gave him a name to distinguish him from the bar's owner, Lou Dene. Mr. Bender, who is retired from the advertising business, has bought a 20-game package every year since 2000.

Until now.

"The prices went up; the seats were going to be worse," he said. "So I have not accepted the Yankees' offer of continuing that plan." Mr. Bender's 20-game package came to $60 per ticket last season. This year, he said, the Yankees offered him $85 tickets in home-run territory instead of inside the foul poles.

Instead, he made a deal to buy tickets to 10 games from his accountant, who has a season package. Mr. Bender said he would continue to go to Stan's, and he suspected that others would as well. "For a lot of people," he said, "it still really is a tradition."

March 29, 2009

PART THREE

Rituals, Rhythms, and Ruminations

26

Please Get Me Out of Here Please

New Yorkers Knew All about the Three-Day Ordeal of the
Chinese-Food Delivery Man Trapped in an Elevator in the
Bronx. They Had Been There, If Only in Their Dreams.

COLIN HARRISON

An image familiar to every New Yorker. *(Hiroko Masuike/The New York Times)*

L AST week, when the news broke that Ming Kuang Chen, a delivery man for a Chinese restaurant, had emerged from a stalled elevator in a 38-story Bronx apartment building after some 81 hours in captivity, not a few New Yorkers skipped accounts of the city's usual mayhem to study the details of Mr. Chen's ordeal.

Who could blame us? New Yorkers, more than any other American population, depend on elevators. The first passenger elevator was built in New York, in 1857 at Broadway and Broome Street, and now millions of us ride them each day. Indeed, we are indivisible from our elevators, being hummingly conveyed within apartment houses, office buildings, schools, bookstores, health clubs, ad agencies, you name it—bing, the elevator stops, the doors open, and there we are.

But even riding an elevator several times a day, one never forgets the unspoken rules of elevator deportment: the attempt not to brush against anyone else, the suppression of the desire to study other people's body parts (attractive and fascinatingly not), the hush of conversation, the mutual agreement not to acknowledge that one is trapped with utter strangers in a metal box hurtling through space. This decorum, we know, is always dependent on the absolute brevity of the ride.

And yet intimate things can and do happen in elevators. Spouses have been known to hiss hatefully at each other in elevators; lawyers reach informal legal settlements in the courthouse elevators around City Hall; newly intimate and often inebriated couples lunge passionately at each other in elevators; important people tweak the details of massive financial deals in private Wall Street elevators paneled in mahogany; formal dinner parties in high-end prewar buildings sometimes receive unscripted beginnings and endings in the classy little boxes in which the invitees ride; and careers can mysteriously unravel in impromptu conversations in corporate office elevators, amid flickering digital floor readouts and gleaming walls of brushed steel.

Yes, New Yorkers know their elevators, and this is why most of us have wondered what it would be like to be stuck in one, if only for an hour, to say nothing of three-plus days. Would the elevator suddenly jolt to a halt? Would it drop and then be caught by some kind of emergency brake? Would the brake hold? Many of us have encountered elevators being repaired and thus been forced to consider the square shaft beneath them that falls into an ominous gloom. A sickening feeling, that. Makes you suddenly appreciate stairs.

In fact, many of us have been caught in elevator mishaps. Most New Yorkers remember the blackout in August 2003, which left many people stranded for an hour or two, and a few New Yorkers of a certain age even remember the previous citywide blackout, in 1977. And while not enduring the miseries of Mr. Chen, a good number of us have our own private elevator misadventures to draw upon.

After entering an East Side apartment building, my wife and I once watched in horror as our two young children, ages 2 and 4, rushed excitedly into an elevator ahead of us just as the door closed. Zoom—up the elevator went. We raced to the lobby security desk and witnessed via the monitor our children's frantic explosion into tears as they realized they were alone. Then the doors opened and they got out—but where in the high building we did not know! We were similarly frantic.

A good Samaritan brought our kids down to the lobby, and so the story has a happy ending, but it will never be forgotten by us, and has even become part of that private primal text all families carry. Other people I know have had to step, crawl, or climb dangerously out of stuck elevators or have collapsed into a fit of weeping even after walking out of one unscathed.

Yet we New Yorkers still stride willingly into those small spaces, and the daily necessity of our provisional faith is precisely why Mr. Chen's imprisonment was so nerve-racking to consider, even from the vantage point of the next day's newspaper. Police had looked for him, going door to door to no fewer than 871 apartments in the building in which he was trapped, using bloodhounds and cadaver-detecting dogs. Yet there he was right next to them, trapped in a tiny express elevator without food or water. They didn't know he was there.

This horrible little fact is the departure point of the New Yorker's imagination, wherein one can't help but mix claustrophobia, big-city anxiety, and plain, old human despair. How would we behave if the elevator stopped? Would we yell out, as did Mr. Chen, bang our fists piteously on the wall or doors? Even after it was clear that no one could hear us? Would we holler at the deaf, dumb, yet presumably all-seeing security camera?

Having ingested too many horror films, wouldn't we wonder whether someone was in fact watching us—yet doing nothing? When would the issue of food and water begin to be a problem? Would we look for a trapdoor in the ceiling or try to unscrew the button panel? What about the most basic of human digestive functions? What about that problem?

•

Do cellphones work in all elevators? One suspects some might not. What if one is one of the few people left in New York who do not have cellphones? What if you needed a cigarette? Who would be worrying about not being able to reach you? What if the kids need to be picked up from school? What if the boss is sitting there wondering whether to fire you? What if you think you hear cockroaches scuttling in the darkness around you? What if one suffers panic attacks in response to lesser stimuli? What is it like to drink or eat nothing for three days?

But wait, the question of "what if" only gets worse. What if you are stuck in an elevator with another person, especially someone you don't know or like the look of? Do you have to smile nervously and make small talk? Share your newspaper or book or hand-held video game? Indeed, things could get very uncomfortably intimate with another person in an elevator, certainly within an hour or so. Again, the issue of bodily functions. What if there are two people and one bottle of water? What if the lights go off and you can hear the other person breathing within the closed box of complete darkness?

The nightmare has endless permutations. Some people need coffee, alcohol or pills to stave off madness and other extreme behaviors. Many human beings emit odors. Some people vomit when anxious. What if the person is violent? What if the air goes bad? What if the other person dies of fright before you do?

Considering these afflictions, perhaps we may offer a collective salute to the weary Mr. Chen, he of the 81 hours, on the theory that, but by the grace of the god of elevator maintenance, he suffered a bit of what we can so easily imagine, while we, thankfully, did not.

April 10, 2005

27

The Starling Chronicles

The Baby Bird Was Small and Smelly, Unlikely to Live Long.
But She Fell from Her Nest into a Cradle of Love,
and Soon She Became a New Yorker, with Wings.

LAURA SHAINE CUNNINGHAM

The author's daughter, Jasmine Cunningham, with the
bird she called Raven Starling. *(Courtesy of the
author)*

WHY is there a wild bird in my apartment?

She fell, as a nestling, from the rain gutter on the roof of my country house. Since then, she has been dividing her time, as I do, between city and country—taking taxis while in town, going to meetings, theater. She has spent quality time in my apartment on East 80th Street, gazing at the street scene and listening to WQXR. She responds to both classical and jazz, is attentive to Jonathan Schwartz.

At the start, there were two baby birds—the one we took to calling Raven Starling and her sibling, a creature that was smaller and weaker from the get-go. The ousted nestlings lay stranded on the grass, looking less like birds than glands, fleshy globs with a suggestion of gray lint over raw red flesh.

The ugly little hatchlings had survived a three-story fall from a roof, and they had luck from the start; they fell at the feet of my 12-year-old daughter, Jasmine. "Oh, look!" she cried. "Baby birds!"

Ugh, I thought. But I dutifully went online to figure out what to do with these creatures, then called a wildlife rehabilitation phone number that I found under "Wild Baby Birds." After listening to my description, the fatigued woman on the other end snapped: "Sturnus vulgaris, a starling. Dog food on a chopstick, every hour."

I set the unappealing twosome on a warm hand towel in a basket in the bathroom. "They'll be dead in the morning," I thought, with some ambivalence.

In the morning, one was dead, but Raven Starling was very much alive.

"One didn't make it," Jasmine said, her voice reedy with grief. "Let's hope for Ravvie."

Thus began the grueling all-day feedings. In the wild, starlings are insectivores, but they can live as omnivores if someone is willing to shop and mash commercial food for them. Ravvie demanded more and more of the recommended meal, which we adapted to cat food, Nine Lives mixed with Mott's natural apple sauce (no sugar for starlings, only corn syrup or fruit sweeteners), ground Tums (for calcium) and mashed hard-boiled egg yolk to meet her "intense protein needs."

Why we were meeting this creature's intense protein needs was another matter. I did not give Raven Starling great odds. I believed that her daily meals were only staving off the inevitable. Every morning, I expected to find her dead in her basket, beak sealed forever.

But when I walked into the bathroom on the fourth day, she stood up and spread her featherless wings, looking like a mini oviraptor escaped from Jurassic Park, demanding to be fed. I did not find the sight appealing, but I was impressed. "She wants to live," I realized. From that moment forth, I found the image of the bird, alone, opening her mouth without anyone to hear, unbearable.

Which explains why I nearly died later that day, feeding her from her chopstick while navigating a turn off the West Side Highway into Greenwich Village, where a play of mine was in rehearsal. She later made it to several performances. With a drape over her head, Raven Starling knew to be still during performances, at least off Broadway. Raven Starling adapted to apartment life; she would even tolerate a car-sit for alternate-side-of-the-street parking, or a quick run into the hot bagel place. Even an insectivore, I noted, was not immune to the charms of a warm sesame bagel.

Our doorman, Manuel Gonzalez, welcomed Raven Starling. With doormanly discretion, he ignored her unattractive appearance and gave her courteous rides, often on his uniformed arm.

In my apartment, two blocks from the Metropolitan Museum of Art, she perched on a houseplant and looked out the window, studying the city pigeons and sparrows and the renovation of the Junior League building across the street. She splattered away, in a box in the powder room. What have I done? I wondered. I've brought the worst of the country; a fecal spray, a wild thing, into what was an oasis of urban civilization. But I did notice she seemed attentive when I turned on WQXR, the classical station, and she clutched a program from the Mostly Mozart Festival at Lincoln Center.

I tried to ignore her odor, her cat-food-encrusted beak, and forced myself to share my daughter's deepening love. "Oh, she's so cute."

But she wasn't cute. Her face was foreshortened, and with her tiny beady eyes, bright with ruthless appetite, and a jaw that compressed when her beak closed, which was rare, she looked like Andy Gump.

*

I WENT to the Web site Starling Talk to check out the origins of starlings and discovered some surprising facts. The starling is a New York immigrant and, if not for Shakespeare, would never have entered our lives.

In March 1890, a New York drug manufacturer named Eugene Schieffelin acted on his love for the playwright by vowing to release into Central Park all the songbirds mentioned in Shakespeare. Mr. Schieffelin loosed several species: thrushes, skylarks and starlings. Only the starlings survived. From the initial 100 birds released, flocks reproduced to the current hundreds of millions, making them among the nation's most abundant and ultimately most controversial birds. They are infamous as pests, accused of corroding buildings with their acid droppings, which is why the joy over their first observed roost, in the eaves of the American Museum of Natural History, quickly hardened into disgust.

What did Shakespeare say regarding starlings that so inspired the 19th-century drug maker? It's a line in "Henry IV, Part 1," in which Hotspur threatens: "The king forbade my tongue to speak of Mortimer. But I will find him when he is asleep. I'll have a starling shall be taught to speak nothing but Mortimer, and give it to him to keep his anger still in motion."

The birds, I learn, are mimics, known in Elizabethan times as "the poor man's mynah." Oddly, they are unlikely to repeat a single word; they require a rhythmic phrase. So Shakespeare is now regarded as having made a mistake. But one billion birds later, with Raven Starling as my constant companion, I live with the result of one man's infatuation with Shakespeare's silver-tongued reference to songbirds. "She's making a mess," I kept saying, but I also kept feeding her, and she grew, not gradually but suddenly, into a midsize blackish bird. "Take a bath!" I ordered her, and she did, in a soup bowl filled with water in my formerly spotless city kitchen.

By this point, the history of the starling had me in its talons. Starlings may be the champion bird "talkers"; they can chorus in the wild by the thousands. Some experts have observed "a murmuration," as a flock of starlings is called, numbering a million or more.

Yet starlings are as despised as they are loved. In September, it was reported that the federal government had killed 2.3 million starlings in 2004 as part of a campaign to get rid of what it described as "nuisance animals." Starling eliminators insist that the birds damage crops, soil buildings, even cause planes to crash, and have resorted to Roman candles, hot wires and a poison called Starlicide to discourage or destroy the birds.

Is the killing justified? Starling supporters insist that it isn't, that the starling kills so many destructive insects; a murmuration should elicit a chorus of praise. Rachel Carson, the author of "Silent Spring," championed the starling: "In spite of his remarkable success as a pioneer, the starling probably has fewer friends than almost any other creature that wears feathers. That fact, however, seems to be of very little importance to this cheerful bird with glossy plumage and stumpy tail." The starling, she continued, "hurries with jerky steps about the farms and gardens in the summer time, carrying more than 100 loads of destructive insects per day to his screaming offspring."

Another admirer was Mozart, who paid dearly for his pet starling, loved it and staged a funeral when it passed away, of unknown causes, at age 3. Some authorities think the starling's song became incorporated into Mozart's composition "A Musical Joke."

·

RAVEN STARLING also began to sing, but would she really be independent someday? Could I release her, perhaps back into Central Park?

No, I could not, I was told by Jackie Collins, who runs Starling Talk. An "imprint" bird like mine, raised from infancy, can never join a starling murmuration. Starling Talk is filled with descriptions of confused imprint birds that have been found injured and emaciated and are unable to join in a flock. Although Raven Starling would one day speak better than a parrot, live to be 20 and play with a whiffle ball, she would have to stay forever among her adopted species—humans.

By then I had ascended into the skies of a cyberculture of starling-keepers, and joined the Chirp Room, where visitors signed off with phrases like "the whisper of wings" and quoted the famous line from Antoine de Saint-Exupéry, "You are responsible forever for what you have tamed." I learned that there are thousands of starling-keepers, the beneficiaries of a legal loophole: Although keeping a native wild bird in your home is illegal, starlings are exempt because of their foreign origin.

Meanwhile, Raven Starling grew prettier. As she matured, she displayed a certain etiquette, wiping her beak after each gooey bite. We shared toast. I played her Mozart's starling song.

Now when I heard the deep chords of Mozart's "Requiem," and Raven Starling sang along, in full throat, I pondered why I had tried so hard to keep this bird alive. Was it simply to keep a promise to a child? Perhaps there was another reason. In my home, we are all foundlings. I was an orphaned child, and my little girl was left on a street in China. Was this why the fallen starling had to be rescued? Because in our family, abandonment is unthinkable?

Whatever my motivation, I was not alone in my demented devotions. At 3 one morning I tried to predict what would become of the three of us by checking on the bird's Web site, Starling Talk. There, I learned about other baby starling "parents" who were struggling with similar issues but also celebrating events such as "Stormy's Fifth Birthday." Tamed starlings were on display, rainbow-hued when loved and cleaned, aglow as they were videotaped: "Plant a kiss on me, liverlips," said a saveling named Techno.

I admit, I had become attached to Ravvie. She flew to me at a whistle, and she groomed my tousled hair. She sat on my head when I played piano. I never thought that I could love an insectivore. Maybe it's possible that someone can love anything.

How far would I go in catering to my insectivore? Could I be like those other starling people on the Web site, who order bags of dried bugs? There was a human murmuration on the Web, especially in the dead of night, composed of bird people like a man living in a city apartment with an adult male starling named Smarty who has learned to take sharp right turns.

But winter would change everything. Winter was when the true trial of caring indoors for a wild bird would begin. Raven Starling would be forced for long periods into apartment life in the city. I have learned that if she walked for much longer on even carpeted city floors, she would develop a deformity, "spraggle feet."

•

ONE dawn, I began to communicate with a woman upstate, who has four starlings and offered to adopt mine. And I begin to wonder, what is best, to maintain Raven Starling as a lone creature, becoming spraggle-footed, commuting to New York and riding elevators, or surrender her to another "mother" who maintains three rooms in her home just for her birds?

So it came to pass that one September Sunday, I found myself driving with my daughter and the bird, in her cage, strapped to the back car seat, to a town five hours north of New York that even on the warm golden day appeared flattened by the memory of blizzards. Fort Plain, just outside Canajoharie.

The town is blanched and beaten, an entire town with freezer burn. Nearly all the factories that once sustained the area closed long ago. Yet it is here I was assured that a warm and loving home with other starlings awaited Raven Starling.

Mary Ann, the "adoptive mother" who is known on the Web as Little Feathers, was sitting on the stoop of a house with a peaked roof when we arrived. At 52, in T-shirt and jeans, with long, flowing hair, she had a fatigued, youthful quality.

Inside her neat but crammed living room, there was a smell, not unpleasant but avian. I think it was the smell of warm feathers.

Mary Ann has three children: an 11-year-old daughter and a boy and girl who are 12. The older girl was robust; her handsome twin brother, who has cerebral palsy, looked five years younger, thin and frail. Mary Ann also had a dozen avian "babies." Her voice quickened as she described the antics of George. "He's just a baby. And Chirp, she was given to me. And Littlefeathers, he was the first. And Trouble, well, his name fits."

In addition to the starlings, there were three pigeons, four society finches, and, the pièce de résistance, a paralyzed sparrow presented in the palm of her hand. I could not help connecting the flightless bird to the child who sits so still on the couch.

How could Mary Ann care for all these needful beings? I was on the brink of saying, "We thank you, but I'll take the bird home." Instead, we recited the chorus of open adoption: I asked and she agreed, "You shall have visitation."

"We can see her again," I said, my voice climbing too high, as Jasmine and I drove back to the city.

I knew we were thinking the same thought. Someone left my daughter somewhere almost 13 years ago. "On Quon Dong Road," her papers report. I recited the rationale that Raven Starling was better off with other birds, with an at-home mother who knew avian medicine and had an avian vet. I had no doubt that was all true, but my hands tightened on the steering wheel.

"We're never coming back," my child said.

We drove along, and then somewhere along the Thruway, above a vast pasture, we saw them, a murmuration of starlings, thousands of birds. Through the open car window, I heard, or more accurately felt, a familiar sound, more vibration or audible breeze than a true noise; the flutter of thousands of wings in unison, combined with a muted mass voice.

Later at twilight in the city, walking through Central Park, my daughter and I caught sight of another flock, or was it the same one? This was the true murmuration, an entity unto itself, to which Raven Starling, had her fate not crossed with ours, would have belonged. I watched the birds dip, then rise and reverse again, an animate banner, starring the skies above the city.

My daughter and I stared upward. We would never see a flock of birds again without noticing and remembering: We knew one in a billion.

February 12, 2006

28

A Chance to Be Mourned

After the Death of One of Its Own, a Homeless Group Searches for Easier Ways to Grieve for New York's Nameless and Unclaimed Dead.

EMILY BRADY

Rikers Island inmates burying babies' caskets at Potter's Field on Hart Island. *(Fred R. Conrad/The New York Times/1991)*

THE trouble began on the subway.

At first he was just another homeless man taking refuge from the bitter New York winter. Then he collapsed. He was unconscious when paramedics pulled him out of the subway car. He died a few hours later at Brooklyn Hospital Center in downtown Brooklyn of an inflamed pancreas and a weakened heart. It was two days before Christmas 2003. He was 48.

In life he was a stocky man with gentle eyes, a short beard and a wide smile. His name was Lewis Haggins Jr., though everyone called him Lou. As it turned out, he had a large circle of friends in the homeless community, along with family in New Jersey. But like many who teeter on the city's edge, this man carried no ID. For weeks, his body lay unclaimed in the city morgue.

Two months after that final subway ride, Mr. Haggins's body was placed in a pine coffin and sent to Potter's Field on Hart Island, east of the Bronx, the city's cemetery for the poor, the unknown and the unclaimed. Over the past 137 years, an estimated 800,000 people have been buried there. On Feb. 25, 2004, Mr. Haggins was placed in a common grave with 149 others.

There, Mr. Haggins joined the thousands of New York's lost and abandoned, the people whose burial there underscores the powerlessness they bore in life.

But Mr. Haggins's burial represented a turning point.

Nine months after his death, the New York police matched the man buried in Potter's Field with a man who had been arrested for trespassing: Mr. Haggins. The police notified his parents of his death and told them where he was buried. His family in turn contacted Picture the Homeless, an advocacy group of which Mr. Haggins was a founder.

Hart Island, members of the group soon learned, was closed to the general public. Only immediate family members were allowed to visit Mr. Haggins's grave, and even they had to navigate a labyrinth of city bureaucracy.

His friends within the homeless community rallied. They wanted to hold a memorial service. They wanted to lay flowers on his grave. More than anything, they wanted Mr. Haggins to know he wasn't forgotten.

What happened next grew into a movement that included religious leaders from around the city. For most of the past year, memorial services were held there every two months. The organization that Mr. Haggins helped to found during his life allowed him and many anonymous others to be memorialized after their death.

•

THE video image is slightly fuzzy, as if someone forgot to wipe off the camera lens. It shows a small group of men standing on a ferry dock and speaking with a pair of middle-aged women. "We're looking to go over and pay our respects," one man says. "So far the city bureaucracy hasn't seen fit to let us."

The men are members of Picture the Homeless who traveled to City Island with a video camera last spring in the hope of joining a Catholic group from the Bronx that was headed to Potter's Field for its yearly Ascension Thursday Mass. The two women they are talking to journeyed from the Midwest to visit a relative long buried.

Bruce Little, a member of Picture the Homeless, is seen peering out across the water. Many of his friends lie underground in the cemetery on the other side. "I just want to let them know I'm still there for them," he says. When the ferry arrives to shuttle the group across the water, the members of Picture the Homeless are not allowed aboard. They didn't have advance approval from the city's Department of Correction.

Mr. Little, 42, first met Mr. Haggins in the late 1990's. At the time, they were both homeless, hanging out near Penn Station. Mr. Little remembers Mr. Haggins as a light within the homeless community. "If you had issues," he said, "you could speak to him about it. If you had a struggle, he wanted to help you with it."

Lewis Haggins Jr. was born in Princeton, N.J., and raised in a middle-class home there. His parents, Lewis Sr. and Geraldine, declined to be interviewed about their son, saying the subject stirred too many emotions, but a short biography they helped write after his death noted that after high school Mr. Haggins had held various jobs at New Jersey universities.

Just why he became homeless is unclear. After a brief marriage, he moved to Harlem, where he played keyboards and worked odd jobs. His younger brother, Brock, remembers that he ended up at a homeless shelter after a fire destroyed his apartment. "We all said you can come back and live with us," said Brock Haggins.

But Lou Haggins never took his family up on the offer. And some who knew him suggest that alcohol may have contributed to his problems. "I know he liked to drink," Brock Haggins said. "I don't know the extent of it."

Whatever the exact circumstances of his situation, Mr. Haggins did not let it prevent him from working on behalf of other homeless people.

He co-founded Picture the Homeless in 1999, after a woman was assaulted with a brick in Midtown. The man accused of attacking her, it turned out, was identified as homeless, and the case was well publicized. Mr. Haggins and a friend named Anthony Williams, whom he had met in the Bellevue Men's Shelter, decided they wanted to do something to change the public perception of the homeless. Picture the Homeless, made up of homeless and formerly homeless people, was the result.

Today, Picture the Homeless operates out of an office on Morris Avenue in Fordham in the Bronx. Visitors are greeted by a framed photo of Mr. Haggins, along with inspirational quotes and posters of cultural icons like Frederick Douglass. In August 2004, Mr. Little was in the organization's office when he learned of Mr. Haggins's death. It had been nearly a year since he'd heard from him; when it comes to life on the streets, no news is often bad news.

After the call came from Mr. Haggins's family, some people in the office began to cry. Mr. Little quickly made up his mind. "We had to have a memorial service in his honor," he said, "so it'll be known he's not forgotten."

Like many of the city's homeless, Mr. Little believes that when he goes, he too will end up at Potter's Field. For him, the saddest part about being sent there is the anonymous burial, and the fact that friends cannot visit. "No one should have to go through that," he said, shaking his head. "To be put in a mass grave where you're forgotten about, where your close friends can't come to visit and remember you."

Kenneth Jackson, a Columbia University history professor who visited the island more than a decade ago while working on a book about graveyards, "Silent Cities," reached a similar conclusion. Of those buried in Potter's Field, Professor Jackson said: "They're isolated, they're forgotten, they're not recognized. The sad thing is that it's very much the same way they lived."

●

NEW YORK is not the only American city to maintain a special cemetery for its anonymous dead. Chicago also has a Potter's Field, which is open to the public. Other urban centers, like Los Angeles, cremate the remains of their lost and abandoned.

New York's mass burial ground is a grassy place surrounded by the waters of Long Island Sound. By the time the city purchased the island, in 1868, there had already been four potter's fields around Manhattan.

In 1869, a 24-year-old woman named Louisa Van Slyke became the first person interred in the island's 45-acre graveyard. The island's southern end continued to accommodate the living; people were quarantined there during the 1870 yellow fever epidemic, and at various times Hart has been home to a sanitarium, prisoners and, during the Cold War, Nike missiles.

Today, Hart Island is abandoned, a ghost town. "It looks like Central Park, with buildings that are decaying," said William Burnett, an organizer for Picture the Homeless. "It doesn't really look like a graveyard."

But a graveyard it is. For 50 cents an hour, inmates from Rikers Island stack the pine coffins in two rows, three high and 25 across. Each plot is marked with a single granite stump. Many of those who are buried are babies; stillborns and infants who die shortly after birth are sent there by the city when their families cannot afford funeral services. Infants are interred in separate plots in miniature pine coffins.

According to the Department of Correction, in 2005 there were 1,419 burials on Hart Island: 826 were of adults, 546 were of infants or stillborn, and 47 were of dismembered body parts.

•

IN many ways, Mr. Haggins's journey to Potter's Field followed the typical route. When an unidentified body arrives at the city morgue, the police check fingerprints for a match in databases of missing persons. If no match is found, dental X-rays are taken, blood is drawn for DNA, and the corpse is photographed. "We try really hard to get the person identified," said Ellen Borakove, a spokeswoman for the city medical examiner's office.

Ideally, the journey from morgue to burial takes two to four weeks. If no one claims a body, or if a body remains unidentified, the Department of Health and Mental Hygiene issues a permit to transport it to Potter's Field.

Sometimes, people fall through the cracks. Fingerprint matches can take three to six months, Ms. Borakove said, at which point the body is long underground. In Mr. Haggins's case, it took the police nine months to identify him through a photograph match. By then he had been buried for seven months.

Sometimes even people who live far from the margins of society end up in Potter's Field. In May 2003, a Brooklyn College student named Charles Guglielmini was missing. His backpack was found near the Queensboro Bridge. It was presumed he had jumped. His family regularly checked with the police to see if the body had been located, to no avail. A year later, the family discovered that the young man had been buried in Potter's Field shortly after his disappearance. The police had never listed him as a missing person.

In the case of Mr. Haggins, there are two accounts of how he ended up in this lonely place.

The police said that at the time he collapsed, Mr. Haggins was traveling with a female companion, who informed the hospital of his identity. Because the woman was notified of his death, the police said, his family and other friends were not.

Mr. Haggins's family and members of Picture the Homeless say they believe that his identity was unknown to officials when he was buried. "He was buried a John Doe," Mr. Burnett said. Brock Haggins said, "I guess he just got lost in the bureaucracy."

Even for family members, visiting Potter's Field is not a simple matter. Though city officials say that no relative wishing to go to the island for what they describe as a closure visit is denied, lack of access is the chief complaint among people familiar with the island.

"I don't view it as a bad thing that the city buries everyone in a very democratic way," said Melinda Hunt, an artist and filmmaker who recently finished a documentary about Potter's Field. Her chief objection is that the island isn't open to the public, and that family members seeking visitation rights or access to records must go through the prison system, an often daunting barrier.

For years, Ms. Hunt has helped families with the arduous task of tracking down their relatives. To find burial records, it is necessary to locate the death certificate at the Department of Health. "It's a needle in a haystack," Ms. Hunt said. In her opinion, the fact that the island is run by the Department of Correction adds to the stigma of being buried there.

Asked about the problem of obtaining records and going there, Stephen Morello, the chief spokesman for the Department of Correction, said: "I don't know if it's as difficult as people say it is. But once they have the certificate, we make arrangements for people to go out to Hart Island."

And for friends of the dead, visiting the island is all but impossible, because they must show proof of relation, or of having been legal guardian, to obtain a death certificate and burial records.

·

IT was a beautiful autumn day as the boat chugged across the water on its short journey from City Island to Hart Island. It was Sept. 30,

2005, and members of Picture the Homeless were joined by Mr. Haggins's mother, his brother and clergy members.

Over the preceding months, Picture the Homeless had persuaded 24 religious leaders from around the city to hold regular memorial services on the island, for Mr. Haggins and the rest of the hundreds of thousands of people buried there.

An imam, a rabbi, priests and ministers from various faiths supported the campaign. After the group met with a former Correction Department spokesman in 2005, Mr. Burnett of Picture the Homeless said, the department agreed to let them hold bimonthly services on the island on a one-year trial, with the condition that no news media would be present. If everything went well, Mr. Burnett understood, the plan was to make the memorials permanent.

According to Mr. Morello, the new spokesman, the visits were suspended as a result of personnel changes in the department. He and members of Picture the Homeless were scheduled to meet soon to talk about resuming the memorial services.

This autumn day, it was a short walk from the ferry dock to the huge granite cross that marks the beginning of Potter's Field. Chairs were set up at the base of the cross. The Rev. Karen Senecal, associate minister of Judson Memorial Church in Greenwich Village, led the reading of the 23rd Psalm. Then Mr. Haggins's brother and two members of Picture the Homeless spoke. Everyone sang "Amazing Grace." Geese flew overhead.

After the service, the group followed a middle-aged woman over to the children's burial site. The woman had come to Potter's Field to fulfill a promise she had made to her dying mother. Shortly after moving to the United States from Italy, the mother lost a baby, whom she was too poor to bury. The promise was to find the baby's grave, which was eventually traced to Potter's Field.

As the woman opened a jar of soil from her mother's grave and poured its contents onto the ground, she and most of the others around her began to weep.

Visitors who come for closure visits are not told exactly where the person they are seeking is buried, and since the children's burial section was the first gravesite that Mr. Little visited, it was there that he chose to say goodbye. At a worn granite marker, next to a bouquet of baby's breath, he left his flowers for his friend.

•

NINE days ago, Lewis Haggins was brought home. His family paid to have his remains disinterred from Potter's Field and buried in a blue casket at a cemetery near their house. A plaque bearing his name marks the spot.

Members of Picture the Homeless say they will continue to push for regular memorial services at Potter's Field.

"His removal doesn't change the fact that homeless people are buried there, and they have a right to be remembered and honored," Mr. Burnett said. "He was just one case, one person."

November 12, 2006

29

Doodles à la Carte

Once a Week the Cartoonists of The New Yorker Assemble
for Lunch in Midtown, There to Enjoy a Little Sketch,
a Little Kvetch, and a Lot of One Liners.

CAROLINE H. DWORIN

(Caroline H. Dworin)

T is a cool, cloudy day in late fall as Sam Gross and Gahan Wilson, both in their 70's and regular contributors of cartoons to The New Yorker, stroll side by side up Seventh Avenue. After a quick Tuesday morning meeting with Bob Mankoff, the magazine's cartoon editor, they and a handful of other New Yorker cartoonists have set out for lunch; more men than women, most in their 70's, each week they are a slightly different bunch.

Mr. Gross and Mr. Wilson lead the way through the crowded nub of Broadway to Pergola des Artistes, a little restaurant on West 46th Street that has, for the past five years or so, been the favored destination.

Mr. Gross, wearing a green baseball cap, swaggering like a schoolboy out to pick a fight, carries a portfolio case by his side. His are the magazine's precocious cats and dogs, their human counterparts outmatched and comparatively unrefined. He has wanted to be a cartoonist since he was a kid.

Next to him, Mr. Wilson walks with an easy stride, tall and black-clad, with fine white hair. His work, fancifully absurdist, morphs the bodies of monsters with those of men. If any adult still takes a pre-emptive peek under the bed or in a darkened closet before falling sleep, it is his creations they will find.

Several paces back, Sidney Harris and John Kane push north between knots of tourists.

Mr. Harris, an artist with a statistician's memory and a child's sense of wonder, was cast by an uncanny penchant for details in the role of Science Cartoonist. He smiles hesitantly, speaks with a careful Brooklyn accent, plays with his knife and fork at the table.

Mr. Kane, who came to the field from advertising, somewhat later than the rest, has taken to cartooning with the superstitious compulsion of a man who plays the slots. He wields a compass and, outfitted in a light hat and a vest packed with pockets, seems as capable of sustaining himself in the woods as on the Web.

Others on their way to Pergola des Artistes this lunchtime are Bud Handelsman, Jack Ziegler, Mort Gerberg (who often stops by a little later, well dressed, as someone with much to do)—men who know well the world of cartooning in New York, as they have, from the front line, defined it. Often there are a couple of youngsters, too, men and women in their late 30's and 40's: Glen Le Lievre, Carolita Johnson, Felipe Galindo. There is also the occasional New Yorker neophyte, one of those who have recently sold their very first cartoons to the magazine: Evan Forsch, Martha Gradisher, me.

I walk with Martha Gradisher, a cartoonist, illustrator, art director and "kitchen sink," as she puts it, for 30 years. Another fresh addition, she sold her first drawing to The New Yorker last March, after a year and a half of faxing submissions to the magazine.

●

PERGOLA DES ARTISTES, a homey French restaurant whose brick facade is painted Swiss Army red, nestles beneath a massive parking sign and the back of the Imperial Theater like a squat little appendix. Its entrance, just east of Eighth Avenue, boasts of the restaurant's "43rd Anniversary Celebration" and "Year Long Lobster Special."

Its walls are pink and white, textured plaster hung with the dated trappings of an old-timey French resort: copper pots, the stuffed head of a goat, murals representing provinces, coat of arms for each. At first glance, it seems an unlikely locus for such a celebrated bunch.

The maître d', Jean-Christian Ponsolle, known as Chris, addresses each person by name. His mother, Marie-Rose, longtime matriarch at Pergola, speaks French to the regulars, leaning in to rest a hand on their shoulders and ask that they enjoy their meal. She often wanders about Times Square wearing a sequin-studded cap and large turquoise earrings, handing out promotional cards to tourists and passers-by.

When Mr. Ponsolle sees the cartoonists arrive, he immediately has two or three tables pushed together along the right-hand wall. As bags and coats and portfolios are stowed, a house red is delivered all around.

The conversation opens up like the fan of a peacock. Whatever starts it, gag or gripe, it tumbles like a pebble from a lofty mountaintop into a landslide of wit.

To the left, how to capture a spit-take: "How many little droplets do you draw?" Ms. Gradisher asks. To the right, how to draw a sneeze.

A waiter delivers a small dish of oil for the bread and places it in front of Mr. Ziegler. "Oh?" says Mr. Harris, with the interrogative upturn of a Brooklynite. "You got the soup?"

●

THERE is a farcical ambiguity among the cartoonists as to the pronunciation of the name of the place. Some Tuesdays, it is PUR-guh-la, other Tuesdays pur-GOH-la, which adds variety, at least, since the setting is the same nearly every week.

On the occasions the group has dined elsewhere, food is judged with caution. On an errant lunch many months ago, away from the faithful default, Mr. Wilson ordered a piece of fish, which he said arrived on his plate tough as boot leather. He took it up speculatively between thumb and forefinger, turned it over and, eyebrows raised, peered at the other side. "I could fix a hole in my wallet with this," he announced. To prove the fish's hardiness, he slapped it against the edge of the table a few times, then passed it on to his neighbor to inspect.

The midday feeding is nothing new, a vestige of a time when cartoonists in this media capital literally took to the streets to sell their work, running into each other on their respective circuits.

From the 1940's to the early to middle 80's—before submissions could be faxed in, before Kinko's made copies for a dime and before the magazine market began to dry up—New York City's cartoonists set out about town each week, on foot, to markets like Collier's, True, Cavalier, The Saturday Evening Post, National Lampoon and Playboy, many now long defunct. Wednesday in New York was the designated day when the editors saw their work.

"We used to spend the whole day going from magazine to magazine," Mr. Gross says. At the time of the Wednesday walk, The New Yorker had a second day, Tuesday, as the day to see its regulars. "Tuesdays they had the elite people come," Mr. Gross said. "And Wednesdays they had the unwashed people come. I came on Wednesdays." (Now, Tuesday is the only day when The New Yorker sees its cartoonists.)

The cartoonists walked a route that lay, for the most part, in the blocks between 42nd and 59th Streets. "A whole day," Mr. Harris says, "starting at the one that paid most." It took tenacity to make art that might not sell, with rejection permitted no greater weight than a testing elbow to the ribs. If a door was locked when you knocked on it, there was a good chance someone had left a window ajar in the back. The dearth of magazines buying cartoons makes current competition even tougher, and those editing more selective.

At the meeting the cartoonists had just left on this cool fall day, The New Yorker's Mr. Mankoff saw them one on one, with hundreds of cartoons reviewed. The cartoonists waited together, chatting, standing about or seated in a tiny lounge.

The first to arrive is the first to be seen. If Mr. Mankoff decides to hold a cartoon, he adds it to the pile on his desk. The rest are handed back—no luck, although a recent book of cartoons spurned by The New Yorker, called "The Rejection Collection," suggests that lucklessness might also sell.

"You gotta be a street rat," Mr. Gross says of the job of selling cartoons. "I'm a street rat. I told Marisa Acocella that once, and she kept her demure outside. But then——" He paused and smiled. "She grew a tail."

•

THE cartoonists' lunch has never been a particularly organized event. "We just wandered until we got tired and hungry," Mr. Harris says. "And then we stopped."

The routine, held together by a few staple gentlemen, furnishes therapy for a week's worth of work, a chance to get good counsel, and a platform for show and tell. Recently released collections make their way from hand to hand, their artists discussed and measured; sketchbooks are flipped through; rejected drawings laid upon the pyre for mass commiseration; ideas held up and shot down, all in good faith, for a laugh.

Lunch is limited by little more than location, its chatter predictably capricious, as a distinctive array of cameos pass through each week like members of a traveling circus.

Recently, Paul Peter Porges made an appearance. Mr. Porges, a Viennese cartoonist who as a young man left Europe after World War II, tucked his napkin directly into his collar and, in an accented baritone above the din of chatter, sang the contents of the menu to the tune of "Moon River."

Another week, Carolita Johnson, an uncommonly lovely-looking cartoonist-slash-model, with dark bangs, large eyes and, if needed, a disarmingly diffident pout, explained the intricacies of her studies in Paris: predoctoral work in historical anthropology, a thesis on the images of rape in political discourse.

She listed for us the contents of her purse: an "idea book," an assortment of pens, the current issue of The New Yorker, a pair of silicone breasts. "They're called cutlets," she said. "They're for when I'm fitting." The table grew curiously attentive, and she removed one from her bag and passed it around.

There is more wise to the wise guy than one might imagine, and just as much wisdom behind the pen as wit: Mr. Gerberg plays the piano beautifully; Mr. Gross knows opera, can talk Mozart as if he knew the guy; Mr. Harris could navigate the Morgan Library in the dark. Nor are they frozen in the past: Mr. Kane has just as many pictures up on Flickr. com as any self-respecting high school kid.

"There are more galaxies out there than there are grains of sand on a beach," Mr. Harris tells us one afternoon. "Can you imagine?" He pauses a beat, then adds: "You can't. Because our brains are too small to grasp this yet."

On the protective paper atop the restaurant's linen tablecloth—another excellent detail suited to this particular gathering—we draw what the edge of the universe might look like. "And what's around it?" asks Mr. Le Lievre, a dark-haired Melbourne import. "Now here's what I imagine."

He takes up his pen and sketches what lies beyond the galaxies. Twin lines contract off into the distance; grass sprouts raggedly on one side. "It's surrounded by a white picket fence," Mr. Le Lievre says. "And there's a gate in it." He draws that next. "And it annoys the hell out of everybody."

Peering at the drawing upside down from across the table, Mr. Gross says: "And on the other side, there's a gated community. It's like Florida."

Mr. Harris declares, "There was no space before the Big Bang." He pauses to intimate that we should consider the statement, which we do.

Then someone asks the obvious question: But how do you draw that?

And the magic is in the digression—the conversation both resolute and ridiculous, a sustained note of humor, choruslike: when one man is off, another is on. Tuesday's lunch is a performance as much as a meal.

What caused the explosion? Says Mr. Harris: Oily rags. Says Mr. Gross: A paint can full of oily rags! And then, Mr. Handelsman asks perfectly, from the end of the table: "How do we know it was a big bang, anyway? What did they have to compare it to?"

Mr. Harris moves bread crumbs about the tablecloth into a design. "Maybe it was a little bang?" he says with a shrug. "If it was the first, how do we know?"

Someone makes an off-color remark, everyone laughs, and the riffing picks up again, tumbling from the celestial into the obscene.

Ms. Gradisher, her cheeks pink, begins to laugh. "You gotta stop this!" she says to the guys.

"No," says Mr. Gross, both hands upon the table. "As a cartoonist, you go to the end, for God's sake! No matter what!"

No topic is exempt: technology's ebb and flow; the price Google put up for YouTube; the Weimar exhibition at the Met.

A waiter puts a plate down on the table. "Don't touch it," he warns. "It's hot." Invariably, everyone nearby touches the plate.

There is a bond among those who do the same work, no matter their age, race or gender. No matter, in fact, if they are living or dead. Personal narratives sweep back on decades ("Were you here when Saxon was here?" someone will ask), a thrill for a youngster, over a glass and a half of wine, to feel so connected, as A. J. Liebling once felt with boxers, by artists who knew artists who knew artists. It is as if James Thurber might show up to lunch one day with his crayon.

•

MR. GROSS works the check. A onetime accountant, he collects the tab in a pile in front of him as if he were presiding over a poker game. "Who had the fish?" he shouts. "It's more!" Everybody throws down a 20. Few have any change.

"I have a $15 bill," Mr. Le Lievre offers, rooting through his wallet. "It's got a picture of Walter Mondale on it."

January 14, 2007

30

Unstoppable

Riding a Bike without Brakes on the Streets of New York
May Sound Insane. But to the Zealous Adherents of
Fixed-Gear Bikes—Fixies for Short—They Are
a Thing of Beauty and a Way of Life.

JOCKO WEYLAND

Fixies, the bikes with no brakes. *(Lars Klove/The New York Times)*

WHEN is a bicycle not like other bicycles? To begin with, when it has no brakes, or at least no visible brakes, or possibly just a front brake. That means you can't ride this bike very well on your first try, and certainly not very gracefully, easily or safely.

The rear cog is bolted directly to the hub, so that whenever the vehicle is in motion, the pedals go around, making coasting impossible. This bike doesn't have a shift lever or extra sprockets, and the chain is shorter and wider than on traditional bikes.

There are no fenders, and the rear wheels are probably bolted onto the frame to deter theft. You slow down by reversing the pedals, or skidding, or doing a skip stop. And that's just the beginning of the differences between your run-of-the-mill 10-speed and a track bike, or fixed-gear bike—fixie for short—as it is also known.

Many fixed-gear adherents contend that their bikes are the ultimate and all others are pretenders. And these fixed-gear zealots are a growing presence on the streets of New York. Perceived by some as nuisances, or as troublesome, anarchist Dumpster-diving punks who happen to ride bikes, they are occasionally reviled, but they are also the subject of curiosity and interest. Just as die-hard skateboarders 15 years ago stood on the cusp of providing a new lifestyle, so the fixed-gear bike culture could be the tip of something that nobody can accurately predict but something that is huge.

Riders of fixed-gear bikes are as diverse as bike riders in general. Messengers are big fixie aficionados, but more and more fixed-gear bikes are being ridden by nonmessengers, most conspicuously the kind of younger people to whom the term "hipster" applies and who emanate from certain neighborhoods in Brooklyn. You see these riders weaving in and out of traffic without stopping, balancing on the pedals at a stoplight and in the process infuriating pedestrians and drivers alike.

In Williamsburg and points south of Grand Street, these bikes are legion. But they are fast gaining popularity, not just in those bastions of trend followers, and not just among 22-year-olds. Fixed-gear bikes are being ridden all over New York, by messengers, racers, lawyers, accountants and college professors—a diverse and not necessarily youthful cross-section of the city's population. They're being ridden by people who work in sandwich shops and don't know or care about gear ratios and bike history, and by people who have been racing these bikes for years in places like the Kissena Velodrome in Flushing, Queens, with its banked, elliptical track. They're ridden by militant vegans who are virtual encyclopedias of arcane bicycle history, by thrill-seeking members of renegade bike gangs like Black Label, by shopgirls, street racers, Critical Mass riders, your aunt.

There's also the phenomenon of city riders returning to fixed-gear biking's roots and getting back to the track, entering races like the Cyclehawk Velo City Tour, to be held at the Kissena Velodrome on May 6.

These disparate riders represent a rainbow coalition, a movement that's about bikes as part of a way of life, as an identity. Although fixed-gear bikes can be seen as a trendy accessory, they also allow a mild form of rebellion against what many of these bike riders see as a wasteful and insipid way of life. Fixed-gear riders embrace the contrary notion of taking a different route.

"We own the streets," the spray-painted stencil reads. Not really, but fixed-gear riders are, in a benign way, promoting an alternative to accepted norms.

So what's the big deal? It's just a bike, right? On some level, yes. Two wheels, a chain, a cog, a seat and handlebars. But in the way that one of Marcel Breuer's vintage Wassily chairs is just a chair that costs $10,000, the top fixed-gear bikes are just custom-made bikes that cost 10 times as much as a regular factory-made bicycle. The pinnacle of two-wheeled transport, they are beautiful objects with simple, clean, stripped-down lines that make them look fast even when they're standing still.

"They're the prettiest bikes out there," said Gina Scardino, owner of King Kog, a store on Hope Street in Williamsburg that sells only fixed-gear bikes. Indeed they are, with a modernist blending of form and function and a look that matches what they're made for, which is going really fast on a banked velodrome track.

But the question arises: Especially in this city, isn't it insane to ride a bike that you can't easily stop? By riding a bike that's meant to be raced around a special track on the chaotic streets of New York, aren't you risking life and limb?

It doesn't make sense. But that may be the appeal, and has been ever since the bikes appeared on the scene more than a century ago.

Fixed-gear bikes have a rich past. Before the invention of the derailleur, the device that made multiple gears a reality, fixed-gears were *the* racing bike. The original Madison Square Garden, built in 1879 at 26th Street and Madison Avenue, was built for a velodrome. Races testing speed and endurance drew huge crowds, with the top riders among the sports stars of their day.

The bike races at Madison Square Garden were all the rage around the turn of the last century. A velodrome circuit flourished around the country, with the best racers earning $100,000 to $150,000 a year at a time when carpenters were lucky to make $5,000. And all this was happening on the forerunners of the bikes being ridden today.

Johnny Coast's Coast Cycles sits at the end of a desolate cul-de-sac in the heart of Bushwick, Brooklyn, near the Myrtle Avenue stop on the J, M and Z lines. Mr. Coast, a 31-year-old with dreadlocks down to the small of his back, is a former squatter and current member of Black Label.

Coast Cycles is not your typical bike store stocked with rows of three-speeds and road bikes, along with locks, water bottles and other doodads. It is an old-fashioned, one-person workshop where chickens wander in from the yard. Here, Mr. Coast builds two or three custom-framed bicycles a month, most of them fixed-gears, "tailored to suit a body's dimensions, to an individual's geometry and affording the maximum of comfort, design and style," as he put it in an e-mail message.

Mr. Coast, who works surrounded by Bridgeport lathes, jigs and blueprints, is a believer in fixies as a metaphorical extension of a squatters' lifestyle that connotes, as he puts it, "living a certain way, subsisting on recycling, not wasting, finding liberation, freedom as a revolutionary act, like in a Hakim Bey sense, primitivist, spiritualist anarchism."

He laughs at the absurdity of a brand like Mountain Dew approaching Black Label with an offer of sponsorship, as he says happened last year, and is wary of exploitation of the fixed-gear bike culture by corporations that have little to do with biking. "I saw what happened to skateboarding and surfing and punk," Mr. Coast said grimly.

•

THE dangers of a small world getting bigger were vividly illustrated a few months ago when a hipster wearing square-frame glasses wandered into King Kog. The store, which sells fixed-gear bikes starting around $800 and going up to the thousands, also carries Jason Chaste's Fortynine Sixteen clothing line, named for a gear ratio, and high-end parts like Sugino cranks, Izumi chains, and Dura-Ace and Ciocc frames.

"Um, I'm looking for a track bike," the visitor said.

"What's your price range?" Ms. Scardino asked.

"Three hundred dollars," the visitor replied.

"Hmmm, you might want to try Craigslist or eBay," she suggested gently.

When Ms. Scardino asked the visitor how he planned to use the bike, he answered, "I'm just going to be cruising around."

You got the sense that this wasn't the place for him, but also that he might come back one day. As he put it when he left: "I like your shop. It's neat."

•

AT Bike Kill, an annual racing event sponsored by Black Label and held in Bedford-Stuyvesant, Brooklyn, nobody seemed worried about the issue of fixed-gear biking becoming too popular; everybody was having too much fun.

Vehicles used in the event, held on a blustery autumn day near the Samuel C. Barnes Elementary School, included tall bikes (two frames on top of each other with a seat about six feet off the ground), bikes with metal rollers as front wheels, tiny bikes and BMX bikes (little single-gear bikes used for tricks) and, of course, fixed-gear bikes.

Mr. Coast was there, along with members of Black Label's Minneapolis and Reno, Nev., chapters and members of other biker groups like C.H.U.N.K. 666, which has footholds in Brooklyn and Portland, Ore.; the Rat Patrol, from Chicago; Dead Baby, from Seattle; and the Skidmarxxx, from Austin, Tex. A lot of unwashed dreads, denim, leather and facial tattoos were in evidence, along with a carnivalesque assortment of voodoo top hats, orange jumpsuits, bunny ears, Mexican wrestling masks and a Pee-wee Herman doppelgänger waving from his Schwinn cruiser.

There were copious drinking, including a contest to see who could ride around in a circle while drinking a six-pack fastest, and the "Blind Skull" event, in which riders wearing big foam skulls over their heads pedaled until they fell over or ran into somebody.

Toward 8 p.m. the drunken tall-bike jousting began, with knights of both sexes armed with padded plastic "spears." The only dissonant note occurred when a cassock-wearing interloper on Rollerblades with a motor attached was expelled by a Black Label member. "Get your motor out of here!" the biker yelled.

That's the cardinal rule. No motors. For environmental reasons. Or practical ones, recalling the West Indian messengers who pioneered urban fixed-gear riding in the 1980's, bringing their ingenuity to New York from the islands, where bikes that didn't have much of anything on them to steal were a decided advantage.

But pinning down what constitutes the fixed-gear movement gets complicated. After all, what does the insanity of Bike Kill have to do with someone like "Fast" Eddie Williams, who runs the bicycle-themed Nayako Gallery in Bedford-Stuyvesant, has published a book of photographs of messengers and competes in Alley Cat and Monster Track street races?

Mr. Williams's scene is the messenger scene, in which he has been a participant since the early 1980's, when he first encountered the West Indian messengers hanging out at Washington Square Park. "I saw them riding," he said. "I liked how they maneuvered, stopped at a red light and didn't step down. And I thought, 'How do they do that?'"

Mr. Williams got a Matsuri, a fast fixed-gear bike, and started working as a messenger. Twenty-five years later, he's still at it, looking incredibly fit and younger than his 43 years. "Track bikes are not made for street," he conceded, "and sometimes I need a hope and a prayer to stop short." But he rhapsodized about their charms. "It's like playing chess," he said. "You think out your moves from a block away."

John Campo, the salty-tongued director of the racing program at the Kissena Velodrome, is another fixie aficionado. As with Mr. Williams, the fixed-gear lifestyle seems to be a healthy one; Mr. Campo looks at least 15 years younger than his 60. Biking isn't his profession—he's a jazz musician who has played with Miles Davis, among others—but it is undeniably his passion.

Mr. Campo missed out on the glory days of the Kissena Velodrome, but he tells tales about the father of Vinny Vella, the actor who plays Jimmy Petrille on "The Sopranos," racing at Madison Square Garden to win enough money to buy a scale for the pushcart he sold fish from, then earning enough to open a fish store on Elizabeth Street. Mr. Campo remembers all the Polish, German and Italian bike clubs, and he remembers Lou Maltese, a member of the Century Road Club who held many cycling records, including the 100-mile national record in a race from Union City, N.J., to Philadelphia.

•

FAR from worrying about fixed-gear bikes getting too popular, Mr. Campo yearns for them to return to their prominence of a century ago, and he welcomes street riders to Kissena. "These kids are lovely," he said. "They come; they win, lose or draw; they have a great time. This is an American spirit thing, to be free, to do what you want to do and express yourself in your own medium, like surfing or skating."

Surfing and skating are mentioned a lot in relation to fixed-gear bikes. Something about these activities prefigures much of what is going on to-day in the bike community. Surfing 50 years ago and skating 25 years ago were small, below-the-radar pursuits with their own rituals and secret codes and vernacular. Now they're billion-dollar industries, popular the world over. And in the opinion of many aficionados, a little bit of soul was lost along the way.

Bicycling is obviously different; there are more bikes than cars in the world, and bikes have a longer popular history, not to mention the fact that fixed-gear bikes predate "regular" bikes. But something about the trajectories of surfing and skating from unexamined, semiunderground secret societies to blown-out cheesy "sports" could forecast the future of the fixed-gear bike.

Surfing and skating retained some of their rebelliousness, in part because of the varied, unpredictable demographic of who is involved: 5-year-olds and 80-year-olds of both sexes, doctors and garbage collectors, law-abiding citizens and criminals. That makes the skating or surfing "movement" hard to locate exactly, just like the amorphous bike movement.

Johnny Coast. Gina Scardino. Fast Eddie. John Campo. The menagerie at Bike Kill. It's a broad swath. The group also includes people like Toni Germanotta, a 42-year-old owner of an art studio that serves the apparel industry. "When you're on a fixed gear," said Ms. Germanotta, who works in the garment district, "it gives you a higher skill level. You have to be constantly aware, always watching the road. You don't just ride, and it feels a little crazy."

And it includes Kyle Fay, a designer for Urban Outfitters who is a relatively new convert. "You take the blame if you get hit," he said. "It's self-reliance, being responsible for yourself. It might sound kind of corny, but it's a Zen thing, being one with the bike."

And it includes Alex Escamilla, a 23-year-old book artist from Fort Greene, Brooklyn.

"I had a couple of friends who made fun of me for riding one because it was trendy," Ms. Escamilla said. "But the problem with looking at bike riding as a trend is that you lose sight of everything that is positive about bikes. You know, the renewable energy source, exercise, convenience, saving money, saving time, community, seeing the city in a whole new way, blah blah blah."

Besides, she added: "Track bikes are fun. And they're beautiful."

April 29, 2007

31

The Urban Ear

New Yorkers Swim in a Sea of Sounds, Most of Them
Reassuringly Familiar. Then Once in a While Comes
a Very Different Noise.

MAX PAGE

Listening to the sounds of the city. *(Kitra Cahana/The
New York Times)*

NEVER slept better than when I lived in a walk-up on Avenue of the Americas, just below Houston Street. The silence of the provinces where I live now, in Amherst, Mass., keeps me up at night, but in New York I was lulled into deep sleep by the endless roar of traffic and the humming music of the C train, punctuated by laughter and boisterous argument.

At least to some ears, city sounds are incredibly soothing. The wealth of sounds that come with too much humanity rooted in too little geography tells us better than anything else that we are in a wonderfully dense urban environment. Each neighborhood has its own particular aural ecology: varieties of sound, quality of echoes, differing dynamic ranges that ebb and flow throughout the day.

We are far better at recognizing our visual environment, but all of us, if blindfolded, would know by the sounds that we were home. The murmurs of sleepy Carroll Gardens in Brooklyn sound far different from the bustle and buzz on the sidewalks of first-generation Jackson Heights in Queens.

Some city sounds are not so comforting. There is the half-heard sidewalk exchange that at first seems spirited but then sounds violent. There is that screech of brakes that seems especially desperate or, worse, ends not in silence and a "phew" but in a crash. Sometimes, the sound is not only unsettling, but in its size and unfamiliarity, terrifying.

That is the kind of sound that roared through Midtown on Wednesday, just before 6 p.m. Workers getting ready to head home during the afternoon rush heard powerful rumblings that exploded into what people variously described as a roar like Niagara Falls, a volcano erupting, a hailstorm that pelted skyscrapers with metal fragments.

Although the roar turned out to be the explosion of a steam pipe, the behavior of New Yorkers was much the same as it was in response to a far different noise, on 9/11. People busy with their lives instinctively stopped in their tracks and looked up because this particular roar, such a common noise in New York, was not just exceedingly loud, but fundamentally, and awfully, out of place.

The deer in the forest instantly knows the difference between leaves crunching underneath a raccoon and leaves crunching underneath a pair of Timberlands. Though humans' hearing is not as acute as that of many animals, we have an ability unique among creatures to hear and interpret multiple sounds and instantaneously sort them, hearing in detail the ones we care about and suppressing the ones we don't.

Like a photographer who focuses in close on the face of a companion, and then shifts focus to the store across the street, we can catch the conversation of the people next to us, then hear the voice of someone yelling from across the street, respond to the honk of a horn, all while pushing out of audible focus the background rush of thousands of cars passing, dogs barking and subways rumbling by.

This sonic editing is no mean feat. Think of the auditory stew New Yorkers place themselves in each day as they wake from the little night music of the city. The shuffling sounds of other New Yorkers preparing themselves for the day, the clack of feet on apartment-building stairs or the groaning of elevators, accelerate as the minutes head toward 9 a.m.

We enter the street as if we are stepping into a river, pulled along by the staccato of feet, and immediacy of traffic sounds, before heading underground to be deafened by the coming growl of our train. Increasingly many New Yorkers tune out the city by tuning in to iPods and cellphones, adding an extra layer of personal sound to the public sound of the city.

Yet through it all, the democratic ear takes it all in—there is no neat flap of skin like the eyelid to turn the sound on or off. Never was there so overworked an organ as a New York eardrum.

●

I HEARD about Wednesday's steam blast on Lexington Avenue as I was headed to Boston to see the Edward Hopper exhibition at the Museum of Fine Arts.

Hopper's images are famously quiet. A lone man reading a paper under a street lamp at night; a solitary woman in an Automat; another woman staring out the window of an apartment building. Yet Hopper's paintings are about not the absence of sound but the quiet moments and places away from the heart of the city's soundstage.

We love "Early Sunday Morning," for example, an iconic image of low storefronts on Seventh Avenue from 1930, because we can almost hear the sounds that will be back on Monday—cars and people passing, stores being opened, wares being hawked. Hopper's figures look, for comfort, out to the sounds of the city.

In 1950, the composer John Cage moved into a tenement building on Monroe Street on the Lower East Side and opened his windows to mingle the city's music and his own. In came the sounds of this immigrant neighborhood and the still-vibrant industrial waterfront nearby. It was here that he composed some of his most famous works, like "Imaginary

Landscape IV" and "4' 33""—all drawing on the indeterminate music made from his neighborhood.

A few years after Cage left (his neighborhood was urban renewed out of existence by Robert Moses), Harry Belafonte was marching down the middle of 42nd Street, right past the future site of the steam pipe explosion on Lexington Avenue, in the 1959 sci-fi doomsday film "The World, the Flesh and the Devil," alone in the city, missing the companionship of people and the urban sounds they make.

Those who heard the jets roar on 9/11 and those who heard the "volcano" erupt from beneath the streets last Wednesday will never forget that sound. The only thing worse would have been silence.

July 22, 2007

32

Children of Darkness

They Plumb Tunnels, Trestles and Other Abandoned Places,
Often Illicitly, and in Those Shadow Cities
Find the Pulsing Heart of New York.

BEN GIBBERD

An urban explorer afoot in the hidden city. *(Miru Kim)*

JOE ANASTASIO, a slim, dark-haired Web designer for a Wall Street publishing company, was standing outside Madison Square Garden, dressed in black work boots, a torn blue check shirt and a bomber jacket. It was a brisk Sunday morning in the spring, and among the swirl of tourists clutching maps and hockey fans in Rangers jerseys, he might easily have been mistaken for a Metropolitan Transportation Authority track worker heading to a shift.

That is how Mr. Anastasio likes it. A 33-year-old native of Astoria, Queens, he is an urban explorer, to use a term he and his fellow adventurers accept somewhat wearily, along with urban spelunker, infiltrator, hacker and guerrilla urbanist. Urban explorers, a highly disparate, loosely knit group, share an obsession with uncovering the hidden city that lies above and below the familiar one all around them. And especially during the summer, they are out in full force.

Alone and with cohorts, Mr. Anastasio has crawled, climbed and sometimes simply brazenly walked into countless train tunnels, abandoned subway stations, rotting factories, storm drains, towers, decaying hospitals and other shadowy remnants of the city's infrastructure the authorities would rather he did not enter. Although he records his adventures on his Web site, ltvsquad.com, anonymity is, for him, a necessary tool.

A few minutes later on this Sunday morning, Mr. Anastasio was joined by a Korean woman in her 20's named Miru Kim, who with her delicate looks and glossy, shoulder-length black hair offered a striking contrast to Mr. Anastasio's grizzled appearance. The two headed off, bound for the netherworld beneath their feet.

A few blocks west, they looked around cautiously. Several trucks were parked behind a wire mesh fence, its gate wide open, but no one seemed about. Beyond the fence lay an entrance to the Amtrak tunnels that run north-south along the West Side. They stepped through the gate and headed for the tunnel's mouth.

Almost immediately, the space became not pitch black, as expected, but a dirty gray, lit by sodium lights and narrow shafts of sunlight from the open street crossings every few blocks above. Faded curlicues of graffiti formed a pattern as dense as wallpaper on the concrete walls.

As the two headed deeper, the sounds of the upper world, of voices and cars, faded. A train thundered past, and the two stepped to one side, averting their faces until its red taillights were dots in the distance. After about 20 minutes, the murky outline of a disused, darker tunnel appeared, and they followed it, holding their flashlights carefully.

This new tunnel ended at a strange contraption, resembling a vast air-conditioner on stilts. Near its base sat the abandoned remains of a homeless person's encampment: bags of filthy clothes, milk crates full of mismatched sneakers, a few swivel chairs and, lying forlornly in the middle of the tracks, a champagne cork.

Only 20 feet above lay Manhattan's busy streets, but it might as well have been 20,000 feet, the sense of human desolation was so intense. For Mr. Anastasio, however, the setting was perfect. He whipped out a digital camera and clicked away. A few days later, the photos were up on his Web site. "Don't you just love this dump?" the text read. "About the only real thing left in NYC is the underground, the dirty, filthy underground."

TRYING to calculate how many urban explorers there are puts one in the hapless position of the reporter who asked Bob Dylan in 1965 how many protest singers there were. "Uh, how many? I think about 136," Dylan replied sarcastically.

Many American cities have urban exploration Web sites, as do British, Canadian and Australian cities. New York, whose vast infrastructure provides a mecca for those drawn to such things, has dozens of Web sites devoted to recording their owner's adventures within it.

At the more extreme end are those like Mr. Anastasio's and nycexposed.com, which is run by a teenager named Sean and contained, until recently, a practical if tongue-in-cheek guide on how to cut through chain-link fences, as well as photographs of speeding subway trains perilously up close.

Not surprisingly, the authorities do not take kindly to such activities.

"Trespassing on the M.T.A.'s infrastructure is not only illegal and extremely dangerous, it's a pretty stupid idea," said Jeremy Soffin, a transportation authority spokesman, echoing the sentiments expressed by officials for Amtrak, the New York Police Department and other agencies. "I personally took a track safety class recently, and then you really appreciate how dangerous it is—how big the trains are, how fast-moving they are, and how narrow the spaces are.

"It's dangerous even for very experienced track workers. There's no place for urban explorers."

While Mr. Anastasio and Ms. Kim, a soft-spoken artist and arts event promoter, have never been arrested while exploring, Mr. Anastasio said he knew some explorers who had been. And many other sites, while they don't thumb their noses so willfully at authority, are extreme in their own way. Ms. Kim's site, mirukim.com, which has made her something of a legend in urban explorer circles, contains a section devoted to a project she calls "Naked City Spleen."

The site features color photographs of Ms. Kim, naked, posed in abandoned tunnels and structures in New York and elsewhere. In one, she crouches like a cat on a vast slab of rusting steel amid the ruins of the former Revere sugar refinery, now demolished, in Red Hook, Brooklyn. In another, she appears, back turned to the camera, squeezed into the narrow heating tunnels below Columbia University, her alma mater. The effect is powerful, not just because of the eroticism, but also because her nakedness seems to emphasize her human vulnerability.

Ms. Kim took considerable risks to obtain her images. A few years ago, she and a friend encountered a body on a trip in Washington Heights. Another time, while she was making a solo visit to the same mysterious tunnel she and Mr. Anastasio visited together, the occupant of the homeless camp appeared just as she had removed her clothes.

Despite her initial fear, she continued with her photography. "In my mind," she wrote later on her Web site, "he is a dweller in one of the darkest rooms in the collective unconsciousness of all the inhabitants of New York and possibly of all modern cities."

THIS sense of communicating with the city on a secret frequency may be what is most appealing to urban explorers.

Steve Duncan is a self-described "guerrilla historian" whose explorations of the city's forbidden structures—among them the old Croton Aqueduct in the Bronx and the long-closed upper viewing platform 216 feet above the 1964 World's Fair in Queens—are documented on his Web site, undercity.org.

"Most people experience their life in the city in a two-dimensional way," said Mr. Duncan, a sandy-haired 28-year-old. "You know, they go from Point A to Point B along streets and don't realize there are these multiple layers to the city. By going 20 feet below or 20 feet above, you can go to a place that is practically unvisited, that maybe 100 people get to see a year."

Seeing something inaccessible, he said, is special. "You experience it differently and more directly," he explained. "The history and city becomes alive."

To prove his point, Mr. Duncan led an expedition around one of his favorite places, the heating tunnels that honeycomb the foundations of Columbia University, a maze he discovered as a student there.

Bent double in their confines one afternoon, sweat dripping from his forehead as the pipes around him wheezed and groaned, he pointed out in a subbasement the remains of the original coal hoppers that fed the boilers before the buildings' conversion to oil. Beneath another building is part of a 19th-century stone wall that Mr. Duncan said was part of a city insane asylum before being demolished to make way for the university.

Mr. Duncan's greatest coup came when he wiggled through a vent in the ceiling and emerged from a door on the other side of a room. A quick step through the door and across the corridor outside led to a densely cluttered room, piled high with cases of ancient electrical machinery.

This, Mr. Duncan announced, was the original Pupin Laboratory, where the university's physics department built a particle accelerator and split the atom in 1939, in an early stage of what would be known as the Manhattan Project. Mr. Duncan said he believed that in 1997 he became the first urban explorer to discover it, although others followed suit, as attested by the graffiti around the room.

The particle accelerator—a circular green mass in the center of the room that resembles nothing more alarming than an enormous food processor—was too heavy and too dangerous to safely remove after the project moved to Chicago, following the attack on Pearl Harbor, he said, so the university decided to keep it here, "in their mildly radioactive junk storage room."

The discovery left him jubilant.

"It's just a great example of how you peel back one layer and you get to old coal hoppers," he said. "You peel back another layer and you find the foundations of an asylum when this area was all grass and farmlands. You peel back another layer, and here's the building where the atom was split."

●

FOR some urban explorers, the search for shadow cities does not entail venturing down tunnels or scaling high walls. Kevin Walsh, the 50-year-old, Brooklyn-born creator of the Web site forgotten-ny.com—a vast cornucopia of facts, photographs, conjecture, mythology and infrastructure—rarely goes urban exploring in the guerrilla sense of the term.

Instead, armed with a camera and the combined knowledge of a small library of books on New York, he stalks the city's streets looking for its secrets hidden in plain view. From faded advertisements to ancient streetlights to streets named after long-obscure luminaries, he obsessively records the ephemera of what he terms "the lost metropolis" on his Web site. Much of this information is collected in his book, "Forgotten New York," which was published last year and is grist for the tours he conducts of forgotten corners of the city.

During a recent stroll with Mr. Walsh around Green-Wood Cemetery in Brooklyn, it became clear that his love of the city's ephemera goes beyond brick and stone. While on a hunt for the gravestone of the infamous 19th-century figure Bill the Butcher, he noticed some ancient lovers' graffiti carved into a tree trunk near the gravestone.

"That's what I love!" he said as he examined the blend of hearts and names, their edges softened and indecipherable with age. "That's what I show people on trips."

Beyond the thrill of seeing what others have not seen, or dare not see, and the sense that it should be recorded for future generations, urban explorers are driven by another motive. It is impossible to visit some of their more spectacular haunts without experiencing a touch of the sacred.

This was apparent one afternoon when Mr. Duncan's good friend and co-conspirator on numerous adventures, Moses Gates, a 31-year-old tour guide and graduate student in urban planning, undertook a journey into the abandoned Red Hook Grain Terminal on Brooklyn's waterfront.

"Generally, climbing urban structures and being high up really allows me to connect with the city," Mr. Gates said, "although I sometimes get that connection from other places, or just from walking around town. I love the feeling of being at one with the city—it's a spiritual experience, I won't deny it."

The grain terminal is one of the waterfront's industrial masterpieces, a series of 54 concrete silos about 12 stories high, built in 1922 to hold grain arriving by barge from the West. The cold gray waters of the Erie Basin lapping around the structure's edges give it the sense of an island fortress.

The terminal was decommissioned in the 1960's and now stands in a small industrial park, surrounded by concrete walls. Recently, a 17-year-old plan to turn it into a recycling center was revived, though its future remains uncertain. Mr. Gates negotiated the walls, then swung himself lithely beneath a rusted steel grating at one corner of the building.

Suddenly he was inside what might at first glance have been mistaken for a cathedral. Fat concrete columns lined up as far as the eye could see, creating a dreamlike procession of naves in all directions. Light filtered in from the sides, casting long diagonal shadows across the floor.

But what really gave the building its rarefied air was the silence. Amid the daily cacophony of the city, where every place is packed with a scrum of people, this space stood empty, a still counterpoint to everything around it.

Mr. Gates began to climb the corroded metal stairs that led to the roof. Graffiti lined the inner walls—a good sign. "Graffiti artists are almost always first," Mr. Gates said. "If there's no graffiti, there's a good chance it's impossible to get there."

At the end of his climb, as he popped his head out of a hatch on the roof, a magnificent—and utterly illicit—360-degree view of the city opened up. In the foreground lay Red Hook's 19th-century industrial sprawl of warehouses and narrow streets lined with row houses. In the distance rose Manhattan's dull gray skyline. Tiny cars crawled along the elevated Prospect Expressway, an F train made its way over the Gowanus Canal, and airplanes banked steeply as they headed for Kennedy Airport.

"Planes, trains and automobiles, you got it all here," Mr. Gates said happily. Pausing to look out at this perspective, seen by so few, he added: "There's no doubt about it. You've got romance here."

July 29, 2007

33

Tunnel Vision

Ever since Childhood, She Had Fantasized about a
Hidden World below the City Streets.
In These Dreams, She Was Not Alone.

KATHERINE MARSH

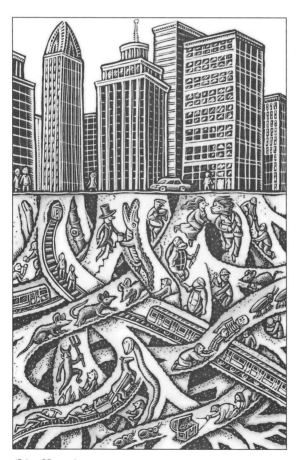

(Lisa Haney)

ONE day, when I was 12 years old, I felt a lump in my throat. It was a year of metaphorical lumps—I had just started a new junior high school and my parents were in the middle of a messy divorce—but this lump was real. A doctor diagnosed it as a cyst, benign but dangerously close to my thyroid gland, and on a December afternoon, my mother took me to see a surgeon in Manhattan.

I don't remember the exam or the decision to schedule an operation, but I do remember getting on the surgeon's tiny elevator to go back home and the doors opening on a place that seemed a physical manifestation of my own bewildered state of mind. In this windowless underground, pipes rattled, steam poured out in gaseous clouds, and mysterious clanking noises filled the air. The elevator had deposited us in the building's basement, but I felt as if I had arrived in another world.

This memory remained with me long after the operation was over and the thin white scar on my neck had faded. The memory is no longer reliable; the basement has grown to mythic proportions, the noise and the heat intensified by time. But it is one I returned to several years ago when I began to write a novel for young adults about New York and the underground world I imagined beneath it. Even in my 20's, when I lived and worked in the city, I always had the strange feeling that one day I might rediscover this room and the universe of fears and possibilities it embodied.

Many cities have a literature of the underground—the Paris of Victor Hugo, the London of the science-fiction writer Neil Gaiman—but New York has been a particularly popular setting for fictional underground worlds. These range from the feasible, the 19th-century basement where the narrator of Ralph Ellison's "Invisible Man" lives literally off the grid, to the entirely fantastical, the fin-de-siècle hotel called the Grand Cosmo in Steven Millhauser's novel "Martin Dressler," where floors open up to inexhaustible worlds of novelty and enchantment.

These can be places of nightmare and shadow, inhabited by monsters like the ones in "Reliquary," the subterranean thriller by Douglas Preston and Lincoln Child. Sometimes they are places of refuge, like the sewers that serve as home to the Teenage Mutant Ninja Turtles.

Part of the allure of New York's underground worlds is that they actually exist. Because of the city's density, much of its infrastructure is tucked beneath it, not only trains, subways and shopping arcades but also electric lines, sewers and water tunnels. New Yorkers journey into this subterranean world every day, casually and almost unthinkingly.

At the same time, the city's underground offers a sense of vastness and possibility. Although the so-called rail-fan window is fast disappearing from the city's subway cars, who hasn't stood looking out the window of the first car of a train and glimpsed enticingly abandoned tunnels and locked doors?

In an island city as small and densely packed as Manhattan, the underground serves as a physical frontier. But it also serves as a psychological frontier, arguably even more so than do the undergrounds of London and Paris. In New York, something about the fantasy subterranean world appeals powerfully to the psyche of the city's residents.

Paradoxically, one of the darker attractions of the underground has to do with its antithesis: tall buildings. New York is a vertical city, one in which socioeconomic status is measured in height: the penthouse in the sky, the bird's-nest office, the pricey restaurant with the panoramic view. The novelist Colson Whitehead plays with this metaphor in "The Intuitionist," imagining a "perfect elevator" that can ferry disenfranchised black New Yorkers to this promised land of social mobility.

And so the underground can represent the failure to thrive in the vertical city, sometimes literally. This is the narrative of the underground homeless society described by Jennifer Toth in her book "The Mole People: Life in the Tunnels beneath New York City."

At the same time, underground worlds can represent a rejection of the city's rat race, even liberation from the pace and the pressure. Over the years, the accuracy of parts of Ms. Toth's book has been challenged. But despite these doubts, and despite the city's efforts to clean out the tunnels, the mole people have only gained a more entrenched place in the popular imagination, showing up as characters in video games, comics, movies and even an episode of "Law & Order."

●

PART of our fascination with this population has to do with the romance of the underground as a place in which the individual can be free, in which he can reveal, without fear of rejection, the strangest, least acceptable parts of himself. This is the thinking that gave birth to Vincent, Linda Hamilton's leonine suitor in the 1980's television series "Beauty and the Beast." Because of his catlike features, Vincent rarely travels above ground, finding shelter and acceptance among a society of other outcasts who inhabit the tunnels beneath New York.

In my novel, the protagonist, Jack Perdu, goes in search of the secret track in Grand Central where Franklin Delano Roosevelt's personal train arrived (a track that really exists), only to find a set of stairs that descend beneath the station into a magical world.

For Jack, underground New York is a place to confront his fears of loneliness and rejection in the world above and, in the company of other lost souls, to learn who he really is. Most of us make that journey in more mundane ways. But one of the remarkable aspects of the city is that it continuously offers that promise of self-discovery, the promise that we can descend into our own dark places and return home stronger, better and more self-assured.

November 4, 2007

34

The Unthinkable,
Right around the Corner

The Convoy of Police Cars Races down the City Streets,
Sirens Blaring, Red Lights Flashing.
They're There to Protect. But They Also Terrify.

FRANCINE PROSE

The "critical response vehicle surge," a fixture of the post-9/11 city. *(Photograph by Ramin Talaie, 2004; photo illustration by The New York Times)*

THE first time I saw it happen, in 2004, I was walking down 14th Street along Union Square on my way home, wondering what we were going to have for dinner that night. A dozen police cars came squealing around the corner, pulled up to the sidewalk, and parked with their back wheels on the curb.

My heartbeat went from zero to 60 (or whatever the actual cardiac equivalent is) in less than 60 seconds. The attacks of 9/11 hadn't been all that long ago, and I wondered: Had something else happened? Was there a "problem" in the Union Square subway station? I thought of my husband, my sons. I ran through a mental list of friends and loved ones. Where were they? Were they in danger? Was everyone O.K.?

By now, I know better. What I witnessed was what the police called a critical response vehicle surge.

Maybe a lot of New Yorkers are already familiar with this term, but I had to look it up. That's the phrase for what you see when you're turning the corner onto Broadway, or Fifth Avenue, and suddenly 50 police cars appear, red lights spinning, all of them streaming in rapid (or slow and steady) formation down the avenue. Or they blare their sirens as they speed along Flatbush Avenue, waking up your children, or they rattle the cobblestones on Hudson Street.

I suppose I knew on some level that all this activity signified anti-terrorist alertness in our toughened-up post-9/11 world. A drill, a show of force, an effort at deterrence, all rolled into one. An unpredictable but firm presence and a speedy response time constitute Homeland Security 101.

But don't try to set your watch by these demonstrations. That's the entire point. Every day, as many as 76 cars, each from a different precinct in the five boroughs, converge in one place, "combat-park" with their backs to the sidewalk, receive a terrorism briefing and get assignments to speed off to multiple locations.

The officers have their Hazmat gear. They have been taught how to deal with chemical, biological and radiation attacks, and have been given special training on how to handle disasters in key locations, like the subway. These drills are never at the same hour of the day, never along the same route as the day before. In fact, they're planned to take place where and when we—and the terrorists—least expect them.

The city is not going to be caught off guard again, as we were on 9/11. Though the strange thing is that the vehicle surge exactly brings to mind my memory of 9/11: streams of police cars racing into the city, red lights spinning, as I rode out to the airport to catch a flight that was about to be canceled.

Now that I know what the readiness drill is called, and what it's designed to do, I can relax and stop being reminded of the time it happened for real. I can calm down and quit asking what any reasonable human being would wonder when several dozen police cars tear by, lights flashing, sirens wailing. Hey, what's going on? Now that I know, I can spare myself the adrenaline rush.

That last sentence is a total lie. Even if you're pretty sure you know what's going on—Hey, whatever, it's probably only a critical response vehicle surge!—some part of you still thinks: Did something happen?

So you watch the police cars speed by. You stand around, you ask someone who asks someone else. Finally, the word goes around. Police drill, or something. Nothing.

Whew. For a few seconds you feel relieved. Then, depending on whether you're an optimist or a realist, you might think: "Great! We're safe!" or "We dodged a bullet this time. Something's going to happen, sooner or later." And that's not a happy moment.

Some people seek out adrenaline: auto racers, sky divers and extreme skiers. Perhaps I'm an oversensitive, overbred urban puppy. But still, if you're not expecting it, a shot of response-vehicle heart-pumping hormones can't be that great for your health. We're Pavlovian creatures. Nature and nurture have conspired to train us to react with fight-or-flight alarm to certain cultural signals: flashing lights and loud noises. First we get the jolt of fear, then the reassurance. Be still my heart; it's only the good guys keeping us safe.

I can't quite remember what the experts ultimately decided about the health hazards of the airborne poisons that residents of Lower Manhattan breathed from September 2001 until that Christmas. So I don't imagine that we will find the time and resources to study how the critical response vehicle surges affect the pulse and blood pressure of ordinary New Yorkers, especially the old and the young.

●

PERHAPS the best thing that can be said for the training drills is that they're probably more enjoyable than many things the police are called upon to do in the course of a normal day. The police do a great deal for us, they lead stressful lives, and I'm all for combining a show of force aimed at deterring Al Qaeda with a challenging, companionable interval in a hard-working officer's morning or evening.

If we're going to have to live with vehicle surges, I hope they save lives. Actually, I hope the surges are never called upon to save lives. I hope they're never tested.

But as a realist, I worry. I hope these surges won't need to save enough lives to stack up against the minutes by which, for all we know, they're shortening the lives of the otherwise peaceful New Yorkers who happen to be strolling down 14th Street, wondering what to cook for dinner, when, suddenly, out of nowhere, police cars screech up to the curb.

January 27, 2008

35

His City, Lost and Found

Raised in Manhattan, He Is Fascinated by the Changes to
His Native Borough. Yet from His Garret across the River,
He Does Not Mourn Its Transformation.

NATHANIEL RICH

Manhattan, as seen from Brooklyn. *(Michael Nagle/The New York Times)*

RECENTLY went into Manhattan with a friend to visit her younger brother's new apartment on 52nd Street and the East River. The brother, Ariel, had just graduated from college and had been hired by a prestigious financial firm in Midtown. His two roommates had followed the same path, and so, apparently, had everyone else who lived on their long, fluorescent-lit hallway on the 32nd floor.

There was a good reason for this. As Ariel explained to me, his firm had negotiated a deal with the building's real estate agents, and every employee who rented an apartment got a 6 percent discount on the brokerage fee. Each weekend, and especially over the summer, the young bankers moved in, while families and elderly people moved out.

The apartment building next door, meanwhile, was filling up with lawyers. Doctors lived in a third building, the one closest to the river. "It's like special-interest housing, but for professionals," Ariel said.

It was Friday night and Ariel's hallway was busy with preparty chatter. One guy no one had ever seen before knocked on the door, inviting us to a party on the next floor. An hour later, two women showed up asking whether we ourselves were having a party.

Ariel and his roommates were elated. They finally had their own place, and one within walking distance of work. Everyone else on their hall was young, friendly and new to the city. It was like freshman year again.

The neighborhood's transformation seemed stark and total. It was as if a new city had erupted overnight, devouring the old one in a panic of hunger. The suddenness of the change came as a surprise to me, because I thought I knew this particular corner of the city pretty well. After all, I grew up there—on East 51st Street, one block from Ariel's apartment.

Later, walking west on 52nd Street, I recognized a grim sushi restaurant on First Avenue. I had never seen anyone eat there, but that night a line of recent college graduates extended out the front door and down the block. The people standing in line probably weren't aware that just a decade ago, the luxury high-rise behind them, on the corner of 51st and First, had been a shelter for homeless and mentally ill women.

Nor is it likely that the throngs on Second Avenue realized that the glossy nightclubs had just a few years ago replaced a row of moribund pizza and taco joints; or that, in the 1970's and 80's, this was one of the city's most widely known gay hustling districts, the inspiration for the Ramones' "53rd and 3rd." ("53rd and 3rd / Standing on the street / 53rd and 3rd / I'm trying to turn a trick.")

I was born in 1980, so my view of the changes that have come to Manhattan is relatively limited. I can't credibly mourn the transformation of the Lower East Side from a wanton, crack-depleted borderland filled with burning trash cans and random knifings into a slick paradise of Avenue C wine bars and Ludlow Street fashion boutiques. I have vivid memories of 1980's Times Square (my parents worked in offices there), but I never got to experience the distinct pleasures of all-night grindhouse double features or live sex shows.

I certainly don't remember the Greenwich Village of the 1950's, or the Bowery of the punk era, or Jean-Michel Basquiat's SoHo, though I'd like to imagine that I passed through the latter, at least in a stroller.

I do remember going to the 24-hour French diner Florent in the meatpacking district in the late 80's, when its pink neon marquee was the only commercial storefront visible in any direction. It was after a dinner there, as my parents searched for a cab, that I saw my first real-life prostitute (also my first real-life transvestite).

Florent is still holding on, but these days it's hard to spot. As the Web site of the new Hotel Gansevoort describes the neighborhood, it is now an "eclectic mix of meat warehouses and retrofit storefronts."

On Gansevoort Street, as well as on West 42nd Street, and to an ever greater extent in Chelsea and Hell's Kitchen and around Columbus Circle, it's impossible for someone like me, born and raised in Manhattan, not to feel like a tourist. Not because these parts of the city feel like a foreign country; just the opposite. From the billboard advertisements to the neon marquees to the new streamlined architecture, Manhattan has embraced the dominant gestures and exclamations of American mall culture.

.

WHEN tourists gaze up at the lights on 42nd Street, they see themselves, and their own towns and cities, but as if through the wrong end of a telescope, the images having suffered some kind of grotesque magnification. I'm not any less in awe myself; I look up, too, mesmerized by the lights.

This used to disturb me, so I understand why there's been a lot of hand-wringing in the past few years about the transformation of Manhattan, particularly over the loss of what some call the city's bohemian spirit.

In an essay in The New Yorker last year called "Gothamitis," Adam Gopnik wrote, "New York is safer and richer but less like itself, an old lover who has gone for a face-lift and come out looking like no one in particular." Inigo Thomas, writing in Slate in 2005, began a week of columns about the history of the city's bohemian past by declaring, "There is no bohemia in today's New York."

New York magazine and Time Out New York regularly run articles about new neighborhoods that promise to be the next frontier of New York cool, now that Manhattan has priced out all artists, youth, ethnic communities and nonbankers ("If You Lived Here, You'd Be Cool by Now" was the title of an article in New York extolling the hipster virtues of Jersey City).

Most of the points made in these reports are valid. Yet the articles often seem plagued by an easily discernible peevishness, irritation and even depression over the way Manhattan has changed. There is also, on the part of those displaced to the poor boroughs, an element of competitive bristling. It's as if Manhattan has to be disgraced and humiliated for any other borough to gain ascendancy.

•

I OFTEN wonder whether the worst of this griping comes not from native New Yorkers but from people who didn't grow up here, the same people who, when they arrived, made immense financial, psychological and physical sacrifices to land a bunk bed in an apartment in Hell's Kitchen. They did it because in their minds, Manhattan was synonymous with the big city.

This is the class of people who moved to New York believing that if they didn't live on the main island, they might as well have stayed in Pasadena, or Raleigh, or even Jersey City. These are the same people who, after enduring a year of Manhattan poverty, decide to move to Brooklyn, or even Queens, and then extravagantly praise the virtues of their new, down-market neighborhood while castigating their old, expensive one. In other words, they secretly wish they could still afford to live in Manhattan.

I don't share that desire, but for the first 21 years of my life I was no less of a Manhattan snob. My own internal map of the city was informed entirely by the subway map. I didn't realize until an alarmingly late age that the map was not to scale but schematic (and highly Manhattan-centric). In other words, I didn't know that Queens continued for another five miles after the end of the F line, or that the little green hexagon of Prospect Park was actually more than two-thirds the size of Central

Park, or that Staten Island was almost three times as big as Manhattan (and was part of New York).

In my teens, my own Saul Steinberg view of the city began at the southern end with the World Trade Center (where I used to go on tedious class trips in grade school) and jumped north to St. Marks Place (where I shopped for used records), then to a friend's apartment in Stuyvesant Town, and finally, taking up the bulk of the frame, the swath that ran from Times Square up to 96th Street. (At the private high school I attended on the Upper East Side, my friends considered my apartment on 51st Street "downtown.")

In the outlying portions of my mental map of the city drifted the continents of Shea Stadium, Randalls Island and the Meadowlands. There was also a small island at East 116th Street where, when my family was stuck in bumper-to-bumper traffic one summer night on the F.D.R. Drive, returning from a visit to some friends in the suburbs, a man threw a large rock through the window on the passenger side and stole my mother's wallet. I was 9 at the time, sitting in the back seat with my younger brother. Glass flew all over the car, and my mother's thigh was bleeding. I remember thinking that it was my first brush with the real New York.

Ever since I moved to Brooklyn five years ago, first to Greenpoint and then to a 300-square-foot garret just south of Atlantic Avenue, I've had a new map of the city. (It's a good thing, too; even metropolises can become claustrophobic.)

Uptown has crept from the Upper East Side down to Union Square; the Upper West Side has moved to Brooklyn Heights (with Zabar's morphing into Sahadi's, the emporium of Middle Eastern food on Atlantic Avenue, and Citarella into Fish Tales on Court Street); the old Lower East Side to Red Hook, or perhaps Sunset Park; Battery Park to Brighton Beach; Midtown to Metrotech.

And Central Park to Prospect Park. My brother, who has just moved to Brooklyn, went into Manhattan with some friends one recent weekend, to play touch football on the field behind the Metropolitan Museum's Temple of Dendur, near 84th Street. It was a 40-minute commute, but they had always played football there as kids.

Yet as soon as they took to the field a park security guard came by and asked them to leave. The park, it turns out, was trying to grow its grass, so park officials didn't want anyone to step on it. After being kicked off four different fields, my brother and his friends headed back to the subway in a state of bewilderment.

"The whole borough of Manhattan is a museum now," he told me that night. "I like that there are fewer murders, but sometimes you want to play catch."

Brooklyn, of course, is changing, too, to no small degree driven by Manhattan. A luxury high-rise goes up on the Bowery, and a Richard Meier luxury apartment goes up in Prospect Heights. Rents skyrocket in Battery Park and then on Myrtle Avenue in Fort Greene.

Fairway has opened in Red Hook; Trader Joe's is coming to Cobble Hill. The construction of the Atlantic Yards development (and the destruction of the prewar residential buildings that now stand on its site) is under way. Neighborhoods like Brooklyn Heights, Park Slope and Fort Greene are nearly as expensive as several areas in Lower Manhattan.

Yet the essential warp of Brooklyn has remained intact. The village-scale neighborhoods bear no resemblance to the canyons of Manhattan. There are still a couple of slaughterhouses within walking distance of my apartment, where I can order the execution of a chicken (or a rabbit), and there is a seaman's bar whose décor (and to only a slightly lesser extent its prices) seems frozen in 1955. What I've lost in Manhattan I've found in Brooklyn, so it seems mawkish to mourn.

•

MOST of the concerts and almost all the parties I attend are in Brooklyn. I often run into friends on the street, which makes sense, because I have only about five friends my age left in Manhattan. If I didn't have to commute to an office downtown, I'd rarely cross the river.

There are still, of course, reasons to do so. Recently I went to Midtown for an event at the New York Public Library. As soon as I came out of the subway, I regretted my decision. The Rockefeller Center Christmas tree had just been unveiled, and a crowd of overjoyed people, perhaps emboldened by the padding of their winter coats, immediately began to coalesce around me.

Barricades had been set up not only along Fifth Avenue, but also along many of the side streets. Police officers ordered the heavy pedestrian traffic to advance through Saks—literally through the department store, passing between the makeup counters and scarf racks—to get from 50th Street to 49th. "Blame the tree," one of the officers shouted, "not me!"

Yet for the most part, the people seemed happy to be there: They had come from all over the world to experience Holiday Season New York.

I was running late, however, and as I tried to make my way through the scrum, I found myself throwing elbows and cursing at the city. Only later that night, when I looked up at Times Square, did I stop to admire the museum that Manhattan has become. The hysterical wattage of the billboards had turned the night sky over Broadway a pale blue—a kind of artificial, perpetual dusk into which the New York I once knew has floated, never to return. I watch that New York float farther away all the time, marveling at the sparkle, but relieved to live in a different city.

February 3, 2008

36

Any Given Monday

These Men Don't Dunk. Yet Every Week for 33 Years,
They Have Sought to Slow the Passage of Time on the
Hardwood Court of a Gym on the Upper West Side.

SAKI KNAFO

Full-court basketball at a school gym on the Upper West Side. *(Christian Hansen/The New York Times)*

FOR New York basketball fans, 33 is either a famous or an infamous number, depending on your age. If you're over 20, you can probably remember when the Knicks were ruled by Patrick Ewing, the dominant center with a blazing 33 on his chest.

Younger fans may be more likely to associate 33 with the number of games a miserable Knicks team won last season in the course of accumulating 49 losses, many of them at Madison Square Garden, on West 33rd Street.

Thirty-three is also the number of years that a group has gathered every Monday for a night of full-court games in a miniature gym at Columbia Grammar and Preparatory School on the Upper West Side.

Anything that lasts for 33 years in this fast-moving, quickly changing city probably deserves a plaque; what's remarkable about Monday night basketball, as the game is called by its devotees, is that it has retained many players for nearly its entire history. The two founding members, Sandy Miller and Nick Macdonald, are still playing at 63; another long-time player, Harry Atkins, is 74.

These men don't dunk. Most of them aren't very tall. On the whole, however, they are exceptionally graceful for guys their age.

"I believe I'm much more coordinated than most 63-year-old people around," said Mr. Miller, a guidebook author and former children's book publisher with a surprisingly quick move to the basket. "And it's absolutely because I never stopped playing basketball."

Mr. Miller, who lives in Boerum Hill, Brooklyn, arranges his travel plans so that he can leave New York on a Tuesday and return on a Sunday, to avoid missing any games. As a rule, he won't meet with out-of-town visitors on Monday evenings unless he hasn't seen them in at least two years.

Eleven years ago, when his first wife, Alice, was dying of cancer, he not only played regularly but found himself competing with greater intensity than ever before.

"I had this incredibly desperate need to play," he said. "Some nights I shot almost 100 percent. I've never seen the basket so large."

Mr. Miller is not the only person for whom the game has inspired devotion bordering on fanaticism: In the 90's, a man whose wife worked as a flight attendant commuted to the Manhattan gym from Puerto Rico.

Mr. Macdonald, an assistant dean at the Brooklyn campus of Long Island University whose father was the writer Dwight Macdonald, has, since the game's inception in late 1974, marked down the name or some other identifying attribute of every participant.

The list, which contains nearly 300 entries, reads, in its apparent randomness, like the dramatis personae of a postmodern play set in New York: Metropolitan Opera baritone, lighting designer for David Letterman's show, architect of the original Times Square TKTS booth, mime who performed almost continuously in front of the Metropolitan Museum of Art in the 80's, house painter, stockbroker, psychologist, Haitian refugee, Macaulay Culkin.

Add to that list my father. Over 15 years, he played in two stages, the first while driving a cab in the early 1980's, the second while drawing pointillist portraits for The Wall Street Journal in the 90's. After games, he and Mr. Miller rode back to Brooklyn on the C and F trains. Our families became very close. When Mr. Miller's wife was in the final weeks of her life, my mother stayed with her on Monday nights so that Mr. Miller could go play basketball.

Most players, though, have nothing to do with one another outside the gym. "I've been playing with some guys for 20 years, and I don't know their last names or what they do for a living," said Ray Leslee, a composer of Off Broadway musicals. "I love that. I think we all do. We come here to play basketball. It doesn't matter if you're a cop or a teacher or a banker."

Or a widower. In perhaps the most striking example of what Mr. Miller considers a peculiarly male social dynamic, a regular once asked my father why Mr. Miller had missed a string of games.

My father replied that Mr. Miller's wife had died after a three-year battle with stomach cancer. The player was startled. He hadn't known that Mr. Miller's wife had been ill. A number of players didn't even know that he had been married.

In the fall of 1973, the Millers were living in a one-bedroom apartment on West 105th Street, a dozen blocks north of Columbia Grammar. She had just started a job as a history teacher at the school, and he suspected her of conducting what he called an "intellectual affair" with one of her colleagues. In Ms. Miller's description, the colleague was "intellectually stimulating." And he was 5 feet 10.

Mr. Miller is 5 feet 5. As a student at Norwalk High School in Fairfield County, Conn., he was tormented by the alphabetical proximity of his surname to that of a 6-foot-7 behemoth with the vaguely intimidating name Urban Mulvahill. Year after year, the two were photographed side by side. Improbably, Mr. Miller got his payback in the gym, where he discovered that he could actually beat his nemesis in a jump ball.

When Mr. Miller learned that his wife's colleague played basketball a couple of nights a week with several other teachers at Columbia Grammar, he saw an opportunity. One evening, he managed to block his rival's shot. This achievement, as he remembers it, was punctuated by a "guttural, piercing, ear-splitting" scream—his own. The same evening, with the ball in his possession, he went up against his rival on the perimeter, jumped, faded backward, fired, and sank the game-winning basket.

In the spring of 1974, Mr. Miller ran into Nick Macdonald outside a screening of Fritz Lang's "Fury" at Theater 80 St. Marks, in the East Village. Mr. Miller knew Mr. Macdonald primarily as a director of "low-low-low-budget" political documentaries. A few years earlier, in an apartment on West 88th Street near Broadway, Mr. Miller and a friend had established Film Forum, now the venerable downtown institution, and screened a film of Mr. Macdonald's, in which the director is seen scrawling antiwar slogans on subway ads for Levy's rye bread.

Mr. Macdonald is 6 feet 2. He hadn't played basketball since the eighth grade at Dalton, the private school on the Upper East Side. Nevertheless, some months after running into Mr. Miller, he showed up at the Columbia Grammar gym wearing a pair of black, high-top PF-Flyer sneakers, a brand that Mr. Miller hadn't seen since about 1960.

Mr. Macdonald's style might be described as thorough. When he has trouble falling asleep at night, he sets himself the task of recalling entire baseball lineups from the 1950's. Within a few years of his return to basketball, he had mastered his signature move, taking a beautiful, high-arching outside shot that hits the mark with astonishing frequency—according to Mr. Miller, about 8 times out of 10. A professional player who could hit half his outside shots in competition would be considered a sharpshooter.

In the early days, Monday night basketball was like New York itself, dominated by lawyers. At a pottery studio in the basement of a brownstone on West 78th Street, Mr. Miller had met a lawyer who, in turn, had recruited several fellow lawyers. Among them was Plummer Lott, a former National Basketball Association forward. He had played on the Seattle SuperSonics with the legendary point guard Lenny Wilkens, a star player from Brooklyn who many years later would coach the Knicks.

The lawyers didn't fare well. As Mr. Macdonald explained, "They argued too much."

Eventually the lawyers migrated elsewhere and new people joined. Word of the game spread beyond Manhattan.

In 1975, the Millers moved to a tree-lined street in Carroll Gardens, Brooklyn, and a few years later they became parents. On a neighborhood excursion, Mr. Miller came across a fellow stroller-pusher, my mother, and introduced himself. Through her, he met my father, a cab-driving artist.

My father is from Israel. He speaks in the gruff voice of a falafel vendor and stands about 5-10. He neither sounds nor looks like much of a basketball player, and by his own admission, he isn't one. But during the 10 years in which he played, he considered Monday nights the highlight of his week.

As his enthusiasm for the game grew, however, something unfortunate happened. He became a Knicks fan. In the mid-90's, at the height of Michael Jordan's tyranny over the Knicks, my dad nurtured a fantasy of going up against the Bulls in the playoffs. He was convinced that the unbeatable superstar would get so shaken by the absurd spectacle of a bumbling 5-10 Israeli in N.B.A. attire that he'd let my father dribble the ball right past him.

•

ONE Monday evening a few weeks ago, I arrived at the gym to find Vinny Akins, 65, the head maintenance worker at Columbia Grammar and a sturdy defender, standing on the sideline, showing off a new knee brace. A few players were offering admiring remarks about its metal reinforcements.

Mr. Miller was wearing a sleeveless shirt imprinted: "It's Miller Time." With his wiry gray hair held back by a blue bandanna, he looked liked someone who had wandered over from a Neil Young concert.

Age and its outer manifestations are the objects of much jesting among players. At one point, Bob Nusbaum, 56, a kettle-bellied construction-netting salesman, joked that he was training for the N.B.A. Mr. Miller replied that Mr. Nusbaum might prefer to try out for the "National Biscuit Association." A former stand-up comedian, Mr. Nusbaum was quick with a comeback: "Sandy and Nick were here when they took down the peach baskets and put up the regular baskets."

Actually, the game has included many young players. Mr. Miller's daughter, Nell, broke the gender barrier in 1997, when she was in high school. This year's regulars include Gustavo Medina, a 19-year-old from Ridgewood, Queens, with a penchant for gold chains.

"I consider all these guys my mentors," Mr. Medina said recently. "I get better competition here than I do in the courts near my house. Over there, it's all flash and no play."

I'm 6 feet 6. When people meet me, they ask whether I play basketball. I usually say no. Thus, to meet me is to experience disappointment.

The truth is that for a few years after college, I frequented whatever Brooklyn playground I happened to be living near. Children two-thirds my size and half my age humiliated me. A special insult, I discovered, had been invented for people like me: "Big for nothing."

Now and again, Mr. Miller encouraged me to come by the gym, but I suppose I preferred losing to people half my age, rather than to people twice my age, because I never took him up on the offer. Then, about a year ago, I stopped playing altogether. One's ego can take only so much abuse.

Last month, I mustered the courage to play again. I went to the gym at Columbia Grammar, where I found Mr. Miller and a few other guys taking practice shots. A ball caromed into my hands. I spread my fingers over the rubber, bent my knees, sprang off my toes, and released.

The ball clanged off the front of the rim. I tried again. Another miss. I took five more shots. All misses. I stepped to the basket and attempted three layups. Three misses. The ball simply refused to go in.

"I can see you won't be getting a tryout with Maccabi Tel Aviv," said Bob Nusbaum, the former comedian, referring to Israel's pre-eminent professional team. In all my years of playground basketball, I had never heard that particular insult.

Once the game got going, things weren't so bad. I concentrated on grabbing rebounds, and I even scored a few points, mostly clumsy shots off the backboard.

The next day, my dad called me to say that he'd received an e-mail message from Mr. Miller: "He says you're dangerous down low!"

He added that his friend had described me as Monday night basketball's David Lee. Mr. Lee is a talented, hard-working power forward on the Knicks.

I was reminded of something Mr. Miller had said to me on the C train back to Brooklyn. The game, he'd pointed out, could comfortably accommodate "a 19-year-old and a 74-year-old, and someone who's 6-5 and a 55-year-old guy who's 55 pounds overweight."

After a moment, he'd added, "It's very forgiving."

February 24, 2008

Lemon Zest

The Scott's Oriole, a Fluffy Yellow Visitor Never Before
Sighted in New York, Had Come to Union Square,
Where It Seemed Utterly at Home.

JONATHAN ROSEN

The Scott's oriole, a rare visitor to New York City. *(Cal Vornberger)*

ON a cold morning late last month, I took a subway to Union Square Park to see a bird I had never seen. The bird, a Scott's oriole, had been noted intermittently behind the statue of Mohandas Gandhi since December, though it took birders several weeks to figure out that it was not in fact an orchard oriole—which would have been unusual enough for winter in Manhattan. Scott's oriole is a bird of the Southwest and has never been recorded in New York. It should be no farther east than Texas, which is why, despite my sluggardly winter ways, I decided it was worth a trip down from the Upper West Side, where I live.

Alongside my excitement, I felt a qualm of embarrassment as I exited the busy subway with my binoculars. It was like taking a taxi to hunt big game: "Let me off near the wildebeest, driver." In Central Park, I can at least conjure the illusion of wildness if I focus on the trees. But when your marker is a metal statue of a man in a loincloth, standing on what is essentially a traffic island, you cannot pretend you are in the middle of nature.

Then again, that's the point of bird-watching. "Nature" isn't necessarily elsewhere. It is the person holding the binoculars, as much as the bird in the tree, and it is the intersection of these two creatures, with technology bringing us closer than we have ever been to the very thing technology has driven from our midst. And, anyway, there are still wild elements in the center of a city. The morning I arrived, the bird had made itself scarce, perhaps because a red-tailed hawk, a Cooper's hawk and a kestrel were all patrolling the park.

I was not the only birder there. Everyone had read the same birding e-mail messages I had, and we were all staking out the southwest corner of the park, scanning the same stunted holly trees and viburnum.

Oranges and banana slices had been scattered on the ground, like votive offerings. The first report I read of the bird had it eating a kaiser roll. Several people had been there for hours, and two men showed me pictures of the bird that they had taken on their digital cameras that very day. They were hoping for a last look and braving the cold in the knowledge that by noon, sunlight would again fall on the building-shadowed corner of the park and entice the lemon-yellow, black-headed bird back into view.

Vagrant though the bird was, it seemed to me that there was also a rightness to its having landed in Union Square. This was not simply because of the statue of Gandhi, suggesting the need for simplicity and putting me to shame in his cotton dhoti and sandals as I shivered in my down jacket. My feelings also had to do with the park itself, named originally for the union of Broadway (then called Bloomingdale Road) and the Bowery.

Bird-watching is all about the coming together of disparate things, not merely earth and sky but the union of technology and a hunger for the wild world. "Imaginary gardens with real toads" is how Marianne Moore described poetry. Birding in city parks evokes much the same sensation. The parks, and the cities around them, may be human-made, but the wildlife that flashes through is no less real.

On the building across from where I stood, high up on the brick wall, there was a metal box that from time to time emitted the cry of a peregrine falcon. It was just a recording, but it roused the pigeons on the windowsills into a sort of lazy panic, getting them to rise and fly a few circles in the air before resettling. Even real peregrine falcons have a hint of the artificial about them, having been brought back from the brink by falconers expert in the ways of an ancient art that involved borrowing a bird from the wild and then turning it loose again.

Like the greenmarket in Union Square that brings apples and vegetables from outside the city, the token bird in the park is a reminder of an older way of life we are still intimately connected to and vitally in need of.

And like birders with their binoculars, we are not necessarily doomed by our modernity to exclusion from wildness. Bird-watching was born in cities—combining technology, urban institutions of higher learning, an awareness of the vanishing wild places of the earth and a desire to welcome what is left of the wild back into our world.

The name Union Square accumulated layers of later meaning, from the great rally held there in 1861 for the Union troops, and the Labor Day marches that took place later that century. In its own way, Scott's oriole belongs with Union Square's famous 19th-century monuments, most especially the 1868 statue of Abraham Lincoln.

•

THE bird was named by Darius Nash Couch, a Union general who was also a naturalist. (There were a lot of army men in the 19th century who used their postings as a way to record bird life.) Couch named the bird in honor of Gen. Winfield Scott, who was known as "Old fuss and feathers," though I feel sure that is not the reason he got a bird named after him; one of the great soldiers in American history, Scott began his career with the War of 1812 and ended it with the Civil War.

The bird is a monument to 19th-century ornithology, but it had defied its label and was doing what creatures with wings do: flying out of range and surprising us with life. It is never enough to know the name of a bird when you are birding. It is the mysterious unknowable animal that lives alongside the named and classified creature that draws us out to look.

By noon on that cold January day, about 20 birders had gathered, craning with increasing urgency into the bushes as the little patch of grass behind Gandhi grew brighter. And suddenly the bird was there. Someone pointed, and then we all saw it. It came down to the ground and, without ceremony, pecked at a piece of banana.

February 24, 2008

38

Tree Proud

The Mayor Pledged to Plant a Million Trees.
Sometimes It Takes Just One to Steal Your Heart.

RANDY KENNEDY

The author's son, Leo, and the fig tree in the family's backyard in Park Slope, Brooklyn. *(Michael Nagle/The New York Times)*

IKE most good Americans, I grew up thinking that figs—or more accurately "fig," as a nondiscrete substance—was something made by
man specifically to fill a soft rectangular cookie, probably manufactured
in the same big Midwestern dessert mill that produced things like nougat
and Twinkie filling and whatever sturdy white confection was used to
make candy cigarettes.

So when my wife and I bought a house in Brooklyn eight years ago
and the woman who sold it to us showed me her (soon to be our) beloved fig tree in the backyard, I had a moment of cognitive dissonance.
Of course I knew fig trees existed. But I guess I assumed that they must
have become largely ornamental by such a late date in human history.
And that the little green bulbs on their branches—it was spring then—
couldn't possibly be edible, much less have any relationship with the inner contents of a Fig Newton.

The woman, Esther, told me that the tree was several decades old (I
think she said 40 years, which in my retelling usually swelled to 60 or
more, though an arborist later broke it to me that the tree was probably
no older than 30).

And it seemed to me that the tree meant almost as much to her as
the house, a narrow brownstone where her Italian-American family had
lived more or less since the 1930's, once arrayed by generations among
the four floors, one of the grandfathers stubbornly residing at the top.
From up there, during his time, he undoubtedly would have been able
to chart the comparative health of dozens of fig trees in the yards neighboring his, planted by people trying hard to smuggle a little dream of
Neapolitan sweetness into a cold Northeastern climate.

When I inherited this dream, my fig frankly didn't look like much of a
tree, any more than the low, gnarled mesquites that passed for trees in the
part of West Texas where I grew up. The tree sat on the eastern side of
the yard and was then no taller than I am. It had either been judiciously
pruned or whittled back by a succession of hard winters.

But it was August when we closed on the house, so the spindly
branches were full of ripe brown figs. And it didn't take long after eating
a few right off the tree—honeylike and fragile, botanically not a fruit but
an enclosed inflorescence, a flower wrapped up in itself—to understand
why someone would try so hard to grow an essentially Mediterranean
tree at such an unfriendly latitude.

When we moved to this part of Park Slope, near Fifth Avenue, you
could still frequently see the battlements of the war between fig and frost

erected by old tree owners in early winter. The trees were cut back and their branches were cinched up next to their trunks. Then the trunks were carefully wrapped, usually in burlap that was sheathed in black tar paper, the whole contraption crowned with a bucket so the snow couldn't get inside. The result looked like a poor man's scarecrow or décor for a Beckett play. My wrappings, which I executed dutifully the first two winters, looked more like a listing pile of trash left behind by a crew of roofers.

But they did the job. In spring, green shoots unfurled from the brown branch tips, extending up and out until their energy seemed to be sapped by the little figs that would start to punch out by June. (It's never warm enough to make a spring crop; the fruit falls off before growing much bigger than marbles.)

As the tree has flourished, owning it has always felt like an outlandish urban luxury, akin to having my own motorboat or squash court. It fulfills so many of what I've slowly come to realize are my needs. Culinary, above all: grilled figs, fresh figs with my Cheerios, figs braised with rabbit and pork and duck, figs baked into pies and cakes, and bags of figs given away with a kingly magnanimity. This summer I'm finally going to learn how to make preserves, partly to try to quell the annual heartbreak that follows when we go away in late August and so many figs are lost, dropping to the ground, doing alarming things to the dog's digestive tract.

For anyone with a literary or quasi-religious bent, few trees can provide the same satisfaction. Sitting in its shade in the late evening as the leaves lift slowly for the last sunshine, showing their pale underbellies, you notice—especially on a brown turkey fig, the kind I have—how perfectly the leaves are shaped for postlapsarian modesty, at least the male kind. You can imagine yourself in a line of fig lovers going back to Adam and Aesop and Siddhartha, at least until a cargo jet on approach to Kennedy rattles the windows and ruins the illusion.

Eight years after I first laid eyes on it, my tree looks much more like a tree now. A few summers ago, an evil pyracantha shrub that blocked some of its sunlight was sacrificed in its honor. Even with years of no winter wrapping, the fig has grown to more than a dozen feet, and I've had to cut back branches that invade the path leading to the back of the yard. Over the last few weeks, the tree has fully leafed out, almost hiding the old compact discs I've strung among the branches to glint and scare off the sparrows that come for the ripening figs, cruelly taking just a few bites and leaving the rest to rot.

More than anything else, the tree has become my timekeeper, the true gauge of summer. The season doesn't really begin for me until I can see that deep, deep green from the kitchen window. It is at its height when the figs fully fit the Spanish proverb, wearing "the cloak of a beggar and the eye of a widow." (The skin grows dark brown and wrinkled when ripe; the little red oculus on the bottom of the fig opens and starts to weep juice.)

And when I find that last lone fig and pull it from the tree sometime in late September, I know the sweet season has come to an end once again.

June 1, 2008

39

Faces in the Crowd

Circling the Jogging Loop in Prospect Park alongside
Skinny Ginsberg, Big Tony, and Other Creatures
Born of a Fertile Imagination.

MAC MONTANDON

(James Hindle)

A FEW years ago, my wife and I moved into a large, friendly, oddly affordable apartment building half a block from Prospect Park in Brooklyn. Soon after we settled in, I began to run on the jogging loop around the park with some regularity, if not sustained enthusiasm. Three or four times a week during motivated moments, less often from December through March.

Part of what keeps me going are the close-up views of the changing seasons. There are few better ways to see the first blooms of spring or encounter the early crunch of fall underfoot.

But what I look forward to most on my runs is seeing the familiar faces stream past me on the path, or the profiles that fade back when I actually pass anyone. I've come to think of these people as characters in my own personal serialized fiction—Dickens, brought to you by Saucony. It's an unusual experience to so frequently see the same strangers with whom I've exchanged plenty of painfully commiserating glances but not a single word.

With the rock soundtrack booming from my headphones, I've begun to construct mini-narratives for some of my favorite characters. Their continuing stories are produced in 10-second bursts—the time it takes to notice them approaching up ahead and then to have them huff past, disappearing in a ripple of air. This being New York, many of the flushed faces I pass possess literary qualities. Others are intriguingly eccentric, or at least they appear that way when seen in such brief installments.

Rushdie—named, of course, for his resemblance to Salman Rushdie, the author of "Midnight's Children," among many other books—is 54, divorced (it was mostly amicable), childless and dedicated to his work as a psychotherapist (we're near Park Slope, after all, and he wears glasses and a sophisticated beard). He began running about two years ago, after his cardiologist noticed an irregular beat or two.

He has taken to the necessary exercise with resigned determination. He looks into the middle distance as he strides, his navy T-shirt tucked neatly into matching shorts. Rushdie runs for his health, yes, but he also runs for his girlfriend, Astrid, a publicist at Simon & Schuster who sometimes pats his remaining paunch with affection. Perhaps her tacit reminders are helping: Rushdie has been looking fit.

When I first spotted Skinny Ginsberg, he struck me as a sad soul. His big, brown, searching eyes peer out behind what may or may not be protective lenses meant for soldering. He wore rumpled sweatsuits, the sleeves pushed up to the elbows, revealing twiggy arms.

Skinny Ginsberg is always alone. But one day he was accompanied by two, three, maybe even four friends: healthy, smart-looking friends with thick, vigorously unmaintained hair, like actors in a Woody Allen movie.

It was suddenly so clear, I couldn't believe I'd missed it. Skinny Ginsberg is the unlikely life of the party. To the writer Malcolm Gladwell, he'd be a connector. Skinny Ginsberg is king of his social empire, finding time to bring artists, intellectuals, entrepreneurs and impresarios together in what he'd call salons, if he didn't think that word sounded pretentious—despite working too-long hours in some vague-sounding field like emerging markets.

Skinny Ginsberg has been underestimated all his life—the last kid picked in street basketball games but the first to knock down that clutch jumper. Sure, he had a slight problem with amphetamines a decade or so ago, but that was just a function of his drive, his work ethic, the tiny terror that he might end up like his father, a pinched man, a high school principal in Paramus.

But now, look at him. Admired by Rita, his wife of 27 years, and their sons, Charlie and Sebastian, he has surpassed the old man and can take comfort in that small fact as he unwinds nightly with Gordon Lightfoot MP3s, cable news and rum raisin ice cream.

Big Tony is not so lucky. Big Tony has been bitten by life and has not yet bitten back. He may never get the chance. A talented outside linebacker at Baylor University in the late 90's, Anthony Ulysses Ferndale once had pro football aspirations. A hyperextended left knee precipitated a junior year rife with injuries, however, and Big Tony was forced to reconsider his dreams.

Turning lemons into lemonade, he recommitted to his coursework in biochemistry, graduating with honors three years ago. In the midst of the economic downturn, though, he was laid off from a great gig at an Upper East Side lab, and so Anthony is now on the hunt for a new job.

In the meantime, he comes to the park to clear his head and strengthen his knee. Because he can't run, he has devised his own workout routine, which involves kicking two red rubber gym-class balls around the loop. Tony knocks one up ahead and then the other; somehow he's able to keep them both more or less on track. I haven't resolved what happens next in Big Tony's story, but I sure hope it ends happily.

•

THERE are minor characters, too, in these aerobic episodes. The Walking Girl, well, walks. Head down, sadly contemplating the pavement as she methodically circumnavigates the park, she is a model of consistency. There isn't much one can count on in this world, but I can be certain that once a week or so, I will see the Walking Girl, and she will be walking, morosely kicking at pebbles.

I will see her, that is, as long as Running Wild doesn't deck me first. Running Wild takes the park clockwise—against the traffic. Most folks who go clockwise defer to the traffic-obeying counterclockwise jogger. Not so, Running Wild. She does not yield, does not slow down; she will, in fact, apparently flatten all comers, should that be required. If, ultimately, that is how I meet my fate—plowed down on the Prospect Park jogging path by a frenzied fitness maniac—I could take some last, gasping solace in this: At least I wasn't done in by the hard-charging and all-too-often-shirtless Sweaty.

October 26, 2008

40

Fertility Rites

As She Traveled about the City in Search of an Elusive Gift, a Remarkable Thing Happened.

JENNIFER GILMORE

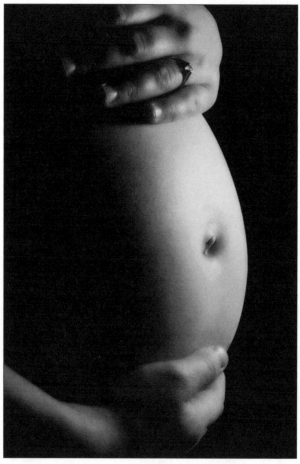

(Fotosearch)

I T was on Sept. 29, the day the first bailout failed, and I was on the train from Carroll Gardens to the financial district—an area I normally hit only for Century 21—for drugs. Not recreational drugs, vestiges of my waning youth, but the outrageously expensive fertility medications not covered by my insurance. (Thank you, national health care system.) I was setting out for the law office of an extraordinarily charitable woman who no longer needed her drugs and whose far more beneficent insurance plan covered them. I had never met her and she was about to hand over a cooler of these medications in the lobby.

Getting off the train at Fulton Street, the unusually blustery wind against me as I walked toward the East River, placed me in the thick of an environment that, as a writer working at home in Brooklyn, I experience only distantly. (The economy has been busted for me and my kind for quite a while.)

I heard snippets of conversations I had only read about: murmurs about A.I.G., rumblings over the bailout. On the corner of Broad and Pearl Streets—the Brooklyn Bridge shining in the distance—someone warned a fellow pedestrian: "Watch out; you're going to get hit by that bus!"

"Who cares?" the man responded, stepping off the curb.

As I waited at the security desk for the woman to emerge from the elevator bank, I realized that I knew her age and her entire medical history, but I had no idea who she was. Illness gives you only a diagnosis, and it was our prognosis that we'd been discussing with hundreds of other women on anonymous Internet message boards for infertile New Yorkers.

We knew what brought us here, the number of in vitro procedures we'd undergone and whether our bodies had responded well to the unthinkable amount of hormones we'd shot into them. We knew the grade of our surgically retrieved eggs, and whether they had been perfect little chickens, fertilizing properly.

We knew how many of those embryos were transferred back in, and we knew whether we were imperturbable women who waited the nerve-racking two weeks for our blood tests to confirm or deny what we've wanted more than anything—we had not previously known the meaning of want—or whether we were completely insane with anticipation and dread and panic, and resorted to early pregnancy tests at home.

We conferred about the toll all this medical intervention took on our bodies and the way it was ruining our relationships, and we bickered over the moral implications of outing celebrities seen at New York clinics. Some, though I cannot claim to be among them, threw imaginary baby dust for good luck. We didn't even know our real names, but this woman knew that I was paying for everything out of my increasingly empty pocket. She had been lucky, and now her extra drugs would be mine.

•

THIS was not my first time at such an encounter. Several months earlier, I had another generous message board friend. Because she lives on Long Island, she had dispatched her husband to bring me her unneeded medications. We were to meet at Penn Station, right by the Long Island Rail Road.

As I waited for him, with police officers in their stiff blue caps and shining badges surveying the commuters, I felt as if I were doing a drug deal true and blue. People rushed by, heading from their jobs in the city back to the Long Island suburbs, discussing their everyday concerns: carpooling, picking up elderly parents, Huntington happy hours.

Who, I wondered, would this man be? And how would he behave, handing over 4,000 bucks' worth of hormones that he had shot into his wife so that they could get pregnant when nature just wouldn't cooperate? How uncomfortable would he be? Should I hug him?

Exactly at our appointed hour, a man in a navy suit stepped off the escalator from 34th Street and out of a line of men in navy suits, a stuffed Gap bag dangling from his wrist. He handed it over, shook my hand and, with feeling, wished me good luck.

I thought of this man as I waited this day, watching women rush out of the lobby elevators—all dressed for the world, all, I imagined, making more money than God despite the tanked economy, each with 13 children, I was sure, and a house in the country, too—wondering what the woman would look like.

Black, white, Latina, Asian? Like any disease or disorder, infertility is race-blind. It doesn't care a bit about class, either; and I wondered, would she be dressed head to toe in Prada (I have this unsupported idea that every high-powered attorney in this city is outfitted as such)? Or perhaps she would be a secretary in crisply ironed Ann Taylor, or a paralegal dressed in H&M's coarser cuts.

I was on my way to teach a writing class; whom did I look like? To me, I had become someone unimaginable, one of those women desperate to have a child, when that isn't the only woman I am. I've had many hopes and ambitions, but each ladybug, every eyelash and every clover, I had been so stupid: I wished for the wrong things; perhaps, I thought, my wishes were all used up.

A woman emerged from an elevator holding a little cooler. She looked like everyone. She looked like me. I have no idea what she was wearing. Thank you, I said with feeling. I have not felt this understood, this given to, by just one look since I was a child.

As I headed away from the river, I faced a gathering of men, their suit jackets open and flapping in the wind, expressions frozen with worry. I felt as if I were sneaking off with an illicit organ, someone's heart.

I felt exposed—to this strange September wind and to this woman, but also to the world, which now seems to distinguish me by what I do not have. I had become so vulnerable to the woman I now was, engaged in a scrappy if mismatched fight against time and my past, an uncertain future.

And then the strangest thing happened. Walking into the subway and out of the wind, I felt something aside from the throbbing ache and lack that has informed my life for the past few years. That man may have wanted to throw himself in front of a bus—that sentiment was now the state of our country—but for the first time in a long while, my own sad want had turned to incredible, soaring gratitude.

January 11, 2009

41

His Kind of River

The Indians Called the Hudson "The River That Runs Both Ways," and Its Majestically Freaky Nature Makes It Easy to Love.

DAVID HAJDU

The Hudson as seen from Riverside Park. *(Nicole Bengiveno/The New York Times)*

UNTOLD numbers of books, articles, love letters, goodbye notes, lists of dog-sitting instructions and poems have been composed in Riverside Park, and I'm hereby adding one more item to the count. I'm writing this on the Riverside promenade—precisely, on the half-length park bench facing the backstop of the ball field around West 103rd Street. That's my spot. I don't come every day—I'm not some kind of outdoors nut. I come to work, because I find the park to be a place equally hospitable to rumination, distraction and procrastination.

When I was growing up, in a steel town in northwestern New Jersey, I could see a sliver of the Delaware River from the top step of my back-door stoop, but only in the winter, when the trees were bare, and only after mill hours, when the air cleared up. A freight line ran along the riverfront on the Jersey side of the Delaware, and my friends and I were forbidden to play there.

With great conspiratorial fervor transparent to our parents, I'm sure, we would bike down to the tracks after school and goof around or sit on the rails and watch the water until the freight-yard guards chased us away. We were bookish, nerd kids, my buddies and I; more than once, we did our homework on the tracks. Then one summer, a boy in our elementary school—Bob Frankenfield, whose older brother later married my big sister—drowned in the Delaware, and the dangers of the riverside no longer seemed so romantic.

Much has been made, in Bruce Springsteen songs, of the import of crossing the Hudson River for kids from New Jersey. When I moved to Manhattan in the mid-70's to go to New York University, I thought of the Hudson in those Boss-ish terms, vainly, as no more than the symbol of a border that I thought I had crossed, an imagined line between youth and adulthood, between provincialism and cosmopolitanism.

Since college, I have lived mostly on the Upper West Side, and I've done a great deal of work in Riverside Park. By work, I mean not just the labor of making sentences; I mean the different sort of effort involved in reading or listening to music that I want to write about. I had the author photos for my first two books ("Lush Life: A Biography of Billy Strayhorn" and "Positively 4th Street") taken in Riverside Park, because the books were essentially made there. The park is where I did the musing that can be the most important part of writing.

Working in Riverside Park, one is reminded from time to time of the porous line between musing and daydreaming. My bench of choice faces the river, and I sometimes find the steady, endless rolling of the water lulling me to dreaminess. I like to think of this state as one conducive to epiphany, although it more often leads, in my case, to naps.

Gazing at the Hudson River can be, by turns, tranquilizing, intellectually nourishing or disorienting. Because the stretch of the Hudson that divides Manhattan and New Jersey is not a typical river but, rather, a tidal estuary; it ebbs and flows. As I understand, the Mahicans called it by a phrase that meant "the river that runs both ways." In wintertime, it's not uncommon to see hunks of ice drifting upstream, toward the river's sources upstate. For self-styled contrarians like me, the majestically freaky nature of the Hudson makes it very much my kind of river.

•

RIVERSIDE PARK was deeply important in the creative lives of two of my idols, a fact that has no doubt informed my own ardor for the park. Billy Strayhorn, the reclusive jazz master who composed "Take the 'A' Train" and other music associated with Duke Ellington, lived for many years in what was once the Master Hotel, a lush Art Deco tower on Riverside Drive and West 103rd Street.

He spent most mornings and a great many afternoons reading books and writing music in the park—on benches somewhere around the one I've chosen, I believe. Strayhorn gave one and only one concert under his own name during his abbreviated lifetime, an event staged at the New School in 1965, not long before he died at age 51, and he called the band he had organized for the occasion the Riverside Drive Five.

Stephane Grappelli, the French jazz violinist, once talked to Strayhorn about what the river meant to him.

"We walked along the Seine," Mr. Grappelli recalled. "I was telling him how much I loved the river and how I loved to look at it as it ran through the city. Billy said it seemed to him to be, he said, the essence of life. It carried life through the city and beyond it, he said." After Strayhorn's death in May 1967, a small group of his friends gathered on a pier at the West 79th Street Boat Basin and emptied an urn of his remains into the Hudson.

About 50 blocks north of the Master Hotel, Ralph Ellison spent most of his own mornings reading and writing on a bench near his apartment at 730 Riverside Drive. There is a striking memorial to Ellison, who died at age 80 in 1994—a figurative sculpture evoking an invisible man, by the artist Elizabeth Catlett—on the small traffic island across the street from Ellison's building.

At the groundbreaking for the memorial, in November 2001, I had the considerable honor of reading a selection from Ellison's prose and saying a few words. I wrote my remarks in Riverside Park, not far from where I'm sitting at the moment. I said that I had not known Ellison as well as I wished I had, but I remembered a little allegory he had told me.

It was about a man whom Ellison used to see picking the newspaper out of a trash bin in the park. Ellison said that when he wrote, he wrote with that man in mind, on the assumption that the fellow might be the best reader he could have. Fine for writing, the park on the river that flows both ways is not bad for reading, either.

March 22, 2009

42

Soul Train

When You're Listening to the Music of the Subway,
It's Easy to Forget Where You Are and Where You're Going.
And You Don't Even Care.

ROXANA ROBINSON

Performing for the passengers. *(Eirini Vourloumis/The New York Times)*

WHAT is it about subway music? Why is it so compelling, so intimate and potent? Why does it reach us in a way that street music doesn't? And why does it interest us so endlessly? It seems there's no limit to our fascination.

Part of its power, I think, lies in the setting. We've left the air and light and freedom of the street, descending into the darkness of the underground. It's a more mysterious place, more complicated. The subway is both suffocating and liberating. We hurtle through the darkness, locked beside strangers, breathing their air. We watch each other like hawks, though we pretend not to see each other, even if one of us is six inches away and singing at the top of his lungs.

For the subway is also concert hall; musicians flock there, drawn by the acoustics and the captive audiences. The music echoes against the stone and in our souls. The music plays in the subterranean reaches of ourselves. We can't ignore it.

I live on the No. 6 line, near the Hunter College station. This season, three men in their 50's have been singing there, in black jackets and berets. They have a keyboard and a rattle for backup, and they sing close harmony: Aaron Neville, Motown. The lead singer has a cherubic face, sunglasses and a big grin. They all have sweet voices, strong and mellow against the stone walls.

"Since you've been gone," they sing. They snap their fingers. "Could it be I'm falling in love?" On the fast songs they clap, smiling at us. When the train arrives and we get on, they're still smiling as the doors close.

We smile back: How can we not? They've made a silver space for us with those bright, sweet voices. As the train pulls away, the lead singer waves; we wave back.

We don't love everyone, though. At 14th Street is a young guy, down on the platform between the express and the local. He sits on one plastic bucket and uses his drumsticks on three others. Fast and dexterous, he gets into a long, complicated, rising crescendo, drumming on the buckets, the metal trash can, the pavement. He's dazzling, he's brilliant. We don't care. He's too loud. Everyone hears him, but no one looks at him. We walk past frowning, as though we've just remembered we left the stove on.

●

SOMETIMES at 68th Street there's a dignified middle-aged man, red sweater, brush cut. He has a deep, full, classical voice, and beautiful posture. He sings "Ave Maria" to an electronic orchestra. We listen respectfully. Some of us put money in his violin case. When the train pulls in, it drowns him out, but he keeps singing. We can see that this is a matter of principle, respect for the music. We can't hear him, but we can see his throat pulsing, the veins in his forehead. As the train pulls away, he's still singing, hands outstretched, Latin words pouring out soundlessly.

It's hard to hold a crowd on the platform. We're a captive audience, but only until the train arrives. The mezzanine floor at 14th Street is a better venue because we don't see the train we're about to miss, and we might linger to listen.

Late one afternoon, there are five guys there, in their early 40's: the Tin Pan Blues Band. They're playing lively, funky jazz on banjo, clarinet, trumpet, saxophone, bass and a silver guitar. The trumpet player sits on a chair in the middle. He has a roundish face, a short, nondescript beard and glasses. They all look like this: friendly, a bit dorky. The clarinetist wears an ochre sweater with red diamonds across the chest.

The trumpeter lowers his horn and begins to sing "St. Louis Woman." He has a strong, bluesy voice, not beautiful, but full of heart. We all feel it. The bass thumps. The crowd thickens. The singer cries, "I wish I could shimmy like my sister Kate." We all wish we could, too.

In an open space, two couples are dancing. A girl with long blond hair, a red sash around her hips, bell-bottom jeans. Her partner is a young guy, with a brown blazer and a soft cap. The other girl, with long hair and bangs, wears a black dress and neon pink tights. Her partner's in a black blazer and a black hat with a red feather. They're dipping and twirling, spinning and sliding. We're rapt. There are about 40 of us. It's nearly 5 o'clock, and we need to get home. We can't move.

The singer belts out "Bill Bailey." The man beside me says, "No mike, right? He must be exhausted!" He's right, there is no mike. It's just us and them. A young mother holds her crying daughter in her arms, swaying to the music. Her daughter turns quiet. The singer picks up his horn and puts in a mute. The dancers switch partners. The woman beside me says, in a thick Jamaican accent: "I love this music! I love the dancing! I love it!"

People coming up the stairs find themselves suddenly center stage, in the middle of a concert. Hurrying past, they turn to look. Some of them quickly throw bills into the open case. The singer lowers his trumpet and leans back against the wall, belting out another song, eyes shut, heart open.

It's long after 5 when I finally tear myself away. They're still singing. I go downstairs, still listening, and get on the wrong train. By the time I realize it, I'm on the wrong side of town. I get off the subway and go up to stand in the dark, waiting for the crosstown bus.

It's worth it. Subway music takes you where you want to go. The train is extra.

May 17, 2009

PART FOUR

Excavating the Past

43

A Mother Lost and Found

Had Some Real Estate God Decreed That the Daughter
Would End Up in the Greenwich Village Town House
Where Her Mother Had Lived 46 Years Earlier?

ELLEN PALL

Josephine Blatt Pall, left, the author's mother, with her
roommate, Debbie, in their West 12th Street apartment.
(Courtesy of the author)

I N 1984, when I first moved to New York, I went to look at an apartment for rent on West 12th Street in Greenwich Village. The building was narrow and old—1848, according to a small brass plaque—with a thick covering of ivy and the house number painted in fat, curving gold numerals above the front door. As soon as I went inside, I felt that this was a place where I could live. Even the tiny ground-floor vestibule was quiet and snug, comfortable and somehow familiar.

From the vestibule rose a set of wooden stairs whose steps tilted alarmingly toward the middle of the building. The apartment I had gone to see was on the top floor, the fourth, in the back, overlooking a small courtyard. The living room had a working fireplace, the kitchen had a skylight. Everything felt just right. Two weeks later, I moved in.

In those times before e-mail, when telephone tolls could mount up quickly, I communicated mostly by letter with my older sister, Steffi, who lived in Maine. Now, when I sent her my new mailing address, she wrote back to say that she thought our mother might have lived in that neighborhood in the late 1930's, in the days before she met our father.

Our mother, Josephine Blatt Pall, died when I was 7. At various times in my life, learning who she was had become a kind of quest for me. I read what papers of hers I could find (I had a box of them that Steffi rescued from oblivion when our father remarried), spoke to my aunts, asked Steffi and my brother, both substantially older than I. Yet my mother remained a ghostly figure lost in a vanished time, vivid only for her sad and early death from a rare form of anemia. I associated her young years with Boston, where she grew up and went to school; I had more or less forgotten that she ever lived in New York.

Now, to my surprise, Steffi announced that she was still in touch with the woman who had been our mother's roommate in those long ago, pre-marriage, New York days. Her name was Debbie Sankey. I had known Debbie myself when I was little, had sometimes stayed overnight at the house in Northport, on Long Island, where she and her husband, Maury, still lived. But shortly after my father's remarriage—which plunged me into a new, blended family—she had gone out of my life. Steffi, who left home soon after our mother's death, had managed to keep in better touch with the past. She wrote to Debbie and mentioned that I had moved to New York and was living on West 12th Street. Hadn't Debbie and Jo lived around there too?

"About West 12th Street," Debbie wrote back in her loose, loopy scrawl. "Wait till you read the next line. We LIVED on West 12th St. Corner of W. 4th, and only a Villager would believe in that possibility."

Debbie's old address books didn't go back far enough to check exactly where their building had been, she added, "but I seem to have the number 288 W. 12th in my head, a narrow building about 3–4 floors, across the street from a restaurant, the Beatrice Inn at that time, with a garden in the back in summer and a cross-eyed, thin, dark, sad-eyed waiter named Romeo whom we both loved." She and Jo had lived on the ground floor, in front.

No. 288 was my building. And the Beatrice Inn was still in business.

The moment I hung up with my sister, I rushed to paw through the carton of our mother's papers for confirmation of her Village address. Jo had made her living as a commercial artist, but she had always wanted to write, and the carton was full of unpurchased radio scripts and unpublished short stories. There were tax records from her various art jobs, rejection letters from The New Yorker and The Saturday Evening Post, scores of scribbled penny postcards from her parents and sisters in Boston and, on yellowing paper, a three-part narrative poem on social injustice called "The Boy with the Auburn Hair." On the cover sheet, these words were typed:

by
JO BLATT
288 W 12th St

IN a matter of weeks, I was having lunch at the Beatrice Inn with Debbie and her husband. Debbie, too, had grown up in Boston, and she had known my mother when she was a young girl. She knew her laugh, her politics (my mother was an ardent Communist), the boyfriend before my father (Jonas, also an aspiring writer and a Communist). From Debbie, over the next 20 years, I learned to know Jo as I never could have if the shared address had not drawn us together.

And truthfully, the building at No. 288 seemed not to have changed so much. In 1938, Debbie told me, the rear ground-floor apartment was occupied by the landlord, Denys Wortman, an artist and cartoonist for The World-Telegram and Sun. A few flights up, Rosalyn Tureck, the great Bach pianist, lived and practiced. During my time there, Emily Prager, who had just published her acclaimed short story collection, "A Visit from the Footbinder," lived and wrote on the third floor. My landlord on the fourth (the building had gone co-op, of course) was the comedy writer Anne Beatts, who sublet the second of her two apartments to the singer Heather MacRae.

In the 1980's, the whole building exhaled a delicious scent of the past, an elixir composed of the smells of working fireplaces and the aging wood of the central staircase. No doubt even in 1938, already 90 years old, the place had exuded a similar aroma. Then as now, the sunny apartments were proportioned to slightly shorter humans and fitted with cunning, handmade carpentry: recessed bookshelves, cubbyholes, window seats.

Debbie gave me a photograph of herself and Jo in their apartment, seated before a blazing fireplace of gleaming, dark stone, their hands joined, their young faces dreamily tilted toward the camera. A few weeks ago, I ate dinner at the Beatrice Inn. The apartment across the street, my mother's apartment, was brightly lighted behind uncurtained windows, the dark fireplace in the picture still intact.

Yet like the world around it, the life my mother lived at No. 288 would soon change forever. She had come to the Village an independent young woman, earning $45 a week as an art director at a magazine publisher, Focus Inc. Her evenings, I gathered, were filled with lectures on Marxism, her weekends with books and poetry, dates with Jonas, visits with friends. Sometimes, under a pen name, she freelanced for a left-wing magazine called The Fight against War and Fascism, once illustrating a story by Dorothy Parker.

In the middle of 1938, though, Focus went out of business. The Depression was not yet over, and among Jo's papers are long, handwritten lists of ad agencies, magazines and department stores, grouped by neighborhood for ease of walking from one to the next to ask for work. In July, she gave up and went home to Boston. The separation strained her romance with Jonas, which ended soon after. A year later, as World War II began, Jo met the young Canadian scientist who would become my father.

My own tenancy at No. 288 was also short. A couple of years after moving in, I married and moved out.

"I got chills and tears and tremors," I wrote in my journal on the night of the great discovery. "It can't be merely coincidence, yet it's unlikely to be anything else." No doubt I had seen my mother's 1938 address on the poem and other papers when I first looked through the carton years before. But had I remembered it? And what real estate god had decreed that an apartment should be available there just when I moved to New York?

However it had happened, learning that my mother once lived where I now lived "comforted and reassured" me that I had landed in the right place, the journal entry from that day went on. "It's one of those rare circumstances that seems to give life some incontrovertible order, and the fact that my mother opened these doors, passed by this railing, pleases me very much."

May 8, 2005

44

Battle in Black and White

Half a Century Ago, the Author's Grandparents Helped
Wage a War to Integrate Stuyvesant Town. Even Today,
Echoes of This Little-Remembered Struggle Linger.

AMY FOX

The author's mother with Hardine Hendrix Jr. at Stuyvesant Town in the
early 1950's. *(Angel Franco/The New York Times)*

WHEN I was a kid, we visited my grandparents in Stuyvesant Town nearly every year. The apartment where my mother had grown up was filled with towers of books and foreign treasures, including a Torah scroll rescued from the Holocaust. I used to fall asleep on a sagging cot listening to footsteps and voices passing underneath my window, something impossible in the quiet Boulder, Colo., neighborhood where I lived. When I dreamed of city life, I saw those red brick structures, the tiled kitchen where my grandmother made meatloaf, the paved circle where we used to wait for my grandfather to pull up in his powder-blue Dodge Dart.

It was hard to imagine my respectable grandma, Diana Miller, her waist-length hair piled on top of her head, or my grandpa, Leo, with his dignified vests, barricading themselves in those same buildings to avoid being put out on the street. But that is what happened in the winter of 1952, when my grandparents were among those white tenants who stood at the forefront of the battle to integrate the housing complex where they lived.

Walking through the brick towers and grassy lawns of Stuyvesant Town three years ago, I stopped in the center of the complex to photograph a plaque, dated 1947, honoring Stuyvesant Town's creator, Frederick Ecker, who "with the vision of experience and the energy of youth conceived and brought into being this project, and others like it, that families of moderate means might live in health, comfort and dignity in parklike communities, and that a pattern might be set of private enterprise productively devoted to public service."

My grandfather had photographed the same plaque 50 years earlier. But neither of us could take its words too seriously. We both knew that for a family to be offered "health, comfort and dignity," the family had to be white.

My grandparents were among 200,000 applicants for the new residential project built in 1947 on the far East Side of Manhattan to offer World War II veterans affordable housing at a monthly rent of $14 to $17 a room. Five years later, they were among 35 families who were nearly evicted from their apartments after fighting their landlord—Metropolitan Life Insurance—over its official policy of rejecting the applications of black veterans. When my grandparents managed to renew their lease, they proudly hung their pale green eviction notice on the wall, with a tiny slip of paper in a corner of the frame bearing the words: "Without Struggle There Is No Progress—Frederick Douglass."

The eviction notice impressed me. Many of my friends were embarrassed by their grandparents' racist attitudes, and I was pleased that mine had fought for civil rights. Unfortunately, I was more proud than curious. I never asked for the whole story, and a few years ago, when I began working on a screenplay about the events, my grandparents were no longer alive.

I was left with my mother's spotty memories of events that happened when she was 5. She remembers walking to school with a black child whose family had moved into Stuyvesant Town. She remembers her father joining other former servicemen standing guard outside the black family's door, ready if necessary to defend the apartment against the landlord. She remembers that when the situation got ugly, she and her baby brother, named Frederick Douglass Miller, in honor of the great abolitionist leader, were sent to their aunt's house on Long Island.

In the cavernous reading room at the New York Public Library, I began slowly filling in the gaps. I learned that my grandparents had been members of the Tenants Committee to End Discrimination in Stuyvesant Town, a grass-roots organization formed in 1948. Stuyvesant Town and the adjacent Peter Cooper Village had been built as part of an ambitious slum-clearance project in which bulldozers tore through 18 blocks south of East 23rd Street to create a solution to the city's postwar housing shortage. But MetLife refused to consider the applications of three black veterans who sought apartments. When these veterans sued the company, a group of Stuyvesant Town residents, including my grandparents, united to support their cause.

Frederick Ecker, chairman of Metropolitan Life Insurance, maintained that as a private landlord, he had the right to define his own criteria for selecting tenants. But although Stuyvesant Town was owned by a private corporation, the city had given MetLife significant tax breaks and financial support. Thus black New Yorkers were paying taxes to support a housing complex they were not allowed to live in.

In public statements, Mr. Ecker described his motives as economic; he said he feared that integrating the complex would lower its value and its appeal to investors. He also said that black applicants could live in Riverton, a MetLife housing complex a few miles to the north on the Harlem River Drive. But Riverton was hardly Stuyvesant Town. While MetLife advertised Stuyvesant Town, with nearly 9,000 apartments, as a "suburb in the city," James Baldwin, writing about Riverton a decade later, called Harlem's housing projects as "cheerless as a prison." In Esquire in 1960, he wrote that blacks hated Riverton "long before the builders arrived."

"They began hating it," he wrote, "at about the time people began moving out of their condemned houses to make room for this additional proof of how thoroughly the white world despised them."

The Stuyvesant Town tenants committee, with 1,800 members, was made up of the families of veterans who believed that after fighting a war for justice overseas, they could not ignore injustice at home. "The courage and sharpshooting of a Negro machine gunner saved my life with a dozen other white G.I.'s," my grandfather had written in a pamphlet issued by the committee. "Can any one of us say he can't be my neighbor? I can't." Surveys of residents conducted by the tenants committee showed that two-thirds of Stuyvesant Town's 25,000 tenants opposed MetLife's exclusionary policy.

In August 1949, the committee invited a black family, the Hendrixes, to move from their overpriced, rat-infested apartment in Harlem into the Stuyvesant Town apartment of Jesse Kessler while Mr. Kessler was on vacation. When he returned, the Hendrixes were moved to another Stuyvesant Town apartment, this one the home of Lee Lorch, a vice chairman of the tenants committee and a mathematics professor who was leaving the city to accept a teaching position at Pennsylvania State College.

The previous April, Dr. Lorch had been abruptly dismissed, without explanation, from his job at City College of New York, and many colleagues, neighbors and journalists believed that the firing was linked to his leadership on the tenants committee.

Hardine Hendrix, an art student who worked by day in a warehouse, along with his wife, Raphael, and their 6-year-old son, Hardine Jr., stayed in these apartments as guests. The young couple did not pay the $76 monthly rent because it was illegal for Stuyvesant Town tenants to sublet. Although the Hendrixes encountered hostile remarks and threatening telephone calls from some neighbors, others were welcoming; one woman apparently introduced them to gefilte fish.

●

WHILE my mother and Hardine Jr. were traipsing through the 12 Stuyvesant Town playgrounds, the battle continued to play out in the courtroom. The black veterans suing MetLife were backed by 29 civic organizations, including the National Association for the Advancement of Colored People and the American Civil Liberties Union. But Justice Felix C. Bevenga of the New York Supreme Court ruled for MetLife, remarking that "housing accommodation is not a recognized civil right."

Appeals did not succeed, and in June 1950, the United States Supreme Court declined to review the case.

The controversy also spilled into City Hall. Councilmen Ben Davis and Stanley Isaacs introduced a bill that would make discrimination on the basis of race illegal in housing projects financially supported by the city. The bill, which would have applied retroactively, was intended to take aim at Stuyvesant Town.

Working behind the scenes, Mayor William O'Dwyer tried to delay action on the legislation, offering instead to facilitate direct negotiations with Mr. Ecker. But although MetLife eventually offered to admit a few token black families, the company refused to change its tenant selection policy. The company also informed 35 families who belonged to the tenants committee, my grandparents among them, that their leases would not be renewed. Dr. Lorch's 6-year-old daughter, Alice, even received an individual notice with her name on it.

Nineteen of the families decided to fight to keep their apartments. They printed a flier whose cover bore the words "a landlord vs. the people" over a black-and-white photograph of the 19; the picture showed my grandfather with his arm around my mother, Betty, a child standing proudly in her short plaid coat. "For the first time in American history," the flier proclaimed, "a landlord has tried to evict citizens from their homes for their social beliefs."

My grandfather kept the flier, along with a typewritten "list of evictees" compiled by the tenants committee. The names of couples are listed with their addresses, and next to each one, my grandfather had scrawled the words "stay" or "go." Next to his own name, he had written the word "stay."

The city marshal ordered the targeted tenants to be out of their apartments by 9 o'clock on the morning of Jan. 17, 1952, and hired a moving company to drag their furniture onto the street. In response, the families barricaded their doors. They sent their children to stay with relatives and passed baskets of food from window to window with ropes.

As word of the evictions spread, civic groups and labor unions called for a demonstration of support for the tenants. Hundreds of New Yorkers picketed at the complex, at City Hall and outside MetLife's headquarters at 1 Madison Avenue, where protesters held a round-the-clock vigil that lasted three days.

Fifteen hours before the city marshal's deadline, MetLife announced that it would postpone the evictions and agreed to negotiate. There followed three days of intense talks, and on the night of Jan. 20, MetLife agreed to drop the eviction proceedings. Several families who were regarded as especially problematic, including Dr. Lorch's, agreed to leave "voluntarily." In return, MetLife rented an apartment to the Hendrixes.

•

A PHOTO of Hardine Jr. and my mother, holding hands and grinning, lay in a jumble of other grainy photos under glass on my grandparents' coffee table. My mother saved it, her only souvenir from her childhood friendship. Hardine Jr. was killed in a car accident, years before his parents died, according to Dr. Lorch, who stayed in touch with the family.

I first contacted Dr. Lorch, now 90 and on the faculty of York University in Toronto, three years ago. Oh, yes, he assured me, he remembered my grandparents.

When I asked what had happened to him after he left the Hendrixes in his apartment and accepted the position at Penn State, he referred me to the front page of The New York Times of April 10, 1950, which reported that the college's officials had declined to renew his appointment, explaining that his decision to let the Hendrixes live in his apartment was "extreme, illegal and immoral and damaging to the public relations of the college."

Dr. Lorch also told me that Albert Einstein, whom he did not know personally, had written to Penn State, "supporting the position I had taken and calling upon them to reinstate me."

Dr. Lorch's political activism continued to hurt his career, he said. After being repeatedly blacklisted by universities and having dynamite placed in his garage, he moved to Canada.

During our conversation, he recalled that one Penn State official asked him directly if he was a Communist. It was not an unexpected question. Many members of the tenants committee were, in fact, Communists, and Councilman Davis, a sponsor of the antidiscrimination bill, was the council's Communist Party representative.

The Cold War was brewing during the Stuyvesant Town controversy, and tenants faced more anti-Communist sentiment than blatant racism. Linking the protesting tenants to Communism was a way to discredit them. Or, as Dr. Lorch remembered an N.A.A.C.P. official commenting wryly, "It's bad enough being black without being Red."

•

THE eviction controversy had dragged out over two years. During that time the City Council housing bill making discrimination illegal in

Stuyvesant Town was reintroduced. Although the bill passed, in February 1951, Stuyvesant Town did not integrate quickly or completely. In the following decades, potential black tenants did not necessarily feel welcome there. MetLife declined to provide statistics on the number of black tenants currently holding leases. Richard Shea, a spokesman for the Stuyvesant Town property, said he had no comment on the matter.

"My perception," said Leo Stevens, an African-American who has lived in Stuyvesant Town for 33 years and raised five children there, "is that excluding celebrities and black immigrants or foreigners, the number of 'average, everyday African-Americans' has been relatively static over the last 30 years. Our sparse number, spread out over this huge complex, makes it difficult to be accurate."

Mr. Stevens, a retired health care executive, does not attribute this situation to the kind of blatant discrimination practiced at Stuyvesant Town by MetLife in the past. Until recently, the complex's mostly rent-stabilized apartments experienced little turnover.

These days, the community is being transformed by MetLife's decision five years ago to renovate newly vacated apartments into luxury units with granite countertops and Kohler faucets, and rent them at market rates: about $3,000 for a two-bedroom apartment.

"With rent stabilization, ethnic and class integration was possible if there was ever the will," Mr. Stevens said. "But now I don't see any hope for meaningful integration."

Most current Stuyvesant Town residents I've interviewed know almost nothing of the complex's troubled racial history. The plaque my grandfather and I photographed was removed from the grounds in the last year or so. As a friend who lives in Stuyvesant Town dryly points out, a market-rate housing complex can't advertise itself as a place for "families of moderate means." My grandfather would shake his head.

When I walk around Stuyvesant Town these days, it is a place soaked in imagination and memory. I wandered these paths with my grandparents 20 years ago, and since then I have wandered them again in my mind, tracking elusive fictional characters from my screenplay whom I have come to know as well as I know my own family. Here are the cold metal monkey bars where I played as a kid, where my 5-year-old mom and the real-life Hardine Jr. played. Here is the daffodil-lined fountain where all of us tossed pennies and wishes.

Though my grandfather, a published author, was a fan of the ice-skating epic I wrote at the age of 11, he did not live to see my more mature work. I don't know what he and my grandmother would have thought of my dramatizing the Stuyvesant Town story. My characters are not directly based on my grandparents, although their memory and spirit were never far away as I wrote.

Recently my family was viewing eight-millimeter movies my grandfather had taken, waxing nostalgic about my mother's childhood. Suddenly the footage shifted to a group of black and white children playing together on the Stuyvesant Town monkey bars as their parents looked on.

On the movie screen, it's just a few minutes of flickering film showing children in a playground, a glimpse of possibility. Then a card appears on the screen, with the date, 10-52, and fat letters my grandfather had drawn in red pen: "As It Should Be."

March 26, 2006

45

Morrisania Melody

Long before Fires and Violence Thrust the South Bronx into
the National Spotlight, One Small Patch of the Community
Played a Critical Role in Forging Musical History.

MANNY FERNANDEZ

McKinley Square, the heart of Morrisania in the Bronx, as it looks today. *(Ruth
Fremson/The New York Times)*

O N a Sunday afternoon in March 1946, you could have stepped into Club 845 on Prospect Avenue in the Morrisania section of the South Bronx—admission $1.25, plus tax—and danced to a goateed, bespectacled trumpet player named Dizzy Gillespie.

A decade later, you could have sat on your stoop on Lyman Place a dozen blocks from the club and passed the time of day with Thelonious Monk, who often visited musicians and relatives who lived on the block.

You could have been at the Blue Morocco on Boston Road on the night in 1959 when a sultry young woman sang "Guess Who I Saw Today," captivating the audience and, more important, impressing one man in particular, the musical agent and manager John Levy, who signed her the next day. That woman would become the renowned jazz singer Nancy Wilson.

There is no trace of this past in the neighborhood today.

The two clubs are long gone; not even their addresses survive. Club 845, so named for its address, 845 Prospect Avenue, has been replaced by a low-slung stretch of gritty shops below the rattling of the elevated 2 and 5 trains. The Blue Morocco, a small, elegant place at 1155 Boston Road that attracted a clientele of mostly dressed-up locals, is an empty narrow lot behind a chain-link fence strewn with rocks and bottle caps.

One of the only ways anyone would know what went on here decades ago is by talking to the people who were there. That is what Mark Naison, a professor of African-American studies and history at Fordham University, has been doing for the past three years. He has been talking to the patrons and musicians of Club 845, the Blue Morocco and other vanished nightclubs, and with their help he is piecing together the fragments of a vibrant but almost entirely unknown chapter of the city's musical past.

Some New York stories tell themselves. Others need a little help. Through research and the memories of residents, Professor Naison has unlocked a secret world, a musical scene that thrived just three miles north of Harlem and one that flourished from the jazz of the 1940's through the Latin music and the doo-wop of the 1950's into the hip-hop of the 1980's. It was a world in which working-class black residents survived in a respectable community long before crime and arson propelled their neighborhood and others near it into national symbols of urban decay.

•

THIS forgotten world has come alive in the most unlikely of places: a cramped, concrete-block office on the sixth floor of Dealy Hall, on Fordham's pristine, decidedly staid Bronx campus. There, in Room 633, is where you can often find Professor Naison, who has invited dozens of people to come to this space and tell their stories as part of the Bronx African-American History Project, which he leads.

The conversations themselves are a kind of jazz: improvisational, loose, melodious. People talk about the time Cute Duke asked the jazz singer Dinah Washington to dance at the Blue Morocco, and was promptly thrown out of the club. They talk about seeing Mr. Monk arrive on Lyman Place in a fancy car, accompanied by the Baroness Pannonica de Koenigswarter, an eccentric British patron of jazz musicians. They talk about the exotic dancers who used to perform at Club 845 and the fellow who used to sing like Nat King Cole at Freddie's at 1204 Boston Road, another bygone club.

On a recent afternoon, Professor Naison was talking to Arthur Jenkins, now living in North Carolina, who used to work as a library clerk in a Manhattan law firm. Mr. Jenkins was speaking slowly and methodically into the microphone of an old Marantz tape recorder, as if giving testimony, which in a way, he was.

Professor Naison was curious about many things concerning Mr. Jenkins, but mostly he wanted to know how this man, a 69-year-old former Morrisania resident, used to spend his Saturday nights. The answer: at the Blue Morocco, where he played piano in the house band, a versatile trio as comfortable with jazz standards as with Tito Puente.

The tape recorder was running. The professor was smiling.

Arguably, few New York historians have taken as enthusiastic an interest in the social lives of black Bronx residents as Professor Naison has. Probably even fewer 59-year-old white Jewish grandfathers from Park Slope can rap the opening lines of "The Message," the pioneering rap song by Grandmaster Flash and the Furious Five.

Not long ago, when Professor Naison gave a speech about the multicultural roots of hip-hop, someone printed up fliers describing him as the Notorious Ph.D., a tip of the hat to the rapper Notorious B.I.G. Or as Professor Naison, who taped one of the fliers to his office door, put it, "I may be old, I may be white, but my flow is funky and my rhymes are tight."

THE erased musical history of the South Bronx has emerged as a subplot to the Bronx African-American History Project, a partnership between Fordham and the Bronx County Historical Society that began in early 2003. This legacy of black residents has been largely overshadowed by a better-known aspect of the Bronx past: the stickball nostalgia of the borough's Jewish, Italian and Irish prewar population. It is often through the prism of the events of the 1970's and 1980's, when arson, drugs and crime helped transform the South Bronx into an urban nightmare, that the borough's black and Latino population is still defined.

"When people think of black history in New York City," Professor Naison said, "they think of Harlem and Bed-Stuy. But there was a whole culture of strivers in the South Bronx."

Professor Naison's first interview was with Victoria Archibald-Good, a social worker, whose family moved from Harlem to the Bronx around 1950. Ms. Good, whose brother is Nate Archibald, the former N.B.A. star, grew up in Patterson Houses, a public housing project in Mott Haven. She told Professor Naison about dancing in the mid-1960's to some of the greats of Latin music—Mr. Puente, Celia Cruz—at the nearby Embassy Ballroom on East 163rd Street at Third Avenue.

For Professor Naison, it was the first of a series of epiphanies: in the multicultural melting pot of Bronx nightlife, black residents were so influenced by their Puerto Rican neighbors that they danced to Latin music at the Embassy, the Hunts Point Palace and other bygone clubs. "I said: 'Oh, boy! I didn't know any of this,'" he recalled. "Little did I know how big the iceberg was going to be."

More interviews followed, each person leading to another, and another. Interview No. 28 was Bob Gumbs, a publisher of books on African-American history and culture who was raised in Morrisania.

Mr. Gumbs, who is 67, lived on Lyman Place, across the street from Elmo Hope, an influential bebop pianist. He also recalled seeing Mr. Monk on the block, there to visit Mr. Hope and relatives of Mr. Monk's wife, who also lived on Lyman Place. Mr. Monk, the great jazz pianist and composer, wore an overcoat, even in August.

"I said, 'Whoa,'" recalled Professor Naison, who had no idea that Mr. Monk was a regular visitor to Lyman Place. "This was the spark for exploring the jazz history of the Bronx."

Many Morrisanians whom Professor Naison has interviewed say he has helped reclaim some of the luster of the neighborhood's past. "The history of the Bronx has not been told from our perspective," Mr. Gumbs said. "We know that the Bronx has always been a borough made up of different ethnic groups. But when it comes to the story of African-Americans in the Bronx, there have been gaps."

To help with some of the research into jazz history, Professor Naison hired Maxine Gordon, the 64-year-old widow of the renowned tenor saxophonist Dexter Gordon and a doctoral candidate in African diaspora history at New York University. Ms. Gordon never spent an evening at Club 845, which saw its popularity decline in 1968 after a club worker was found fatally beaten inside, but one of the first things she discovered when poring through old newspaper ads about the place was that her late husband regularly played there in the 1940's.

•

THE project got another boost last year when Professor Naison came into possession of a historical gold mine that had been hidden away in a New Jersey attic. David Carp, a 55-year-old freelance orchestra librarian who was researching the history of Latin music and social dance, had amassed an extensive collection of articles, ads and memorabilia on Bronx nightclubs, including Club 845 and the Blue Morocco, and he offered to donate the material to the Bronx County Historical Society.

To collect it, Professor Naison drove his silver Mazda minivan to Mr. Carp's house in Leonia, carried more than two dozen 50-pound boxes down from the attic, and accidentally backed his vehicle into a wall on the way out, causing auto damage that cost $1,500 to repair.

He remembers it as a great day for the project.

The documents painted a vivid picture of a little-known chapter of South Bronx history, the moment in the 1940's and 1950's when Latin music thrived alongside jazz in nightclubs in Morrisania and the surrounding neighborhoods. Latin bandleaders such as Mr. Puente, Tito Rodriguez and Johnny Pacheco all lived here at one time, and local clubs such as the Hunts Point Palace and the Tropicana fueled the rhythms of mambo and salsa.

Several black Morrisania residents remember dancing to Latin rhythms at the Royal Mansion, a dance hall at 1315 Boston Road. Mr. Jenkins, the pianist at the Blue Morocco, who lived around the corner from the club, played his first gig there.

The Royal Mansion occupied the second floor of a building that also included a movie theater. But the original structure was torn down two years ago. In its place sits a three-story tan-brick building, its bright red awning announcing a soon-to-open Family Dollar store.

More than a physical structure was lost when the Royal Mansion was destroyed. "That's one of the sad things about it," said Elena Martinez, a folklorist at City Lore, a nonprofit arts group, who has researched the history of the borough's Latin clubs. "That's why it's important to hold onto the history in other ways. You don't have the physical spaces to hold onto as a reminder."

•

ON a recent afternoon, Professor Naison pulled his minivan over near the intersection of East 168th Street and Boston Road, got out of the car, and stood on the sidewalk to trace yet another chapter in the history of the music birthed in Morrisania. It was on these blocks, in the mid-1950's, that doo-wop became one of the big sounds.

Inside the majestic neo-Gothic building that is Morris High School, now occupied by five small schools, a young man named William Lindsay performed in 1954 at the school's senior talent show. He went on to sing with the Crickets, the original members of which were from Morrisania, and were a favorite of doo-wop fans for their 1953 ballads "You're Mine" and "I'm Not the One You Love."

Another popular doo-wop group from the neighborhood, the Chimes, got their start winning talent shows at Public School 99, an institution on Stebbins Avenue in Morrisania that Arthur Crier, a onetime member of the group, called "the Motown of the Bronx."

The Chords, the group that recorded the 1954 doo-wop classic "Sh-Boom," attended Morris High. And the Chantels, who went on to record the 1957 hit "Maybe," grew up singing together in the choir of St. Anthony of Padua, a few blocks away.

When Professor Naison returned to his minivan, he put on an old Nancy Wilson CD. Her voice provided an unlikely soundtrack, filling the van with sweet harmony, while outside the windows, the sweetness evaporated into the grating harshness of city life: car alarms, sirens, the rumble of the elevated railroad.

The hilly, graffiti-pocked neighborhoods south and east of Yankee Stadium—Morrisania, Hunts Point, Melrose, Mott Haven, Longwood—are known more for the fires that raged in the 1970's and the random violence that still explodes there today than for the music they gave birth to. Yet musical creativity grew out of—in spite of—such violence. Or, as Professor Naison put it, "The Bronx is more than the sum total of its tragedies."

It was in the late 1970's, at the asphalt playground of Public School 63, known as 63 Park, at Boston Road and East 169th Street, that a skinny teenager named Joseph Saddler, later more famous as Grandmaster Flash, used to set up his turntables and stereo equipment for parties known as park jams. Grand Wizard Theodore, an early hip-hop innovator credited with inventing scratching—the rubbing of a record to a beat by a D.J., the squeaky sound of which has become synonymous with rap—once told an interviewer that the first time he ever "got on the turntables" in public was at 63 Park.

Occasionally, the D.J.'s used electricity from the light poles outside park jams, borrowing the city's high voltage to create some of their own. Had these outdoor concerts taken place in a wealthier neighborhood, it's likely that the police would have moved fast to stop the al fresco improvisations. But given the gravity of the neighborhood's problems, the police had far more serious things to worry about than noise, and the music had a chance to thrive.

The parties soon moved indoors, to Morrisania clubs like the Black Door and the Dixie. Charlie Ahearn, an independent filmmaker whose cult movie "Wild Style," filmed largely in the Morrisania area in the early 1980's, captured hip-hop culture in its infancy, said it was important to remember that the global phenomenon of rap had its roots in the despair of the South Bronx. "It came up in a very hard atmosphere," Mr. Ahearn said of hip-hop. "Everyone that I knew from the hip-hop scene were survivors and strugglers."

A few years later, in the mid-1980's, the men's shelter in the Franklin Avenue Armory, off Third Avenue, was the meeting place of two men who would eventually form an influential rap duo called Boogie Down Productions: the social worker Scott Sterling, a.k.a. Scott La Rock, and the homeless rapper Kris Parker, now known as KRS-One and considered an intellectual in the rap world. Mr. Sterling was fatally shot outside the Highbridge Garden Homes on University Avenue in 1987.

On a recent afternoon, the only person causing a scene at 63 Park was a harried-looking woman selling $1.25 cherry ices in tiny cups from a cart. The schoolyard behind the red-brick building looks no different from hundreds in the city: white basketball backboards, a bright blue mural of a diploma painted onto a nearby wall.

These days, as the music of choice—Latin-flavored reggaeton—blares from car stereos, it is difficult to imagine such musical innovation coming from these gritty streets. Sneakers dangle from block after block of power lines. Curls of razor wire decorate the fences surrounding apartment buildings. The old plastic bags that get caught in their grasp flap in the wind like flags. People walk quickly, carrying bags of groceries, picking up their children from school, talking on their cellphones.

On Lyman Place, the little street where Mr. Monk used to show up in his overcoat, a mural has been spray-painted on a concrete-block wall, a memorial to someone who has died. People line up their empty liquor bottles at the base of the mural in tribute. The spray paint reads, "R.I.P."

April 30, 2006

46

BoHo, Back in the Day

In the 70's, the Bums on the Bowery Were Gallant,
and an Impressionable Young Woman
Could Rent a Sun-Drenched Loft for a Song.

DOROTHY GALLAGHER

The studio apartment on the Bowery where the author lived more than three decades ago. *(Courtesy of the author)*

A FEW weeks ago, for old times' sake, I wandered over to the Bowery. It is booming over there. And I noticed that real estate developers are trying to obliterate the very name of the street, referring to their offerings as being in trendy BoHo.

I'm not surprised. The free market has trickled down way below Astor Place, and where the free market takes root, we must be prepared to say goodbye to the past. Still, I'm a little resentful; I feel territorial about the Bowery, just as a native of a small fishing village might feel when the summer folks take it over.

In 1973, I answered an ad for a Bowery loft. It was a sweltering July day, as I remember. The moment I turned downtown from Houston Street, my steps began to drag. It wasn't so much the heat that slowed me as the need to pick my way over and through the men we used to call bums and winos, who littered the sidewalks of the street also known as Skid Row. One man, covered in vomit, stretched his hand out to me, asking not to be given money but to be helped to his feet. If I couldn't bring myself to touch him, how, I wondered, could I possibly live here?

I walked past the Sunshine Hotel and the Bowery Mission, and then I was looking at the building I had come to see, 215 Bowery, on the northeast corner, just where Rivington Street begins. It was five stories, veneered with brownstone on the Bowery side, red brick where it wrapped around Rivington. A postwar building, if you happened to be thinking of the Civil War. I rang the bell. At least there was a bell.

The loft I'd come to see was on the third floor, with an enticing rent of $199 a month. Apart from that, however, the loft had some problems. Like the fact that one basin served as both kitchen and bathroom sink. There was no bathroom, as I understood that space: A stall resembling an outhouse enclosed a toilet, and a second stall contained a jury-rigged shower. At the east end of the loft was a crude platform rising halfway to the ceiling; you climbed a shaky ladder to a mattress. Frankly, the place looked dismal. The splintery floors were painted black, and black roller shades were pulled down over the windows.

Then I raised the shades. Even through the fogged sheets of plastic that were duct-taped to every window, nothing blocked the sunlight that flooded in through the seven tall south-facing windows, and into the far corners of a space that was almost a thousand square feet. The ceilings were pressed tin and 13 feet high. Yes!

The Bowery seemed as wide as a Paris boulevard. The buildings were low, the light wonderful. On the west side of the street, I could see three tiny Federal houses, dilapidated, yes, and used as storehouses for the kitchen supply business, but with their lovely lines still intact. Directly south, I looked out at One Mile House, a bar and flophouse, true, but a historic building, constructed at the site of the old stone One Mile marker from City Hall. Farther downtown, I could see the towers of the newly finished World Trade Center. I didn't like them. I never knew anybody who did. But I got used to them. Everybody did.

I moved in during that summer of 1973. With help from friends, I painted the floors and walls white, built a counter for the kitchen, installed a larger sink and bought a new mattress, of course. Best of all, when winter came and I complained about freezing, my landlord Dale gave me a wood-burning stove.

I lived in that loft for eight years. I loved it, the light, the space. I liked the fact that the Bowery was a working street, busy, noisy with trucks, with men loading and unloading restaurant supplies, display cases, pizza ovens, lamps. On the ground floor of my building, a cash register and typewriter repair shop opened, and this came in very handy.

•

EXCEPT for the bedbugs, which must have ridden in on one of the many treasures I picked up at the Canal Street Flea Market, and the rat that galloped below my loft bed all one winter night, nothing bad ever happened to me on the Bowery. No break-ins, no muggings. From time to time, a drunk fell asleep in my doorway; when that happened, getting into and out of the building presented a problem. But, you know, those winos had an old-fashioned gallantry: Women were seldom panhandled, and when those men were momentarily upright, they always made me a little bow as they stepped out of my path.

I shopped for food in Little Italy, and what food could be better than that? I liked all my neighbors: Tom, who lived on the second floor, and brought me wood for my stove; Dale and Jim, my landlords, who lived together on the fourth floor and created a wonderful roof garden, planting flowers and bushes in the wooden barrels they collected late at night from the fish market on South Street.

I wrote my first book in that loft, and started another. I came of age in that loft, not of legal age—I had reached that long before—but the time of life when you grow into yourself and finally give up the struggle to become someone else.

I remember everything about that loft: the winters when the nights were so cold that the cat's water froze in her bowl; the hot summers when, with my windows wide open, music from the Dominican social club on Rivington Street filled my room. I even remember my phone number: 260-1896.

Everything changes. Dale and Jim split up and decided to sell the building floor by floor. In 1981, they offered to sell me the entire third floor, not just the half I lived in, for $25,000.

I didn't have $25,000. I moved out. And now I see that the second floor at No. 215 is available. For about $2 million, give or take a couple of hundred thousand, you can live in Tom's old loft. Poor Tom. Poor me. BoHo, indeed. Boo hoo is more like it.

October 1, 2006

47

Was He the Eggman?

A Dashing Turn-of-the-Century Wall Streeter May Have
Invented Eggs Benedict. Or Maybe Not.

GREGORY BEYER

Eggs Benedict, the mystery dish with a New York past. *(Theo
Coulombe/The New York Times)*

THE story of eggs Benedict is a hard one to tell. The beginning is shady at best, the main character has a hangover, and there are decades when nothing much happens. But the genre is certain, and the setting clear: Eggs Benedict is a mystery rooted in a long-vanished version of New York. Despite the dish's twisted history, it provides a link to one of the city's more glamorous eras.

Of eggs Benedict's origins, much has been said, but little has been settled. Key witnesses are long dead. One cookbook contradicts another. Even the Oxford English Dictionary shrugs: "Origins U.S." What remains is a recipe that for about a century has come to represent something greater than the sum of its ingredients.

The dish—poached eggs and Canadian bacon on an English muffin, all topped with hollandaise sauce—remains a brunch staple in the city's most luxurious restaurants, and far beyond, prepared by the most accomplished chefs, keeping the distinguished company of the bloody mary and the mimosa.

And while there are several eggs Benedict creation myths, some of which may be the subject of discussion among aficionados on National Eggs Benedict Day, a little-known observance celebrated on April 16, they share decidedly genteel roots: rich and distinguished New Yorkers, fabulous New York restaurants and an adventurous 19th-century dining culture unfettered by contemporary concerns about trans fats and cholesterol.

If there is a starting point to the debate over the provenance of this quintessential brunch dish, it would be 1942. That was the year The New Yorker published an article about a stockbroker named Lemuel Benedict and a breakfast order he had placed nearly 50 years earlier, in 1894, at the old Waldorf Hotel at Fifth Avenue and 33rd Street. By 1931, when the hotel, renamed the Waldorf-Astoria, moved to its current location on Park Avenue, eggs Benedict had been enshrined as a classic American dish and a fixture in a hotel that served presidents, movie stars and foreign dignitaries.

By all accounts, Lemuel Benedict was a dashing ladies' man, typically outfitted in fine dark suits and high white collars. The New York Stock Exchange archive has a caricature depicting him as a slick purveyor of Wall Street gossip. His name appeared often in newspaper society columns, and he had a reputation for leaving huge tips in New York's finest restaurants. When attending football games at Princeton, where his nephew Coleman Benedict was a student, "Uncle Lem" drew attention by donning a raccoon-skin coat and carrying a cane that contained a liquor flask.

Understandably, Lemuel's flamboyant man-about-town persona alienated him from the rest of the aristocratic and reserved Benedict family. In 1908, when he married Carrie Bridewell, a New York opera singer who was one of the first American-born women to sing at the Metropolitan Opera House, his family objected on the grounds that his new wife worked for a living.

Although Lemuel Benedict had a hangover that morning in 1894, the New Yorker article recounted, he didn't shy away from breakfast. He ordered two poached eggs, bacon, buttered toast and a pitcher of hollandaise sauce, a rich, egg-based sauce flavored with butter, lemon and vinegar. Then he built the dish that bears his name.

Lemuel's innovation attracted the attention of Oscar of the Waldorf, as the maître d'hôtel there was widely known. He promptly tested it and put the item on the menu, although Oscar's version substituted ham for bacon and an English muffin for toast.

After that history-making morning, Lemuel Benedict reveled in the attention and prestige that resulted from his breakfast order. But his original request had specified toast, and he never warmed to the idea of English muffins.

"Lemmy would be upset if they made it other than the way he first ordered it," Ethyle Wolfe Benedict, his nephew's widow, said. "Or if the hollandaise wasn't just right."

•

LEMUEL BENEDICT died at age 76 in 1943, less than a year after the New Yorker article was published. The article had, however, caught the attention of Jack Benedict, a real estate salesman from Colorado who was the son of Lemuel's first cousin. As other stories about the creation of eggs Benedict surfaced, Jack Benedict's interest in the dish grew into full-fledged activism and, eventually, obsession. He became dedicated to the task of making sure that his dead relative got credit for his famous breakfast order.

Jack Benedict was particularly upset by an article published in March 1978 in Bon Appetit magazine titled "Perfect Eggs Benedict," which credited a Mr. and Mrs. LeGrand Benedict as the founders of the dish.

According to Bon Appetit, the couple requested the ingredients one morning around the turn of the last century at Delmonico's, the financial district restaurant famous for its eponymous steaks and heavy-hitter clientele; apparently the couple, who were regular Delmonico's patrons, were bored with the menu. The article noted that one account credited the dish's creation to a young man with a hangover at the Waldorf, but in an error that must have further inflamed Jack Benedict, it referred to the young man not as Lemuel Benedict but as Samuel.

And in 1894, the year Lemuel placed his order at the Waldorf, the legendary Delmonico's chef Charles Ranhofer published a huge cookbook called "The Epicurean" that included an almost identical recipe, Eggs a la Benedick.

The LeGrand version of the eggs Benedict creation story came to eclipse the account offered in The New Yorker in many cookbooks and food reference books. It also prompted Jack Benedict to begin a campaign to reinstate the Lemuel Benedict version.

"As long as the delectable dish is enjoyed by an increasing number of persons," he wrote to Bon Appetit after its article appeared, "I don't suppose it really matters to whom is given credit for its innovation. But to set the record straight, it all began in New York City, at the old Waldorf Hotel, in 1894."

By coincidence, the Bon Appetit article appeared just as Jack Benedict was poised to realize a long-held dream of starting a restaurant. In August 1978, he opened L. C. Benedict Restaurant and Tavern, in Winter Park, a ski resort near Denver. The initials in the restaurant's name stood for the venerated relative's first two names, Lemuel Coleman.

Jack Benedict's purposes at the restaurant were culinary but also historical; by offering both Eggs Benedict Lemuel's Way (with toast and bacon) and Eggs Benedict Oscar's Way (with an English muffin and Canadian bacon), he hoped to educate his customers about the origins of the dish.

Having collected as much material as he could find on eggs Benedict, he installed a storyboard near the restaurant's entrance that traced the complex history of eggs Benedict from Lemuel's initial order up to the present. By discrediting the opposition, he hoped to restore his cousin's claim to culinary immortality.

●

AT this point, the tale moved to New York, to the Chelsea apartment of Lemuel's nephew Coleman, a classics professor at Columbia University who grew up in his uncle's care, and his wife, Ethyle, a classics professor and provost at Brooklyn College. The couple's apartment is decorated with elaborate tea sets, a collection of silver spoons encased in glass and a Benedict family sofa dating to 1830.

One day in the late 1980's, Coleman Benedict announced to his wife: "Some nut has been pestering me. He says he's my cousin. He wants to know about Uncle Lemmy."

The caller, of course, was Jack Benedict. The couple had never heard of him and had no real way—or even a desire—to verify his claim that he was a relative. For all they knew, the man was an impostor eager to cash in on the family name.

After that initial phone call, however, Jack Benedict's enthusiasm only grew. "He wouldn't let go of us," Ms. Benedict said. A deluge of phone calls and letters followed, as Jack began to forge a bond with the couple, despite the fact that they did not share his passionate interest in eggs Benedict.

Jack was thrilled not only to have connected with his newfound relatives, but to learn that they were historians. He informed them that he had begun work on what he hoped would be the definitive article on eggs Benedict, and hoped that the couple, with their editorial experience, could help.

His jovial sincerity—his letters simultaneously begged for their help and apologized for boring them—overcame their initial skepticism, to the extent that they stopped referring to him as "Crazy Cousin Jack." His letters kept coming, written on stationery engraved with the words "The family that gave the world eggs Benedict." He sent along every article he could find mentioning the dish, filling the margins with responses and lamenting instances in which credit was given to anyone but the person he deemed the dish's one true inventor.

In 1988, a decade after Jack Benedict took up the cause, Ethyle and Coleman Benedict found themselves in Denver, where Ms. Benedict was to give a lecture. The couple agreed to meet Jack Benedict at his home in nearby Littleton, where he hoped to enlist them as allies in his campaign to settle the eggs Benedict question once and for all.

When the couple arrived at Jack's home, Ms. Benedict recalled, he hugged Coleman and exclaimed, "You look just like my father!" The couple were still unsure about Jack Benedict's claim that he was their relative. But on arriving at his house, Ms. Benedict noticed that the family photographs on the walls were the same as those that hung in the couple's New York apartment. The man might be a character, she concluded, but he didn't seem to be a liar. And his interest in eggs Benedict seemed genuine enough.

Family photographs were only the beginning. One room was filled with eggs Benedict memorabilia: menus, photographs, restaurant signs.

"His house was a shrine," Ms. Benedict said. "We spent that day going through everything on the walls."

As it turned out, Jack's culinary venture, L. C. Benedict Restaurant and Tavern, had closed its doors in 1984 after six years in business. The eggs Benedict memorabilia that now furnished his home had once decorated the restaurant that had been his dream.

The next morning, Jack joined the couple for breakfast at their hotel. Nobody ordered eggs Benedict. Ms. Benedict, for one, doesn't particularly care for the dish. Her husband, after a lifetime of hearing about it, was sick of brunch-related celebrations of his family name. And Jack, though a tireless advocate for the cause, had inherited Lemuel's pickiness. "He thought nobody made it authentically," Ms. Benedict said.

After that meeting, Jack wrote to his relatives, "Thank you for coming to the house for an historical visit." The experience had revitalized his writing efforts, he added, and he looked forward to their editorial guidance.

Still, it was an overwhelming task, and one that Jack, then 64 and suffering from emphysema, was not sure he would live to see to completion. He continued to send the couple letters brimming with passion, but they were laced with frustration; the Bon Appetit article had done insufferable damage to his cause. "The facts are that people did read Bon Appetit in 1978," he conceded, "and LeGrand is winning, not Lemuel."

Jack continued to explore different ways of telling Lemuel's story. He sent a detailed business proposal to McDonald's suggesting a breakfast sandwich called Eggs McBenedict, and he designed an intricate place mat featuring an image of Lemuel and the story of his Waldorf order. He was too late; the Egg McMuffin, which helped McDonald's introduce its breakfast menu in the mid-1970's, had already taken eggs Benedict as its model. Dejected but determined, Jack Benedict continued work on his article and kept up his correspondence with his relatives. Fifteen magazines had rejected him.

"The funny thing is, it's pointless and a waste of almost two years' time unless the true story is finally published," he wrote to the couple. "I think it will be, however, which is why I keep on with my thinking and writing."

•

ONE seeming hitch in the version that credits Lemuel Benedict is that Oscar of the Waldorf, who plays such a key role in that account, never confirmed the story, despite ample opportunity to do so. Oscar had no aversion to publicity; in his biography, "Oscar of the Waldorf," published in 1943 by Karl Schriftgiesser, and in magazine articles that Oscar wrote, he notes that his creations include the Waldorf salad and Thousand Island dressing.

But Oscar never mentions eggs Benedict, either by name or by description. In 1947, three years before he died, Oscar wrote an introduction to "The Gold Cook Book," written by a chef named Louis Pullig DeGouy. The cookbook includes a recipe for eggs Benedict, but neither the introduction nor the recipe itself mentions any connection to Oscar.

Some food historians are also skeptical about Jack Benedict's claims.

"It's not a 100 percent invented dish," said Gerald Gliber, a culinary expert at the Art Institute of New York City, formerly the New York Restaurant School. "It's an evolution, not a creation." That a dish called eggs Benedict took New York restaurants by storm a long time ago, Mr. Gliber added, doesn't necessarily mean the dish was anything new.

Even the American Egg Board, the promotional arm of the egg industry, is not sure where the dish originated.

"Food history is so muddy," said Linda Braun, the board's consumer services director. "It's kind of like that telephone game, with somebody whispering in someone else's ear." Nevertheless, Ms. Braun's organization endorses the version that credits Lemuel with the invention of the dish. As for the rival claims of the Waldorf and Delmonico's, Ms. Braun offered a conciliatory theory.

"What if we're talking about the same person, and he simply got his two favorite chefs to make him his own special dish?" she suggested. "Couldn't he have walked into two different places with the same request?"

•

WHEN Lemuel Benedict died, the paid death notice in The New York Times cited his membership in the New York Stock Exchange but made no mention of a culinary legacy. His survivors hadn't forgotten. They were simply ashamed.

"It was undignified," explained Ms. Benedict, who at 88 has become the family's unofficial historian and the sole surviving teller of the eggs Benedict tale. "It's all in the context of an aristocratic family." To talk about breakfast, let alone the hangover, in the same breath as a career on the stock exchange would have been an embarrassing misrepresentation of Lemuel's genteel roots.

Such an explanation would not have satisfied Jack Benedict, who died in 1993 at age 69 without publishing his article. But one publication did give Lemuel the posthumous credit his cousin Jack always dreamed he would get.

When Coleman Benedict died in 2005, his widow had a decision to make. Though she is sure her husband would not have approved, she included, high in a paid death notice published in The Times, a mention of his relation to Lemuel Benedict, who, as the notice put it, "is incidentally renowned as the eponymous creator of 'Eggs Benedict' for his breakfast order at the Waldorf Hotel in 1894," which Oscar of the Waldorf "prepared at his request, and named in his honor."

April 8, 2007

48

When He Was Seventeen

You Could Almost Buy a Legal Drink. Parents Didn't Hover So Much. And If You Were Not Really Tougher than Kids Today, You Certainly Felt like Your Own Man.

CHRISTOPHER SORRENTINO

The author, seated at center, at seventeen with friends atop the High Line in Chelsea. *(Patrick Adams)*

EARLY on the morning of April 1, 1980, the month before I turned 17, members of the Transport Workers Union walked off their jobs and my adolescence began in earnest. I don't remember the particulars surrounding the strike, but because I couldn't get from my Greenwich Village home to the High School of Music and Art on West 135th Street, Easter Vacation (the seasonal breaks from public school then still retained their nonsecular designations) extended into Transit Strike Vacation.

Serendipitously, around the same time, the mother and stepfather of my friend Patrick set out on an African safari, leaving Pat and his sisters alone in their Bleecker Street town house for however long an African tourist safari circa 1980 can be expected to have lasted.

For maybe a dozen of us, the house became home base. We assembled there, ate there, slept there. We kibitzed and played cards and listened to records and watched TV (regular broadcast TV, I should add). We drank beer and smoked cigarettes, lots of both. People lost their virginity, fell in love. Hearts were broken. Friendships and animosities were formed. More important, none of us ever went home, or if we went home it was just to change clothes.

For me, the 11-day transit strike marks the true beginning of a critical shift: from the existence I had until then, one shared mostly with my parents (nurturing, comfortable, semiclaustrophobic), to one that I would fill with friends, girlfriends and my own interests, a life full of exhilarating, scary and sometimes awesomely boneheaded decisions.

I know that for some, adolescence is a process of breaking up with one's parents. The guiding equation of childhood is need, and whether your needs have been met or gone wanting, upon adolescence they're replaced wholesale by the entirely different condition of desire, of the kind that parents, qua parents, are inherently unequipped to address. The resulting struggle between parent and child can fall anywhere on the spectrum between "An American Tragedy" and "Portnoy's Complaint."

Both of those novels, though, situate their coming-of-age narratives in far more parochial places and far more restrictive times than New York in the early 1980's. My parents took most of the changes I underwent in stride: Hip town, hip kids—that much seems exactly the same today.

But some things have changed a lot over the past 27 years. The level of permissiveness, for one. For example, until I was 16 I'd been subject to a somewhat arbitrary curfew, unless I could persuade my parents that I'd be "spending the night at a friend's," that dubiously reassuring pitch.

Then I'd presented them with a radical proposal: that I be subject to no curfew at all.

My logic wasn't impeccable, but it was persuasive. Rather than complain that none of my friends were subject to curfew restrictions (which was true, but who wanted to encourage the old "I don't care what so-and-so's mother lets him do; I'm not so-and-so's mother, I'm your mother" routine?), I told them honestly that leaving wherever it was that I happened to be in order to arrive home at the designated time meant that I was traveling alone throughout the city.

What, I argued, was the difference between midnight and 4 a.m., except that if I were allowed to stay out until whenever with my more liberated friends, I would be traveling within the safety of a large group? My parents thought about it—and agreed.

Never mind that I was often just traveling the three blocks from Pat's. My parents probably knew that. Not much got by my parents. They probably also knew that Pat's house was kind of a gateway drug; that I also was going, or very soon would be going, to bars, clubs, and parties all over the city, sometimes even—gasp!—across the river in Brooklyn.

I should confess that I can't imagine making a similar arrangement with my own kids, the oldest of whom is two years from high school. Are you kidding? The kid's going to be 12, and my heart's in my mouth if I send her out for a quart of milk.

When you have kids of your own, Channel 5's "It's 10 o'clock—do you know where your children are?" isn't quite the fodder for hilarity that it was once upon a time. It should also be acknowledged, though, that in allowing me to keep my own hours, my parents were adhering to the norm as fully as I would be violating it by permitting my kids to do as I was.

•

IT'S time to speak a little of the nature of my relationship with my parents during this period, and of the relationships most kids I knew had with their parents. My folks could be strict, even inflexible, but mostly concerning some aspect of my behavior that impinged directly upon them. When it came to what I chose to do outside the house, they had a single word they frequently directed at me. That word was "big"—as in "You're big," usually delivered with a kind of verbal shrug.

"Big" as a concept was just nebulous enough to be meaningless if defined outside the specific context in which it was meant to be applied: Certainly you could be "big" at 4, meaning that you weren't supposed to blow bubbles in your chocolate milk; you could be "big" at 10, meaning you wrote your own thank-you notes.

But apron strings were untied a lot younger then, and as you grew up it became a word that, when used by your parents in reference to you, signified that as far as they were concerned you were both capable of and responsible for making your own decisions, even if they were stupid ones.

The first time I went to a party, for instance, I made the monumentally stupid decision to sample every type of alcohol available, in immoderate quantities. I returned home, greeted my parents as nonchalantly as I could manage, and threw up all over myself. "Scucciamens," my father said, not unaffectionately employing a Sicilian insult, as he put me to bed after cleaning me up. "Here's a pot if you have to puke again. Grab the wall if the room starts to spin."

"Big" took for granted that things that are now considered taboo to varying degrees (for example, teenage experimentation with cigarettes, alcohol, drugs, peculiar music and clothing, and sex, to name them in the order I discovered them) were necessarily the very things with which kids were going to court encounters, and that such encounters weren't avoidable accidents but had been sought out, preceded by curiosity and that desire I was talking about earlier.

The idea was to let the hormonal fires raging at the core of adolescence consume some of the fuel that fed them, while putting it all in a kind of useful perspective. I remember my mother talking frankly to me about her various drug experiences. "Heroin, ugh," she told me. "I threw up." I never tried it.

•

I'M sure some variation of "big" exists now, but as far as I can tell, the social conditions that defined it when I was 17 no longer obtain among the members of what I shall call, for lack of a better term, the educated middle classes of New York. Things were—let's face it—different then. I will admit to a degree of geezerdom in declaring that New York in 2007 isn't nearly as interesting a place as New York in 1980.

For that matter, New York wasn't even as interesting a place in 1985 as it was in 1980. Despite New York's reputation then for dangerousness, even lawlessness, nobody walked around saying: "My! What a bankrupt and anarchic city! Raise the drawbridge! Another day, another struggle to survive!"

The city went about its business, and in many ways the place was heady and wide open in ways that just aren't possible now. It's not just that huge swaths of town have become wall-to-wall enclaves of the well-to-do, with their attendant intolerance for heterodoxy and disorder. In 1980 there were still the vestigial remains of the various downtown revolutions that had reinvigorated New York's music and art scenes and kept Manhattan in the position it had occupied since the 1940's as the cultural center of the world.

CBGB hadn't yet closed (or become a tourist trap); it was then one of the few places where interesting new bands could perform. Max's Kansas City (for live music) and the Mudd Club (for dancing) were still thriving, as well as lesser-known joints like TR-3 and the Rock Lounge. A generation of New York kids was introduced to reggae at Tramps's "Mod Mondays." British bands whose United States record sales numbered in the thousands headlined at clubs like Hurrah and Irving Plaza.

No one worried about H.I.V. (granted, that was a fool's paradise). There was no such thing as crack cocaine, and pot didn't provide the elephant-gun dose of THC that today's hydroponic stuff does. The country's divorce rate peaked around 1980 (I was one of three kids I knew whose parents stayed together), which put something of a crimp in the ideal of parental oversight à la "Father Knows Best"—it wasn't unusual to run into a friend's father or mother dancing the night away at the same club you'd gone to.

Maybe most important, I'm one of thousands of aging New Yorkers who took their first legal drink while still in high school. The banishment of the 18-year-old drinking age—and the relegation of American adults of that age to Junior Grown-Up status—meant that certain behaviors were abruptly criminalized. Close readers of this article may have gathered that some of the pertinent laws were mostly honored in the breach to begin with, and that is indeed the case (I had no trouble obtaining alcohol at 14), but when the drinking age rose to 21 in the mid-80's, with concomitantly tougher enforcement, the handwriting was on the wall.

Above all, I lament the loss of this majority, this legitimacy of behavior, this legal bestowal of the idea of "big." But the point is that many of the places we gathered, and many of the activities we took part in, abruptly became verboten.

At 17 my friends and I didn't partake of sanctioned, homogenized "teen culture." We participated in culture, period, meaning that often we made it ourselves. We were perfectly aware that certain aspects of Western civilization, whether or not they would appear on network television or play on Top 40 radio, had their point of origin in the fertile brains of teenagers.

I'm happy to provide an unscientific postmortem on the casualty rate sustained by those of us raised according to those bygone mores, in those pre-AIDS, pre-crack, pre-Reagan (and pre-Giuliani) times. Most of us survived, and prospered. Many of us are raising our own children.

True, one guy died of complications arising from alcoholism—at 28. Some people struggled with substance abuse. A couple of girls had children while they were still arguably children themselves. There was some anorexia. Not everybody got into the college of his choice. And some kids, running loose on the streets at all hours, fell victim to crime.

Riding the subway early one morning in 1981, I was the victim of an attempted mugging. The attempt failed—they were younger than I—but I was shaken up, and when I got home and found my father reading in his study, which it was his habit to do until late at night, I startled him by lighting a cigarette. It was the first time I'd smoked in front of him. "You really shouldn't," he said, "but you're big."

September 16, 2007

49

A Long Day's Journey into Lip Gloss

How Sephora Ate Her Theater, and Why She Hates to See Blusher Displays Where Sam Shepard's Losers Used to Slouch.

LESLIE NIPKOW

(Juliette Borda)

'M walking north on the Upper West Side, listening to my iPod's power mix, my musical antidepressant. I pass the tae kwon do school and pause to admire its new buttercup-yellow sign. Then I stop short.

The sushi place is there, but where I expect to see the Promenade Theater there is a marquee announcing the grand opening of—Sephora?

To someone looking out from within the newborn temple of applied beauty, I must resemble a before picture: hair spiking wildly around the edges of my cap, Chucks worn down at the heels, raccoon circles ringing my tired eyes. I squint into the cosmetic wonderland and wonder: Where did they put the theater?

The Promenade wasn't one of the gilded Ziegfeld palaces of bona fide Broadway. Its lines were square, its walls an indeterminate quarry color that went well with dirt. It was an achievement of the drywallers' union rather than the cherub carvers' or the chandelier makers'. But it was a legit theater, not a movie multiplex given an extreme makeover, retrofitted to house performances like "Naked Altar Boyz Blowing Bubbles on Ice." (Not that there's anything wrong with that.) The Promenade was Off Broadway Uptown, and more often than not, when you went there to see a play, it stuck with you.

But here is a Sephora that looks eerily like the one that ate the Scribner's on Fifth Avenue. The theater is as gone as if the curtain had rung down and the crew had come in and struck the set—no, the building—overnight.

Yet the ghosts of the Promenade still have a hold over me. When I moved to New York in the mid-80's, I volunteered as an usher for Promenade productions in exchange for seeing the plays free. As I tore tickets, I'd ask theatergoers to please silence their pagers out of respect for the actors. Pagers begat cellphones begat BlackBerrys, but one thing remained the same:

When I said "respect for the actors," my heart swelled, because I was one of them, or hoped to be. I believed that one day I would be backstage in my Promenade dressing room, flaying my emotions raw in order to give my best performance for the next generation of actors who I knew were out there ushering and wanting more than anything to be in my shoes.

In 1985, six months after moving to the city, I nearly exploded with joy as I sat in the audience for a preview of Sam Shepard's play "A Lie of the Mind." I wanted to spend a few hours inside Mr. Shepard's head, so I sat close: third row on the aisle. I chose a preview, so Mr. Shepard would be in the house, and I would be in the same "room" with my favorite living playwright, and just feet from two of my actress/idols: Geraldine Page and Amanda Plummer.

It was an incandescent moment, and there were many more like it: Harvey Keitel, Christopher Walken and William Hurt in "Hurlyburly." Edward Albee's "Three Tall Women." And my personal hero, Kathy Bates, alongside Athol Fugard in his play "The Road to Mecca," and in Mr. Shepard's "Curse of the Starving Class."

The Promenade is now quarantined behind the Philosophy Hope in a Jar moisturizer display. It looks oddly as if the theater had opened its mouth to yawn, and somebody had stuffed a superstore inside. Taking a deep breath, I enter the maw of makeup, passing a sign that reads, "Beauty Bestsellers: Get Addicted." I think they're talking lipstick, but I hark back to Mr. Shepard's grizzled, alcoholic father figures lumbering through this space, somewhere between Dior's Midnight Poison and Diesel's Fuel for Life Pour Homme.

It's not as if I don't know what I'm getting into here. I love Sephora, an institution that carries the tools I need to play my many parts. I'm one me at the holiday dinner table with my family (pink eye shadow and Xanax), quite another out to dinner with my boyfriend (shimmer powder and pheromones), at the dog run (dog saliva and ChapStick) or any place I may run into an ex (mascara and a satisfied smile).

●

WHEN you come offstage, that's when you put on your mask. This is why I am drawn to the Benefit display, featuring Bad Girl Betty, the cosmetic version of "Grease's" Rizzo as interpreted by Quentin Tarantino. This chick carries nunchucks in her glitter purse and ninja stars in her cleavage. The Betty in me fondles lipsticks with names like Nice Knickers and Frenched.

As I examine a tester of pink Champagne shimmer shadow, a mom with a New Jersey accent stops a sleek, black-clad Sephora employee with perfectly plucked brows and asks, "Where's the Britney perfume?" I hold my breath, writing the next line in my head. Something like, "It's under 'S' for Skanky." Instead I hear, without a touch of irony: "We sold out over a week ago. I'm so sorry."

A Sephora employee is suddenly at my side. "Do you need help finding anything?"

"Actually, yes, I do. Where is the Promenade Theater?"

Blank stare.

"Seriously. It was right here. We'd be standing in the lobby right now."

No recognition whatsoever.

"They did great plays here. Great plays."

She can't wait to get away from me.

If this had been the Sephora that ate the sticky floors and mottled seats at the old Criterion Times Square multiplex, I'd hit the Urban Decay aisle. A spritz of Opium, a little Orgasm on the apples of the cheeks, a swath of Hotpants across the eyelid, finished off with lips stained Kinky, and I might be good to go. But I'm standing in the shell of the Promenade, and no new bronzer is going to make it any less gone.

I don't want any of this stuff. Not today. My younger self is calling me. I want to sit in a theater seat and lose myself in somebody else's imagination for a few hours. I want to be reminded that my world does not stop at the front of my face. I want to forget the way I look so my soul can come out to play with those of Shepard, Fugard, Feiffer, Rabe, Durang, Baitz, Albee, Stoppard and all the actors who sat here, like me, dreaming their futures. Alone in the dark with great minds like that, you don't need protective covering.

August 17, 2008

50

Always, the Crack of the Bat

Stadiums, in the End, Are Just Window Dressing. The Play's the Thing.

WILLIAM ZINSSER

An early photograph of Babe Ruth on the wall of the author's office. *(Rob Bennett/The New York Times)*

HANGING on my office wall is a baseball photograph taken in 1926. I bought it from an antiques dealer many years ago because I had never seen a picture that so perfectly distills the essence of the game; it almost looks staged. The setting appears to be Fenway Park, home of the Boston Red Sox, and the central figure is Babe Ruth, who was then a Yankee, batting against his former employers.

Ruth's still-slender body is coiled in readiness, his bat raised high behind his head. The pitcher has just delivered the pitch, his arm at the low end of its trajectory. The ball is halfway to the plate, its flight tracked by Ruth, by the masked catcher and by the umpire, hands clasped behind his back in the classic stance of impending judgment. Farther away, the shortstop is crouched forward expectantly, though the Babe wasn't known for hitting grounders to the left side of the infield.

I have no trouble willing myself back into that summer afternoon 83 years ago, tracking the ball as intently as Ruth and the catcher and the ump. Time has stopped; nothing can happen until something happens to the ball. It's only one moment in one game in the long history of baseball. But it's also every game ever played in the ballparks of America. The symmetries are absolute.

That photograph keeps catching my eye in this spring of 2009 as New York's two major-league teams prepare to take up residence in grandiose new stadiums. My Mets are moving into a park named for a bank that I'm helping the government to bail out. The Yankees' new stadium comes wrapped in a vocabulary that has no connection to baseball: luxury boxes, bond issues, cost overruns. My fellow taxpayers and I are also footing that bill, though the announced prices will dissuade many of us from going there to enjoy the fruits of our charity.

I assume that the new stadiums will feature the newest advances in audio-visual assault. I stopped going to Mets games at Shea Stadium when my friend Dick Smolens and I could no longer hear each other talk between innings—such was the din of amplified music and blather from the giant screen in center field. But baseball is also a game of silences. After every half-inning, it invites its parishioners to meditate on what they have just seen and to recall other players they once saw performing similar feats. Memory is the glue that holds the game together.

RESENTFUL of the noise at Shea, I wrote to the Mets explaining that I wouldn't be coming back. I reminded them of the game's historic tranquillity. "Dare to leave us occasionally to our own thoughts and conversations," I said. In reply I got a note saying: "Dear Mets fan. Thanks so much for your nice letter. We are happy that you have such an active interest in our team. We hope you will enjoy adding our photo cards to your collection of Mets memorabilia. Thanks again for writing, and we hope to see you at Shea Stadium during the season." Enclosed were three photos of current Mets stars.

Some of the newer stadiums, like Camden Yards in Baltimore, have made an effort to honor the emotional longings of their fans. They are quirky and irregular, as ballparks used to be, built in obedience to existing street patterns, often enshrining those streets in local mythology. Bedford Avenue, in Brooklyn, which ran behind the short right-field fence of Ebbets Field, was woven into the hopes and dreams of fans listening to Dodgers games on the radio. "There's a long fly to right and it's . . . it's . . . in Bedford Avenue!" was the best or worst of sentences.

But the only thing that finally matters about a baseball stadium is what happens on the field that it encloses—that immaculate expanse of grass. My brain is an echoing warehouse of ballplayers' names, many of them linguistic gems, as perfect as the photograph on my wall: Eppa Rixey, Smead Jolley, Wayne Terwilliger, Cletus ("Boots") Poffenberger, Van Lingle Mungo, Edd Roush, Vinegar Bend Mizell.

And nicknames! Dizzy and Daffy and Dazzy, Catfish and Cookie, Gabby and Goose, Pee Wee and Pie, Scooter and Schnozz, the Sultan of Swat, the Georgia Peach, the Wild Horse of the Osage, the Arkansas Hummingbird, the Splendid Splinter, the Iron Horse, the Fordham Flash, Big Poison and Little Poison, the Meal Ticket, the Brat, the Man, the Lip.

Most of those ballplayers were farm boys and mountain boys, descendants of early English and Scottish-Irish settlers; it's probably safe to guess that the Terwilligers came from England. Since then, new tides of immigration have brought new names, wholly different in shape and sonority but equally resonant: Clemente and Concepción and Carrasquel, Marichal and Martínez, Ramírez and Reyes, Ichiro and Matsuzaka and Chien-Ming Wang.

Whoever they are and wherever they came from, I watch them on television all summer long, night after night, no less absorbed than I was as a boy watching Carl Hubbell and Mel Ott and Bill Dickey in the Polo Grounds and Yankee Stadium.

Surprisingly often, I find myself staying up late to follow a deeply uninteresting game between two going-nowhere teams, and I ask myself, "Why am I doing this?" Then a situation occurs on the field that I've never seen before. How can that be? The announcers are equally astonished. ("You ever see anything like that, Keith?" "Can't say I have, Gary.")

Stadiums will continue to come and go, artifacts of their allotted moment. But what happens on the field is beyond the reach of time. That's the point of the picture hanging on my office wall.

March 29, 2009

About the Contributors

ALEXANDER ACIMAN is a student at the University of Chicago and the co-author of the book "Twitterature."

JAMES ANGELOS is a former reporter for the City section of The New York Times. He now lives in Berlin, where he has received a fellowship to work on a collection of stories about the city.

KEVIN BAKER's works include three historical novels, "Dreamland," "Paradise Alley," and "Strivers Row," his "City of Fire" trilogy about New York City. He is currently at work on a history of New York baseball.

JOHANNA BALDWIN is a writer whose work includes film, theater and short stories. Her screenplay "Venus and Mars" was produced by the BBC. She is currently writing a novel with the best-selling author Raymond A. Moody.

HELEN BENEDICT, a professor at Columbia University, is the author, most recently, of "The Lonely Soldier: The Private War of Women Serving in Iraq" and the novel "The Edge of Eden," both published in 2009.

GREGORY BEYER is a former reporter for the City section of The New York Times.

KATHERINE BINDLEY is a former reporter for the City section of The New York Times.

EMILY BRADY, a former reporter for the City section of The New York Times, is a freelance writer based in New York.

MARK CALDWELL is a professor of English literature at Fordham University whose books include "New York Night: The Mystique and Its History."

LAURA SHAINE CUNNINGHAM, a novelist and playwright, is the author of two memoirs, "Sleeping Arrangements" and "A Place in the Country," the novels "Beautiful Bodies" and "Dreams of Rescue," and the play "Beautiful Bodies."

EDWIDGE DANTICAT's novels and story collections include "Breath, Eyes, Memory," "The Farming of Bones," "Krik? Krak!," "After the Dance," "The Dew Breaker," and "Brother, I'm Dying."

VYTENIS DIDZIULIS is a reporter for The Miami Herald.

CAROLINE H. DWORIN, a published cartoonist, is a former reporter for the City section of The New York Times.

ADAM B. ELLICK is a journalist for The New York Times who reports in video and print.

CASSI FELDMAN is an associate producer at the CBS Evening News.

MANNY FERNANDEZ is a reporter on the metropolitan staff of The New York Times.

RICHARD FIRSTMAN's books include "A Criminal Injustice: A True Crime, a False Confession, and the Fight to Free Marty Tankleff," with Jay Salpeter.

AMY FOX, author of the screenplay for the 2005 movie "Heights" and the play "Summer Cyclone," is on the faculty of the Tisch School of the Arts of New York University. She is writing a screenplay about the integration of Stuyvesant Town.

DOROTHY GALLAGHER is the author of four books, including two memoirs, "How I Came into My Inheritance" and "Strangers in the House: Life Stories," and most recently the text for "The Mural at the Waverly Inn." She is currently working on a book about Lillian Hellman.

BEN GIBBERD is the author of "New York Waters: Profiles from the Edge," with the photographer Randy Duchaine.

JOHN FREEMAN GILL is a former reporter for the City section of The New York Times. His writing has appeared in "The New York Times Book of New York" as well as in The Atlantic Monthly, The New York Observer, Premiere, The Washington Monthly, and The New York Times Magazine. He is at work on a novel set in 1970's Manhattan.

JENNIFER GILMORE's first novel, "Golden Country," was published in 2006. Her new novel, "Something Red," was published in April 2010.

SARA GRAN is the author of the novels "Dope," "Come Closer," and "Saturn's Return to New York."

DAVID HAJDU is a professor at the Columbia Graduate School of Journalism and a critic for The New Republic. His books include "The 10-Cent Plague: The Great Comic Book Scare and How It Changed America" and the essay collection "Heroes and Villains."

COLIN HARRISON is the author of seven novels, including "The Havana Room," "Manhattan Nocturne," "The Finder," and "Risk." Since 2001 he has been a vice president and senior editor at Scribner.

ROY HOFFMAN's books include "Back Home: Journeys through Mobile" and the novels "Almost Family" and "Chicken Dreaming Corn."

MITCH KELLER is the supervising editor of The New York Times News Service.

RANDY KENNEDY, a reporter for The New York Times who writes about the art world, is the author of "Subwayland: Adventures in the World beneath New York."

FRANCES KIERNAN, who worked at The New Yorker magazine for 20 years, most of that time as a fiction editor, is the author of "Seeing Mary Plain: A Life of Mary McCarthy" and "The Last Mrs. Astor: A New York Story."

MARK KINGWELL is a professor of philosophy at the University of Toronto and the author of 12 books of political and cultural theory, including "Nearest Thing to Heaven: The Empire State Building and American Dreams" and "Concrete Reveries: Consciousness and the City."

SAKI KNAFO is a former reporter for the City section of The New York Times. His work has appeared in The New York Times Magazine and in the anthology "Lost and Found: Stories from New York."

LAURA LONGHINE is an editor at Youth Communication, a nonprofit that trains teens in journalism and narrative writing and publishes their stories.

KATHERINE MARSH is the Edgar Award–winning author of two New York City–based fantasy novels for children, "The Night Tourist" and "The Twilight Prisoner."

REBECCA FLINT MARX is a staff writer for The Village Voice.

DAVID MASELLO is senior editor and men's fashion editor of Town & Country magazine. He is the author of two books, "Architecture without Rules: The Houses of Marcel Breuer" and "Art in Public Places: Walking New York's Neighborhoods to See the Best Paintings, Sculptures, Murals, Mosaics and Mobiles."

DAVID McANINCH is the deputy editor of Saveur magazine.

SUKETU MEHTA, the author of "Maximum City: Bombay Lost and Found," is working on a nonfiction book about immigrants in contemporary New York. He teaches journalism at New York University.

MAC MONTANDON is the author of "Jetpack Dreams: One Man's Up and Down (but Mostly Down) Search for the Greatest Invention That Never Was" and the editor of "Innocent When You Dream: The Tom Waits Reader."

JAKE MOONEY is a former reporter for the City section of The New York Times and the author of the section's Dispatches column.

LESLIE NIPKOW is an Emmy and Writers' Guild Award–winning author. Her one-woman play, "Guarding Erica," was published in "Talk to Me: Monologue Plays."

MAX PAGE is a professor of architecture and history at the University of Massachusetts in Amherst and the author of "The City's End: Two Centuries of Fantasies, Fears, and Premonitions of New York's Destruction." He is currently at work on a book about historic preservation.

ELLEN PALL is a novelist whose works include "Among the Ginzburgs" and "Slightly Abridged."

FRANCINE PROSE's most recent book is "Anne Frank: The Book, the Life, the Afterlife." She is currently a Distinguished Visiting Writer at Bard College.

NATHANIEL RICH is the author of the novel "The Mayor's Tongue."

ROXANA ROBINSON is the author of four novels, three story collections, and a biography of Georgia O'Keeffe.

ALEX ROSE is a co-founding editor of Hotel St. George Press and the author of "The Musical Illusionist and Other Tales." His story "Ostracon" was included in the 2009 edition of "Best American Short Stories."

JONATHAN ROSEN is the author of the novels "Eve's Apple" and "Joy Comes in the Morning" and two works of nonfiction, "The Talmud and the Internet" and "The Life of the Skies: Birding at the End of Nature." He is editorial director of Nextbook.

CHRISTOPHER SORRENTINO is the author of three novels, including "Trance," a National Book Award Finalist in 2005. His short fiction has appeared in Esquire, Harper's, Playboy, Tin House, and other publications.

ROBERT SULLIVAN is the author of numerous books, including "The Meadowlands," "How Not to Get Rich: Why Being Bad Off Isn't So Bad," and "Rats: Observations on the History and Habitat of the City's Most Unwanted Inhabitants."

JOCKO WEYLAND is the author of "The Answer Is Never: A Skateboarder's History of the World."

WILLIAM ZINSSER's 18 books include "On Writing Well" and the memoir "Writing Places: The Life Journey of a Writer and Teacher."

About the Editor

CONSTANCE ROSENBLUM, the longtime editor of the City section of The New York Times and former editor of the newspaper's Arts & Leisure section, is the author of "Boulevard of Dreams: Heady Times, Heartbreak, and Hope along the Grand Concourse in the Bronx," available from NYU Press, and "Gold Digger: The Outrageous Life and Times of Peggy Hopkins Joyce" and editor of "New York Stories: The Best of the City Section of the New York Times," also available from NYU Press.